MOSCOW
AND THE GOLDEN RING

To Moshka and The Lenin Sisters

ACKNOWLEDGEMENTS

Finnair & Ilkka Mitro; Lindblad; Angliiski Misha; James "Toshiba" Burke; Robert Trent Jones, II; Jeff Kriendler, Pan American; Herb Caen; Jando; Eleanor, Len, Gorsky & Karen; Lyoni Craven; Bolshoi Bob Mac Dougal; "Multimate" Winters; Dan Hays; Belka; Babushka Anna & Dedushka Mitro; Leningrad Circus & Nikulin; Sasha, Tanya & Andrei— The Frishkadelkamis; Tolya Valushkin & Katya Jharkovskaya; Shigeru-san; Valentin, Volodya & Viktor; Slava; Govard Green & Vatrushka; Ivan "Lodka"; Markski; Yuko & Ari, Dave Pleiman; Andy; Geriakaka; Muffett Kaufman; Carlichka Gottlieb; Rich Neill; Bashkaus Bill; Karen Montgomery; John Porterfield; David Fineman; Peggy Burns; Matt Valencic; Barb Penningroth; Dywa Puziri Mashahari and Medvyed Philip. Special thanks to Dikii Deke, Tovarish Tobias and Magnus Bartlett.

Masha Nordbye is a writer and film producer who has traveled through more than 70 countries, and has studied and worked in the Soviet Union on a regular basis over the past fifteen years. Her films in the USSR include National Geographic's *Inside the Soviet Circus* and her own *Villages of the North*, filmed in the Arctic Circle region. Nordbye has traveled across the country with the Soviet Circus many times, and helped organize the Moscow Circus' American Tour in 1989. Her current projects include an ABC Network film on the Trans-Siberian railroad and a National Geographic film on Leningrad. She now lives in San Francisco.

Patricia Lanza has been a freelance and contract photographer for the National Geographic Society for the past eight years, with over 600 published photos to her credit. She contributed to the book *A Day In The Life Of The Soviet Union* and provided all the still photography for the National Geographic film *Inside the Soviet Circus* and the US Tour of The Moscow Circus, among other projects. An exhibition of Lanza's Russian photographs was recently mounted at Radio City Music Hall in New York. She lives in Alexandria, Virginia.

MOSCOW
AND THE GOLDEN RING

Masha Nordbye
Photography by Patricia Lanza

On with the journey!...
Russia! Russia!
When I see you...my eyes are lit up
with supernatural power. Oh, what a
glittering, wondrous infinity of
space.... What a strange, alluring,
enthralling, wonderful world!

Nikolai Gogol

PASSPORT BOOKS
a division of *NTC Publishing Group*
Lincolnwood, Illinois USA

Published by Passport Books in conjunction with
The Guidebook Company Ltd.

This edition first published in 1992 by Passport Books,
a division of NTC Publishing Group, 4255 W. Touhy Avenue,
Lincolnwood (Chicago), Illinois 60646-1975 U.S.A.
originally published by The Guidebook Company Ltd.
Library of Congress Catalog Card Number: 91-61557

Grateful acknowledgement is made to the following
authors and publishers for permission granted:

Stanford University Press for
Moscow Diary by Walter Benjamin, edited by Gary Smith
translated by Richard Sieburth, © 1986 by President and Fellows of Harvard.

Ardis Publishers for
'The Barsukov Triangle' from *The Two-Toned Blond and Other Stories* by Nina Katerli,
edited by Carl R Proffer and Ellandea Proffer, © Ardis 1984.

Grove Weidenfeld Inc, for
Heart of a Dog by Mikhail Bulgakov, translated by Mirra Ginsburg

Peter Owen Ltd for
Adventures in Czarist Russia by Alexandre Dumas,
edited and translated by Alma Elizabeth Murch

Excerpt from *In Plain Russian* by Vladimir Voinovich, translated by Richard Lourie,
translation ©1979 by Farrar, Straus and Giroux, Inc., reprinted by permission of Farrar,
Straus and Giroux Inc. and Georges Borchardt Inc.

Editor: Deke Castleman
Illustrations Editor: Caroline Robertson
Map Design: Bai Yiliang
Design: John Ng
Cover Concept: Aubrey Tse
Photography by Patricia Lanza, with additional contributions from Cary Wolinsky,
Trillium Studios (Pages 80, 81, 85, 88, 89, 92, 93 and 96); Masha Nordbye (pages 108,
121, 132 bottom left, 133 bottom left, 148, 153, 160, 161, 185, 196, 197, 212, 213 and 225);
Altfield Gallery (page 37).

Production House: Twin Age Limited, Hong Kong

Printed in Hong Kong

Contents

Excerpts

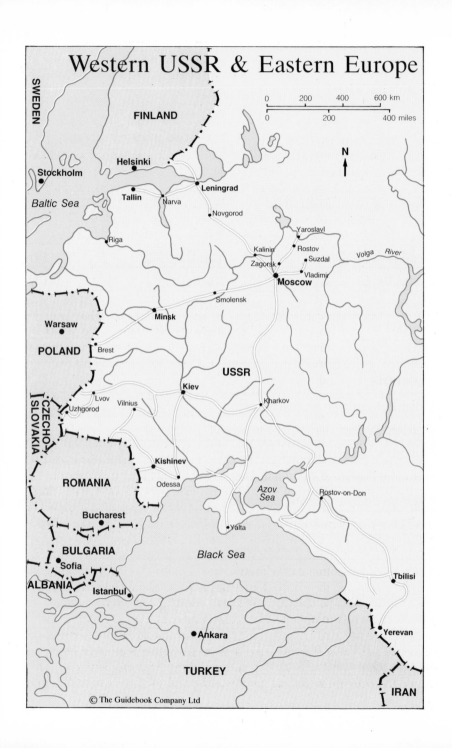

Introduction

Perhaps no other place in the world has ever captivated the traveler's imagination as much as the Soviet Union. Throughout the centuries, visitors to Russia reported phenomenal and fanciful scenes: from golden churches, bejewelled icons and towering kremlins to mad-cap czars, wild Cossacks and prolific poets. Russia was an impressive sight for any beholder. A travel writer in the early 20th century remarked that Russia's capital, Moscow, "embodies fantasy on an unearthly scale...Towers, domes, spires, cones, onions, crenellations filled the whole view. It might have been the invention of Dante, arrived in a Russian heaven."

The largest country in the world, the USSR, or as the Soviets refer to their homeland, SSSR, (*CCCP* in Cyrillic), for *Soyuz Sovyetskikh Sotsialisticheskikh Respublikh*, spreads across 11 time zones and two continents from Europe to Asia, encompassing one-sixth of the planet's total land area. Its inhabitants number 289 million in 15 republics, and speak over 200 different languages and dialects. Russian, the official language, unites 92 different nationalities.

It would be impossible to take in the diversity of the entire country on one (or even two or three) visits, but there's no better way to learn about the Russian character and way of life than with a trip to Moscow. The Soviet Union's largest city, Moscow is the capital of both the country and its largest republic, the Russian Federation. It's the center of politics, industry and culture, the heart of this giant nation. *Moskva* is also the core of the Russian spirit. The Russian poet Alexander Pushkin wrote of his first trip to Moscow: "And now at last the goal is in sight: in the shimmer of the white walls...and golden domes, Moscow lies great and splendid before us...O Moscow, have I thought of you! Moscow, how violently the name plucks at any Russian heart!"

The true enchantment of Moscow begins in the city's center, where you can gaze upon the gilded domes of the palaces and churches of the former czars that rise up from within the Kremlin, the old protective walls of the city. From the citadel, paths lead out to the fairy-tale creation of Ivan the Terrible, St. Basil's Cathedral, that looms up from the middle of *Krasnaya Ploshad*, Red Square. *Krasnaya* is an old Russian word meaning both "red" and "beautiful." Long lines of visitors stretch around the Kremlin walls, patiently waiting their turn to be admitted into

Historical Chart

A.D. 700-882: The Vikings begin to leave Scandinavia and establish trading settlements with the Slavs in northwestern Russia. Kievan state in the south is formed and named after the Slavic Prince Kii. In 862, the Norseman Rurik defeats the important Slavic town of Novgorod and becomes one of the first Vikings to rule in Russia. In 880, Rurik's successor, Oleg, conquers the Slavic-ruled Kiev, unites the two states and makes Kiev his capital. The ruling class is known as **"Rus"** (thought to be derived from the Viking word *ruotsi*, meaning rower or oarsman). This term is later applied to the people of Eastern Europe; eventually the areas are united into the Russian states.

977: Novgorod gains its independence from Kiev.

978-1015: Rule of Prince Vladimir, who introduces Byzantine Christianity into Russia.

1015-54: Rule of Yaroslav the Wise. Kiev becomes the first center of the Orthodox Church.

1113-1125: Rule of Vladimir Monomakh. The two principalities of Novgorod and Kiev are united again under his rule. The crown of Monomakh is worn by the later rulers of Russia. The decline of Kievan Rus begins after his death.

1147: Prince Yuri Dolgoruky "Long Arms" founds Moscow. He builds a kremlin and defensive walls around the city.

1169: Prince Andrei Bogoliubsky transfers the capital from Kiev to Vladimir.

1223: First Mongol invasion of Russia.

1237: Batu Khan, grandson of Genghis Khan, invades Moscow and goes on to conquer many of Russia's other regions. The Mongol Tatars dominate Russia for the next 250 years.

1240: The Prince of Novgorod, Alexander Nevsky, defeats the Swedes in an important battle along the Neva River. Nevsky rules as Grand Prince in Vladimir from 1252-63.

1299: The Church Metropolitan flees Kiev and takes up residence with the Grand Prince in Vladimir.

1325-40: Reign of Ivan I, nicknamed Kalita "Moneybags" because of his strong economic hold over the other principalities. Ivan is named Grand Prince in 1328, and chooses Moscow as his residence. The seat of the Orthodox Church is also moved from Vladimir to Moscow. In 1337, St. Sergius founds the Monastery of the Holy Trinity in Zagorsk.

1353-59: Reign of Ivan II.

1362-89: Reign of Dmitri Donskoi. In 1380, the Grand Prince defeats the Tatars in the Battle of Kulikovo on the Don, becoming the first Russian prince to win a decisive battle over the Mongol army. Two years later the Mongols burn Moscow to the ground.

1453: The Ottoman Turks conquer Constantinople, which releases the Russian Orthodox Church from Byzantine domination. Less than a decade later, the head of the Orthodox Church takes on the title of Metropolitan of Moscow and All Russia and receives his orders from the Grand Prince.

1460-1505: Reign of Ivan III (Ivan the Great). He marries Sophia, the niece of the last Byzantine Emperor, in 1472 and adopts the crest of the double-headed eagle. Moscow is declared the Third Rome. During his rule, Ivan the Great rebuilds the Kremlin and annexes the city of Novgorod. He refuses to pay any further tribute to the Mongols and defeats their armies. Two centuries of Tatar oppression in Russia come to an end.

1533-84: Reign of Ivan IV (Ivan the Terrible) who is crowned in 1547 in the Moscow Kremlin with the title of Czar (derived from Caesar) of All Russia. He organizes the *"Oprichniki,"* a special bodyguard to prosecute the *Boyars* (landowners). He defeats the Tatars in the far eastern territories. Russia loses the Livonian War and access to the Baltic.

1584-98: Reign of Fyodor I, son of Ivan IV. Establishment of Moscow Church Patriarch.

1598-1613: The Time of Troubles. Boris Godunov rules as Czar from 1598 to 1605. Claim to the throne by two false Dmitris. Second false Dmitri seizes the throne with Polish support. Battles with Polish armies.

1613-1645: Mikhail Romanov is elected Czar. The Romanov Dynasty continues to rule Russia until 1762.

1645-76: Reign of Alexei I.

1676-82: Reign of Fyodor III. When Fyodor dies, his feeble-minded brother, Ivan V, and half-brother, Peter I (Peter the Great), are proclaimed joint czars. The *Streltsy* (Marksmen) briefly gain control over the government. Sophia, Peter's half sister, acts as Regent.

1689-1725: Reign of Peter the Great. During his enlightened rule, Peter adopts the Julian calendar, transfers the capital from Moscow to St. Petersburg, introduces Western culture and customs to his country and builds the first Russian fleet along the Baltic. In 1721, he assumes the title of Emperor of All Russia.

1725-27: Reign of Catherine I, the widow of Peter the Great, who becomes Czarina with the help of her guard Menshikov.

1727-30: Reign of Peter II, Peter the Great's grandson.

1730-40: Reign of Anna Ivanova, daughter of Ivan V and niece of Peter the Great.

1740-41: Reign of Ivan VI.

1741-61: Reign of Elizabeth, daughter of Peter the Great and Catherine I. In 1755, the first university is founded in Moscow.

1761-62: Reign of Peter III, grandson of Peter the Great.

1762-96: Reign of Catherine II (Catherine the Great), German-born wife of Peter III. The first foreign woman to rule as Czarina. Russia becomes a major power.

1796-1801: Reign of Paul I, son of Catherine the Great.

1801-25: Reign of Alexander I, son of Paul I. In 1812, Napoleon's armies flee Moscow. Rise of the Decembrist movement.

1825-55: Reign of Nicholas I, son of Paul I. On December 14, 1825 the Decembrists attempt to overthrow the Czarist autocracy and gain freedom for the serfs. Bolshoi Theater opens in 1825. In 1851, the first railway opens between St. Petersburg and Moscow.

1855-81: Reign of Alexander II, son of Nicholas I. In 1861, Alexander signs a decree to emancipate the serfs.

1867: Sale of Alaska to the United States; Karl Marx's *Das Kapital* is translated into Russian.

1881: Alexander II is assassinated by members of the Peoples' Will group.

1881-94: Reign of Alexander III. The brother of Lenin, Alexander Ulyanov, along with four others, attempt to assassinate the Czar.

Nicholas marries the granddaughter of Queen Victoria. In 1895, workers hold public rallies to celebrate May Day, day of worker Solidarity. In 1903, the Social Democratic Party splits into two factions: Bolsheviks and Mensheviks. The first revolution takes place in 1905 (known as Bloody Sunday) in St. Petersburg. World War I breaks out in 1914. Second revolution begins in February, 1917. Czar Nicholas abdicates and a Provisional Government is formed under Kerensky's leadership. In October 1917, Lenin and the Bolsheviks overthrow the Provisional Government and establish the Socialist Soviet State.

1918-24: In 1918, Lenin moves capital from Petrograd to Moscow. First Soviet constitution is adopted. Switch to Gregorian calendar. The Communist Government nationalizes industry, introduces censorship of the press and forms the Cheka police force. Lenin introduces the New Economic Policy (NEP). When Lenin dies in 1924, St. Petersburg (Petrograd) is renamed Leningrad.

1924-53: Joseph Stalin. In 1927, Trotsky is expelled from the Party. In 1928, Stalin introduces the First Five Year Plan and Collectivization. A widespread famine sweeps the nation, eventually killing ten million people.

1934-41: Stalin's assassination of Leningrad Party Chief Sergel Kirov signals the beginning of the Great Terror. Half the delegates of the 17th Party Congress are purged, along with 90 percent of the country's generals. Of approximately 20 million people arrested, seven million are shot immediately while the rest are sent to gulag camps for rehabilitation.

1941-5: World War II. Hitler invades the USSR in 1941, and the siege of Leningrad lasts for 900 days until 1944. The Soviet Union suffers 20 million casualties.

1945-53: Occupation of Eastern Europe.

1953-64: Stalin dies and is succeeded by Nikita Khruschev, who founds the KGB in 1954. Two-thirds of the Orthodox churches and monasteries are closed down. In 1961, the Soviets send the first man into space, and the Congress votes to remove Stalin's body from its place of honor alongside Lenin in the Kremlin Mausoleum.

1964-82: Khruschev's forced resignation is engineered by Leonid Brezhnev, who immediately rescinds Khruschev's Rule 25 restricting Party officials to 15 years in office. The discovery of large gas and oil reserves boosts the economy, but these benefits are undermined by poor planning and lack of incentives. Alcohol consumption quadruples in 20 years.

1968: Invasion of Czechoslovakia.

1979: Invasion of Afghanistan.

1982-84: Brezhnev dies and is succeeded by Yuri Andropov.

1984-85: Andropov dies and is succeeded by Konstantin Chernenko

1985-present: Chernenko dies and is succeeded by Mikhail Gorbachev

Lenin's Mausoleum to view the "Father of the Great October Revolution." Jutting out like arteries from the heart of the city are the long thoroughfares with names like Gorky Street, Kalinin Prospekt and the Boulevard Ring that carry you through various passages of history to the present. These avenues and rings around the city lead to an abundance of sights that include the Bolshoi Theater, Novodevichy Monastery, Tretyakov Art Gallery and the Exhibition Park of Economic Achievements.

The Arbat district embodies all the changes currently sweeping the Soviet Union. Here is everything from *babushki* (grandmothers) carrying their net bags filled with cabbages and potatoes, to long-haired musicians jamming on their guitars and saxophones. Nowadays, Moscow, while basking in the beauty of past splendors, is also dancing wildly, for the first time in decades, to the tune of a different drummer. Mikhail Gorbachev's *perestroika* (restructuring) and *glasnost* (openness) have become the watchwords for the new generation.

The towns and villages surrounding the city's outskirts, known as the Golden Ring, reveal a quieter and quainter country lifestyle. The Golden Ring area is considered the cradle of Russian culture. The small towns, like Zagorsk (the center of Russian Orthodoxy), Rostov, Vladimir and Suzdal (the most ancient Russian towns), were built between the 10th and 17th centuries and are still magnificently preserved. Antiquated villages, onion-domed churches, the frescos and icons of the 15th-century artist Andrei Rublev, colorful wooden *dachas* (country homes) and endless groves of birch trees provide a fine contrast to the bigger cities.

With the dawning of Gorbachev's "second revolution" comes a virtual explosion in communication, culture and national awareness—there has never been a more interesting and exciting time to visit the Soviet Union. In what is called "the new Russian Renaissance," Soviet people are experiencing greater freedoms than ever permitted throughout the entire history of post-revolutionary Russia. Yet, aside from all the new and stimulating developments, the Soviet Union is still a place filled with paradoxes and limitations, and a traveler cannot anticipate a relaxing or luxurious holiday. "First-class socialist style" can be a little different from what you may imagine; it doesn't include piña coladas by the pool or sumptuous breakfasts in bed!

Most travelers enter the USSR through the Soviet Tour Agency, Intourist, which provides hotels, meals and sightseeing. Even though the

USSR, through the years, has boasted large-scale production of rockets and ballets, it has not yet produced a surplus of food or clothing, let alone stocked a warehouse with tourist amenities. Soviets do not enjoy a variety of fruits and vegetables, nor sometimes even the basics, such as toilet paper or soap. The average Russian must still stand in long lines to buy most things, including ice cream, and there is currently a rationing of common items such as sausage, sugar and tea. So, in any moments of slight frustration, remember that the traveler is receiving all that the country can most readily provide, and probably much more than is available to the average citizen. A sure remedy for the lack of certain supplies is simply to bring anything you cannot do without—from prescription drugs to peanut butter.

If you do not read Cyrillic or speak the Russian language, bring a Russian phrasebook; it's amazing how far a smile, some patience and the knowledge of a few Russian words will go. So far, in fact, that you may even find yourself being invited to someone's home for dinner, where you will quickly discover that Russians are some of the warmest and most hospitable people that you will ever meet.

The country has come a long way from being "a riddle wrapped in a mystery inside an enigma," as Winston Churchill once observed. Russia has changed. Now with just a little of your own *glasnost*, and curiosity, your trip to the Soviet Union will surely be one of the most fascinating and memorable adventures of your life.

Perestroika

On March 11, 1985, 54-year old Mikhail Sergeyevich Gorbachev was elected the new General Secretary of the Communist Party. Following in the footsteps of such past rulers as Ivan the Terrible, Peter the Great, Stalin and Brezhnev, Gorbachev inherited a stagnating economy, an entrenched bureaucracy and a population which had lived in fear and mistrust of their previous leaders.

His first actions were to shut down the production and sale of vodka and ardently pursue Andropov's anti-corruption campaign (one of the first to go was Leningrad party boss, Grigory Romanov) and in 1986, he introduced the radical reform policies of *perestroika* (restructuring), *demokratizatsiya* (democratization) and *glasnost* (openness), now household words. Gorbachev emphasized that past reforms had not worked because they did not directly involve Soviet citizens. *Perestroika* introduced the profit motive, quality control, private ownership in agriculture, decentralization and multi-candidate elections. Industry concentrated on measures promoting quality over quantity; private businesses and cooperatives were encouraged; farmers and individuals could now lease land and housing from the government and keep the profits made from produce grown on private plots; hundreds of ministries and bureaucratic centers were disbanded. A law was passed that allows individuals to own small businesses and hire workers so long as there is "no exploitation of man by man."

In a powerful symbolic gesture, Andrei Sakharov and other political prisoners were released from internal exile. (After winning the 1975 Nobel Peace Prize, Sakharov, the physicist and human rights activist, was banished for nearly seven years to the city of Gorky. He died in Moscow on November 14, 1989.) One hundred Soviet dissidents from 20 cities were allowed to form the "Democratic Club," an open political discussion group. Glasnost swept through all facets of Soviet life.

For the 40 million Russian Orthodox and people of other religious beliefs, Gorbachev stated that "believers have the full right to express their convictions with dignity." On December 1, 1989, Gorbachev became the first Soviet leader to set foot in the Vatican, where he declared that: "We need spiritual values; we need a revolution of the mind... No one should interfere in matters of the individual's conscience.

"Christians, Moslems, Jews, Buddhists and others live in the Soviet Union. All of them have a right to satisfy their spiritual needs — this is the only way toward a new culture and new politics that can meet the challenge of our time."

As Peter the Great had understood, modernization means Westernization, and Gorbachev reopened the window to the West. With the fostering of private business, about 5 million people are now employed by over 150,000 cooperatives. After April 1, 1989, all enterprises were allowed to carry on trade relations with foreign partners, triggering the development of joint ventures. Multi-million-dollar deals have been established with Western companies such as Chevron, Pepsico, Eastman-Kodak, McDonald's, Time-Warner and Occidental.

At the 1986 Iceland Summit, Gorbachev proposed to sharply reduce ballistic missiles, and in December, 1987, he signed a treaty with U.S. President Ronald Reagan to eliminate intermediate nuclear missiles. In January, 1988, plans to withdraw all forces from Afghanistan were announced. Nine months later Andrei Gromyko retired and Gorbachev was elected President of the Supreme Soviet.

During a visit to Finland in October, 1989, Gorbachev declared that "the Soviet Union has no moral or political right to interfere in the affairs of its East European neighbors. They have the right to decide their own fate." And that is what they did. By the end of 1989, every country throughout Eastern Europe saw its people protesting openly for mass reforms. The Iron Curtain crumbled, symbolized most poignantly by the demolishing of the wall between East and West Berlin.

Elections and Economy

On March 26, 1989, there was a general election for the new Congress of People's Deputies — the first time since 1917 that Soviet citizens actually had a chance to vote in a national election. One thousand five hundred delegates were elected together with an additional 750, who were elected by other public organizations. The 2,250-delegate body then elected 542 members to form a new Supreme Soviet.

Ousted a year earlier from his Politburo post for criticizing the reforms, the Congress candidate Boris Yeltsin won 89 percent of the Moscow district vote. As Moscow crowds chanted, "Yeltsin is a Man of the People" and "Down with Bureaucrats," a surprising number of bureaucrats had, in fact, lost to people like the Church Metropolitan of Leningrad. Andrei Sakharov was also elected. One interesting aspect of the election rules was that even candidates who ran unopposed could lose, if over half the votes pulled a lever of "no confidence," a privilege not enjoyed by voters in most Western countries, including the United States!

At the beginning of 1990 Soviet citizens once again headed for the polls to elect their own regional and district officials, this time with the additional opportunity to choose candidates from other independent and pro-democracy movements. Scores of Communist Party candidates suffered defeat at the hands of former political prisoners, adamant reformers, environmentalists and strike leaders. Yeltsin was voted in as President of the Russian Federation, the Soviet Union's largest republic, which has more than half the country's population and Moscow as its capital. In June 1990, Yeltsin resigned from the Communist Party, declaring that "in view of my...great responsibility toward the people of Russia and in connection with moves toward a multi-party state, I cannot fulfill only the instructions of the Party."

Yeltsin's ascent underscores the fact that, for all his unprecedented reforms and innovative policies, Gorbachev has not been able to bring the country's economy out of stagnation and he is losing his popularity at home. In an extensive poll conducted in the Soviet Union, the survey found more than 90 percent considered the economic situation in the country critical. Some of the disheartened have commented that "glasnost has produced more copies of Solzhenitsyn than salami." Food and fuel are in critically low supply, and the population is expecting the worst food shortages since World War II. Ration coupons are being issued for meat, sugar, tea and soap. After a recent launching of a probe to Mars, graffiti in Moscow appeared, exclaiming "To Mars for Soap!" Modernization does not approach Western standards, there are few computers, and most areas still use the abacus. It is estimated that 40 percent of the crops are wasted because of poor storage, packing and distribution methods. Many Soviets feel that their living conditions have worsened: "We live like dogs. The leash has become longer but the meat is a bit smaller, and the plate is two meters further away. But at least we can now bark as much as we want."

Gorbachev is also faced with a budget deficit of over 100 billion rubles. The severe shortages have created a virtual black-market economy, providing goods for up to 85 percent of the population.On November 1, 1989, the government drastically cut the bank ruble exchange rate by 90 percent in order to curb black-market exchanges (up to 20 times

above the official rate) and to bring the ruble closer to an open exchange on the world market. The Prime Minister has stated that 43 million people (15 percent of the population) live below the poverty level. There are also an estimated 23 million people unemployed, the new paradox of modern Soviet society.

Compounding failing measures and political contradictions, the nation has been rocked by a series of disasters: Chernobyl, the earthquake in Armenia, ethnic unrest, and extensive strikes in mines and factories across the country (a 1989 law legalized strikes). But Gorbachev remains confident and presses on with *perestroika*. "This is a turbulent time, a turbulent sea in which it's not easy to sail the ship. But we have a compass and we have a crew to guide that ship, and the ship itself is strong."

The New Revolution

The Bolshevik Party, formed by Lenin, began as a unified band of revolutionaries whose 8,000 members organized the mass strike of the 1905 St. Petersburg revolt. By October 1917, the Bolshevik Party (soon renamed the Communist Party) had over 300,000 members, many of whom became the leaders and planners for the newly formed Soviet State.

Today there are 20 million Party members, a third of them women. Membership is open to any citizen who "does not exploit the labor of others," abides by the Party's philosophy, and gives three percent of her monthly pay as dues to the Party. Members are also required to attend several meetings and lectures every month, provide volunteer work a few times a year and help with election campaigns. Approximately 200,000 of these members are full-time officials, *apparatchiks*, who are paid by the Party. The Komsomol, or Communist Youth Organization, has 40 million additional members, while 25 million school children belong to the Young Pioneers. Eligibility for party membership begins at age 18.

On February 7, 1990, after 72 years of Communist rule, the Soviet Communist Party's Central Committee voted overwhelmingly to surrender its monopoly on power. On March 15, 1990, the Soviet Congress of People's Deputies amended Article Six, which had guaranteed the Communist Party its position as the only "leading authority" in government. In its revised form, Article Six states that the Communists, together with other political parties and social organizations, have the right to shape state policy. During the 28th Party Congress, the Party voted to reorganize its ruling body, the Politburo, to include Communist Party leaders from each of the 15 republics, in addition to the top 12 Moscow officials; it is expected to grow to as many as 23 voting members. Instead of being selected by the Central Committee, the Party in each republic will choose its own leaders, guaranteeing a voice in the Party to even the smallest republic.

Other amendments revised the Marxist view that private property is incompatible with Socialism. Individuals may now own land and factories as long as they do not "exploit" other Soviet citizens. New economic policies replace direct central planning, institute new price reforms and even create a stock exchange; farmers may soon sell their produce on the open market. Additional new laws decree that "the press and other mass media are free. Censorship of the mass media is forbidden," and that "all political movements will have access to the airwaves with the right to establish their own television and radio stations." The Communist Party no longer has a monopoly on the State-run radio and television. These historic votes pave the way for a multiparty democracy and a free-market economy.

In one of the most important changes in this country's political and economic system since the 1917 Bolshevik Revolution, Mikhail Gorbachev was elected by the Congress as the Soviet Union's first executive President. This new post, replacing the former honorary chairmanship of the Supreme Soviet, has broader constitutional powers; the President now has the right to propose legislation, veto bills passed by Congress, appoint and fire the Prime Minister and other senior government officials and declare states of emergency (with the approval of the republics).

Facts for the Traveler

Planning Your Trip

Traveling to the USSR requires careful, advanced planning. Read some literature on the cities you plan to visit and talk to people who have been there. Locate travel agents or other special organizations that deal with travel to the USSR.

Intourist

Most travelers organize their stay in the USSR through Intourist, the official Soviet travel agency for foreigners. An Intourist branch is located in each of the approximately 150 cities that are officially open to tourists. Under most circumstances, visitors stay in Intourist hotels, which have an Intourist service desk. All hotel reservations must be prepaid before entering the country. Visas will not be issued by a Soviet embassy or consulate without a confirmed reservation. It often takes up to one month for reservations and itineraries to be confirmed.

Group Tours or Independent Travel

There are a multitude of package and special-interest group tours from which to choose. The advantage of a group tour (especially if it is your first trip and you do not speak the language) is that everything is set up for you. Travel agencies handling USSR excursions have a list of package tours available. Most group tours have preset departures and a fixed length of stay, and usually visit Moscow and Leningrad. The group rate includes roundtrip airfare, visa processing fees, first-class Intourist accommodations, up to three meals a day, all transportation within the USSR, sightseeing excursions and a bilingual Intourist guide. Special-interest groups offer trips that include some sightseeing, but focus more on specific issues such as sports, ecology, the arts, citizen diplomacy, religion or world peace. Independent travelers can also organize a stay through Intourist, but have to accept that the visit cannot be completely spontaneous as the route, cities to be visited and exact length of stay must be fixed before departure. Reservations can be made through a travel agency that has connections with Intourist. Any slight change made in the itinerary can delay the process by weeks. A cancellation after payment can take up to six months to be refunded by Intourist. However, once there, the traveler can set out and discover each city on his own.

Visas

All travelers to the Soviet Union must have a visa. There are three types of visa: Tourist, Business and Visitor. The travel agency supplies each person with a Tourist visa application (or it can be picked up at a Soviet embassy or consulate). A processing fee may be charged. Four passport-size photos and a xerox of the information page of your passport are also required. The host agency telexes Intourist, requesting your itinerary. Once a confirmation is received, your visa is issued. Independent travelers are advised to book at least six to eight weeks in advance to guarantee space and the best rates in hotels. Once the bookings are confirmed, all hotel costs and internal transfers must be prepaid. Individuals may also apply directly to the Soviet embassy or consulate for a visa, but must show a letter from a travel agency confirming Intourist reservations before a visa will be granted. The travel agency will issue an Intourist voucher — a prepaid confirmation booklet for hotel and transfers.

Once in the USSR, you can lengthen your stay or visit additional cities by making arrangements with the Intourist desk at your hotel.

If you are sponsored by a Soviet organization, relative or friend, you can enter the Soviet Union on a Visitor's visa. You must send your host a visa application filled out in duplicate (not a xerox copy). The host must then take it to his own travelers' organization, OVIR, which will issue a Visitor's visa after several months. The traveler is only allowed to travel to the cities and stay with the persons designated on the visa.

When to Go

The season of travel affects itineraries and hotel prices of many of the tour programs. Peak season is from May to September. Alternatives are to go in the spring (April 1-May 15) or fall (Sept. 1-Oct. 31) when prices are lower and the cities less crowded. Summer in Moscow can be humid and dusty; at the same time, the White Nights in Leningrad are spectacular. Indian summer in the fall is quite pleasant. If you do not mind the cold and snow, the winter season is cheapest, and accommodation most readily available. The rainiest months for both cities are July and August.

International Flights and Connecting Trains

Most major airlines fly to Moscow (Airport Sheremetyevo II) and Leningrad (Pulkovo II). Moscow is connected with 121 cities in Europe and 70 countries around the world. Inquire at travel agencies and call around the different airlines. The advance-purchase (APEX) fares give the best rate. A **Pan Am** (in the U.S., tel. 800–221–1111) non-stop flight to Moscow from New York and Washington, D.C. (and other U.S. cities with a stop in Frankfurt) with a 14-day advance-purchase starts at roundtrip $885. The Soviet airline, **Aeroflot**, also flies from most major cities to Moscow. **British Airways** (U.S. tel. 800–247–9297; London tel. 897–4000) offers a fare with a 28-day advance purchase roundtrip London-Moscow (twice weekly to Leningrad) for £270/$430.

Aeroflot is the largest airline in the world, carrying 100 million passengers each year. You can fly from and to destinations in Asia and Europe on Aeroflot with stopovers in Moscow (a Transit visa and hotel confirmation are required). Since flying, especially from points outside Europe, involves large time differences, consider a stay in a European city for a day or two. Stopovers are sometimes included or provided for a minimal extra charge.

Another pleasant way to travel is to take a train from a European city to Moscow or Leningrad. **Finnair** (U.S. tel.800-950-5000; London tel. 408-1222) flies daily from New York to Helsinki (21-day advance-purchase from $745 roundtrip) and on Thursdays and Saturdays non-

The Trans-Siberian Railroad

Construction of the Trans-Siberian Railroad was started in 1891 and only completed 25 years later in 1916. Linking Chelyubinsk in the Ural Mountains to the Pacific port of Vladivostok, it facilitated the settlement of sparsely populated regions in southern regions of the Soviet Union.

Today, one hundred years after the first tracks were laid, the Trans-Siberian is one of the cheapest ways of traveling from Europe to Asia. It also is one of the great travel adventures and mind-bogglingly boring—endless stretches of birch forest clacking by.

The main section of the railroad stretches from Moscow to Beijing. The five-day Chinese Trans-Mongolian train via Ulan Bator leaves every Wednesday, while the six-day Russian Trans-Manchurian via Manzhouli leaves Friday and Saturday. Starting in Moscow, the departure days are Tuesday and Friday, respectively.

Reservations are essential, and must be made at least two months in advance. The train is heavily booked during the summer, and the wheels of Soviet bureaucracy grind slowly all year round. The nearest Intourist office will provide you with a list of travel agents that book Soviet tours. (In Hong Kong, try Monkey Business at 723-1376, fax 367-2447). Fares begin at US$250, and can be much more. You can either travel with a group or go individually (note that only a few travel agents book solo tours). Tourists have the option of reserving a berth in a two- or four-berth compartment, which almost always is in a car set aside for foreigners. If you travel alone, you may be booked into a compartment with Russians. Avoid buying open tickets, as they are virtually impossible to book and expire after two months. Russian and/or Chinese visas are required for both trains, and an additional Mongolian visa is needed for the Trans-Mongolian.

From May to September, trains travel from Moscow all the way to Nakhodka near Vladivostok on the Pacific Ocean, and from there you can take a Soviet cruise ship to Yokohama, Japan. You can stop overnight in Novosibirsk and Irkutsk, and all passengers spend the night in Khabarovsk, where they change trains. On the stretch between Khabarovsk and Nakhodka, the train runs along the Chinese-Russian border, and you can see the lights of numerous mysterious military installations.

Popular connecting destinations to the west include Berlin, which can be reached in less than 28 hours, Budapest (34 hours) and Helsinki (14 hours). If you're a real train fanatic, you can extend this journey all the way to Paris on the East-West Express via Berlin and Warsaw. Tickets on the East-West Express can be reserved through Germanrail.

Solo travellers on the Trans-Siberian should try to pay for meals in advance; if you don't, a large tour could eat up all the food and your hunger will be met by shrugs from the waiters. The Russian restaurant car has an impressive menu but a limited supply due in part to selling food stock at high prices on the Siberian black market. All travelers should note that the food is generally terrible and alcohol is not available on the train nor in stations along the way. Bring your own stock of snacks and booze (and lots of books!).

stop from Los Angeles (from $965 roundtrip). After a few relaxing days in Helsinki, take the train to Leningrad or Moscow. (Finnair also flies daily from Helsinki to Moscow or Leningrad.) The train leaves daily from Helsinki at 1 p.m., arriving the same day in Leningrad at 8:45 p.m. (one hour time change). The Moscow train leaves each day at 5 p.m. and arrives the next morning at 9 a.m. (you cross the border the day you depart), costing $110 ($160 first class) each way. You can even book and pay for the train through your travel agency. Return trains leave Moscow at 11:20 a.m. and arrive in Helsinki at 12:30 p.m. the next day (cross border the following day). Trains from Leningrad depart at 11:45 a.m. and arrive in Helsinki at 5 p.m. the same day.

Time Zones
The Soviet Union has 11 time zones. Moscow and Leningrad are in the same time zone. Many train and plane schedules are listed throughout the country as Moscow time. Always check to see what time is actually meant by the listing. It's an 11-hour time difference from the U.S. West Coast, eight hours from the East Coast, and three hours from London.

Packing
For your own convenience, travel as light as possible. Most airlines allow up to two pieces of luggage and one carry-on. Baggage allowance is very strict when exiting the USSR. Often, all bags are weighed, including your carry-on. Anything over 20 kilos (coach class) and 30 kilos (first and business class) gets charged per additional kilo! This is usually the procedure for internal flights as well.

Documents
Keep your passport, visa, important papers, tickets, vouchers, money, etc. in your hand luggage at all times. Also carry a xerox of your passport and visa. Keep in mind that you will need to show some ID to get into certain places. Serious photographers with a lot of film should have it inspected separately—Soviet X-rays are not always guaranteed film-safe.

Clothes
The season of the year is a major factor in deciding what to bring. Summers are warm, humid and dusty, with frequent thunderstorms, especially in Moscow. Bring a rain parka or an umbrella. Summer

evenings with the White Nights are delightful in Leningrad, but you will occasionally need a sweater or light jacket. Winters are cold and damp, with temperatures well below freezing. It can snow from November until April, when, especially in Leningrad, the cold Arctic winds sharpen the chill. Be prepared with your warmest clothes — waterproof boots, gloves and long underwear. Interiors are usually well heated, so dress in layers. It is best to bring everything with you, since Soviet clothing is mostly of poor quality—except for the Russian fur hats (*shapki*) found in the *Beriozkas*, (foreign-currency shops). Bring slightly smarter attire for ballets and banquets. A must is a good pair of walking shoes. Wearing shorts or sleeveless shirts may prevent you from entering a church during services.

Medicine
Take a good supply of medicine, prescription drugs, and remedies for flu and minor illnesses. Recommended: aspirin or Tylenol, throat lozenges, cold formulas, a course of antibiotics against a very bad cold or infection, vitamins (especially C), laxatives, lip salve, travel sickness pills, water-purifying tablets, contact-lens cleaners. For an upset stomach: indigestion tablets, Alka-Selzer, Pepto Bismal. If the "dreaded belly" strikes, cut out heavy foods, drink plenty of fluids and ask for rice in the restaurants. Take Lomotil, if necessary. Each hotel has a resident nurse or doctor and a small apothecary stand with a few medications for sale.

Personal Articles
Remember that the Soviet Union lacks many supplies that we take for granted.

Bring: cosmetics, lotions, shampoo, conditioner, razors, shaving cream, toothpaste, lavatory paper, Kleenex, feminine products, water bottle for long trips, soap, washing powder, flat bathtub stopper, pantyhose, sewing kit, scotch and strong wrapping tape, pens, extra pair of glasses or contact lenses.

Film
Film is expensive and hard to find. Bring whatever you plan to use. Since flash is prohibited in many museums and churches, have high-speed film on hand. New photo-developing centers are opening up, for example on the third floor of Moscow's Mezhdunarodnaya Hotel and the Pribaltiickaya in Leningrad. You must pay in foreign currency. If you can wait, it is advised to have your film, especially slides, processed at home.

Gadgets
Voltage varies from 220 to 127. Sometimes hotels have plugs for 220/110. Pack an adaptor/transformer. New hair dryers, travel irons and electrical shavers are now made with safety ends that don't fit into many adaptors — check before you go. A duel voltage coil is useful for boiling water and brewing tea and coffee in hotel rooms. Use with *extreme caution.* A walkman may be welcome. Bring plenty of batteries, for your camera, alarm clock and watch, too. Also handy is a pen-knife with a bottle opener and corkscrew.

Sightseeing
A Russian phrase book and dictionary are necessary. Try to master the Cyrillic alphabet before you leave. It will be especially helpful in places like the Metro. Bring reading material and travel literature. (The Soviet government is the largest book publisher in the world, though most books are in Russian.) Check in the Beriozka or kiosks in your hotel for books or maps printed in English. Giftgiving is a part of Russian *gostyepriimstvo* (hospitality). Buy a small supply of gifts for your Intourist guide and new friends: paperbacks, travel picture books, fashion magazines, T-shirts, music cassettes, cosmetics, colognes. Cigarettes and Scotch can be found in Beriozkas. Small souvenir items such as disposable lighters, pantyhose, boxes of herbal teas, perfumed soaps, bubblebath, and felt pens are good gifts for taxi drivers and maids. Bubblegum, baseball cards, etc. are terrific for children, who will trade them for *znachki* (pins).

Customs

Visitors arriving by air pass through a passport checkpoint in the airport terminal. Those arriving by train do this at the border. Uniformed border guards check passports and stamp visas. (A passport is never stamped. One page of the visa is removed upon arrival. The rest of it is turned in upon leaving the country.) Soviet customs declarations are issued during your flight or train ride, or one can be picked up from stands, located near the baggage claim area in the airport. Fill in exactly how much foreign currency you are bringing into the country (there is no limit unless it is ridiculously high). Declare your valuables (gold, silver, jewelry, etc.). An inspector will look at or through your luggage in varying degrees and stamp your declaration. Do not misplace it. You need it to exchange money and leave the country. Your valuables could be confiscated if you cannot prove that you brought them into the country. On departure, another declaration (same format) must be filled out, which is compared to your original. Make sure you are not leaving the country with more foreign currency than you declared upon arrival. Even though Soviet customs has become considerably easier and faster than in past years, your bags may be thoroughly searched when you leave. Do not overwrap items, which may be picked for inspection.

It is forbidden to bring in what is considered anti-Soviet material and pornography. You may be asked to show all your printed matter. Drugs, other than medicinal, are highly illegal. Any video or small-film camera, VCR, personal computer, or typewriter should be noted on the customs form. You must exit with these items (unless you have official permission to leave them) or else pay a huge duty up to the full worth of the items in question. In addition, any exposed movie film or pre-recorded cassettes may be confiscated upon arrival and held a few days for review. You cannot leave with antiques, icons, or expensive works of art, unless you have permission from the Ministry of Culture. A law states that any Soviet book printed before 1975 cannot be taken out of the country. This is not stringently upheld, but books have been confiscated; it is advisable not to pack such printed matter right at the top of your suitcase.

Currency Exchange

It is illegal to bring in and take out Soviet currency. (Small change is accepted as a souvenir.) Officially, foreign currency can only be converted into rubles at exchange offices at fixed rates. You can convert some currency to rubles at the airport or in your hotel. The customs declaration form must be presented when money is exchanged. The date and amount converted is noted on the form. You can re-exchange your unused rubles at the end of your trip (not before) at the airport or border. Remember when exiting that you cannot convert more rubles than you officially exchanged. As it is illegal to change foreign currency on the black market, if the opportunity presents itself, be discreet, and forewarned that you can be arrested. An interesting note is that the Soviet government, in a major move on November 1, 1989, devalued the ruble by 90 percent. The ruble, for many years, was worth about $1.60; now it is worth about 16 cents. This was to bring the ruble closer to its actual value and discourage the huge black-market exchanges. It also provided a further step in bringing the ruble closer to an open exchange on the world market.

Traveler's Checks And Credit Cards
Traveler's checks and foreign cash are accepted at banks and Beriozkas, the foreign currency stores. It's advisable to bring cash, especially small notes and change. Very often the Beriozkas will not have your currency and will give change in a mixture of other foreign currencies. Also, foreign-currency bars and restaurants found in hotels do not often accept traveler's checks. And it is very difficult to change traveler's checks into foreign cash. Major credit cards are accepted at Intourist hotels, Beriozkas and some hotel restaurants. You should have rubles for regular stores and local transportation.

Valuables
Hotels usually have safety deposit boxes by the front desk. It is advisable to lock up your valuables, money, passport and airline tickets. In case of loss or theft, notify the Service Bureau at your hotel.

Health
Immunizations are not required, unless you are coming from an infected area. The Soviet Union does not have many health risks, except for the cold and food! Some people may have trouble adjusting to Russian cuisine, which includes heavy breads, thick greasy soups, smoked fish and sour cream. Vegetables and fruit are in low supply. Bring indigestion or stomach-disorder remedies. If you are a vegetarian or require a special diet, bring along what you need, even if it is instant, freeze-dried

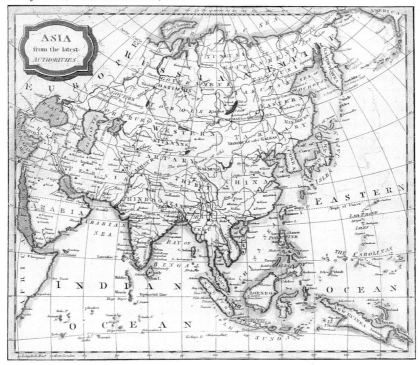

mixes or nutritional supplements. In the wintertime, be prepared for a possible cold. Do not drink the water, especially in Leningrad, where it is highly polluted. The parasite, *giardia lamblia*, can cause severe illness. Drink bottled or boiled water. The bottled water does have an enormously high salt content; you may prefer soda or tea. Juices or flavored sugar waters cannot always be trusted, and watch out for iced drinks. In case of any illness, medical care in the Soviet Union is free of charge. Each hotel usually has its own resident physician. For a serious illness, contact your embassy or consulate and consider leaving the country for proper care. If you have a health ailment, consider purchasing some type of travel medical insurance before the trip. Do note that even though some areas of the USSR are experiencing unrest, it is considered safe to walk around Moscow and Leningrad any time during the day or evening. As in any big city, just take care of your valuables.

Getting Around

When arriving in Moscow, group travelers are automatically taken by bus to their hotel. Individual travelers should hold a transportation voucher issued at home before departure. For those without transportation, inquire at the Intourist desk. Or bargain with drivers of taxis or individual cars for a ride into town. Remember to reconfirm your departure flight. This can be done through the Intourist desk at your hotel or by phoning the airlines directly. Reconfirm internal flights as well, for they tend to be overbooked.

Inter-City Movement
Most of your bookings have been taken care of before your arrival. Report any changes in plans to Intourist. If you would like to extend your visa, visit another city that is not on your itinerary or make train or plane reservations, check at the hotel's Intourist desk. Always do this as soon as you can.

By Air
The airports used for internal flights are much more crowded and chaotic than the international airports. Special preference is usually given to foreign groups at check-in, and Intourist waiting areas are provided. Passports and visas are required at check-in. Boarding passes are issued, either with open seating or with seat numbers, and rows written in Cyrillic. Groups are usually seated first on the plane. Remember that the locals are quite assertive and will push vigorously to get on the plane, especially with open seating. On internal flights, there is one class and no non-smoking sections. Sometimes the only meal consists of seltzer water, bread and cucumbers! Bring along some snacks. There is no airport departure tax.

By Train
Trains are much more fun than flying. The Red Arrow trains between Moscow and Leningrad are a wonderful way to travel. Board the sleeper at night and arrive the next morning for a full day of sightseeing. Since there are several train stations in each city, make sure you know which one you are departing from. In Moscow, trains for Leningrad leave from the *Leningradski Vokzal*, the Leningrad station. In Leningrad, they leave from the *Moskovski Vokzal*, the Moscow station. The trains always leave on time with a broadcasted five-minute warning before departure — and that is all! So do not miss the train! First class has two berths to a compartment and second class has four. This is an excellent way to meet Russians. A personal car attendant will bring tea (brewed in the car's samovar) and biscuits, and wake you up in the morning. Remember to

turn off the radio at night or the National Anthem will blast you awake at 6 a.m. The compartments are not segregated. If there is a problem, the attendent can usually arrange a swap. Foreigners cannot buy train or plane tickets at stations or ticket counters. Tickets must be bought through Intourist, and each city you visit must be listed on your visa.

By Bus and Coach

Group tourists are shown around Moscow and Leningrad by coach. Often the buses are not air conditioned, but all are heated in winter. Individual travelers can sign up through Intourist for city sightseeing excursions; check at Intourist for a listing. Comfortable coach excursions are also offered to areas in the Golden Ring. Always remember the number of your bus; parking lots tend to fill up quickly.

Local Buses, Trams and Trolleys

Local transportation operates from 6 a.m. to 1 a.m. and is charged by distance. A short hop is five kopeks. Rides run by the honor system. Either you put five kopeks into a machine and roll out a ticket by hand or you must pre-purchase tickets at a special kiosk. These get stamped with a device on the wall. Sometimes there are control checks; the fine is three rubles. You may find someone muttering *"peredaitye pazhalsta"* ("please pass this on"), and thrusting a few kopeks into your hand! This is meant to be passed back to the ticket machine where a ticket, in turn, will find its way back to the donor. Even if you do not speak Russian, people will help to direct you to the proper bus or stop. Never be afraid to ask, even if in sign language! Many Russians understand a little English, German or French.

Metro

The Metro is the quickest and least expensive way (five kopeks to any destination) to get around Moscow and Leningrad. More than eight million people ride the Moscow Metro daily. Trains run every 50 seconds during rush hour. Central stations are beautifully decorated with chandeliers and mosaics. Metro stations are easy to spot; entrances on the street are marked with a large "M". Even the long escalator rides are great entertainment. Metro maps can be purchased in the hotels and are posted inside each station. Automatic machines change 20, 15, and 10 kopek coins to five-kopek coins. Deposit a five-kopek coin in the turnstile. Wait for the green light — the doors do close, with a ghastly

thrust, if nothing has registered. All stations and transfer areas are clearly marked in Russian. If you do not read Cyrillic, have someone write down the name of your destination in Russian. People are always most helpful and will point you in the proper direction. It is time to be adventurous!

Taxi

Taxi service desks are located in the lobbies of most hotels. Here you can order a taxi — but at least one to two hours in advance, if not the night before! A service fee of one ruble is charged. If the desk says *nyet*, no taxis available, simply walk to the front of the hotel. Many times a taxi or private car can be found. Payment is made directly to the driver in rubles; each taxi should have a meter. Hailing taxis on the street can be a problem and some will request some other form of payment, like Marlboro cigarettes (try to carry a few packs at all times). It is illegal to pay in foreign currency, but some travelers do so in order to get a ride. Use your own judgement. Hitching is quite common also, since taxis are not always available, and private cars are eager to earn a few extra rubles by picking up paying passengers.

Car Hire

Many hotels offer car service with a driver. A guide can also be hired for the day. This must be paid in foreign currency. Outside the hotel, you will usually find many cars and off-duty taxi drivers who will be open to a suggestion. Some can be hired for the day to take you around town. Make your own payment agreement beforehand. Moscow and Leningrad have a few rent-a-car companies. Driving in Russia is worse than Rome! In addition, all signs are written in Russian and gas stations are hard to find (and have huge lines). It is best to hire a car or use public transportation. It is also possible to drive your own car in from Europe. This requires advance planning and permits, since a few borders are crossed and special insurance is necessary.

Being There

Hotels

Most group tours are provided with first-class hotel accommodation. Intourist hotels usually offer deluxe, first-class or tourist accommoda- tion. For individual travelers, hotels are the most expensive part of the stay. To visit Russia, you must pay the fixed rate for Soviet Intourist hotels, which are expensive, costing up to $200 per person a night. (Note that in most instances it costs only a few rubles extra for a double room.) Cheap hotels, hostels or dormitories are virtually non-existent. (One can "camp" at designated campgrounds, but this must be set up before entering the country and arranged far in advance.)

Upon arrival, hand in your passport and visa. The hotel registers you and returns everything within a few days. (Notice that the hotel dates are stamped on the back of your visa. If you exit the country and have not been stamped, you may be pulled aside for questioning. Make sure a hotel stamp appears on the back of your visa.) You will also be issued a hotel card (*propusk*). Keep this with you at all times. You need to show it to the doorman, who might block your entrance until the card is shown. This is because Soviets are not allowed to enter the Intourist hotels, unless they are registered guests.

If you have Soviet visitors, they must register in the hotel and leave by around ll p.m. (You can try meeting them outside and walking in past the doorman speaking to them in English. If they go unnoticed, usually they can go "unregistered.") They could get in trouble for spending the night.

The name of the hotel is written in Russian on the hotel card, which can be shown to taxis, etc. Most hotels still have a *dezhurnaya* (hall attendant) on each floor. When you show her your hotel card, she will give you the key. (Some "westernized" hotels just issue the key at the front desk.) The *dezhurnaya* is also positioned to notice all that is happening in your hallway. She is very helpful and friendly; if you have a question, she is the one to ask. Most rooms are quite adequate, but they sometimes do not match your conception of a first-class hotel, particularly those outside Moscow and Leningrad. They have a bathroom, TV and phone, but many lack room service. A laundry bag is provided in each room; dry-cleaning services are not often available. Give your clothes to the maid or *dezhurnaya*. It's usually same-day or two-day service.

A word of warning: Housekeepers in the USSR often lack a respect for privacy, and enter the room without knocking, or bring back your laundry at midnight. Use the chain lock! Most hotels do not have a central switchboard — which means someone calling the main number of the hotel will not be able to contact you. Each room has a phone with a corresponding seven-digit number. Only if the caller knows this

Maybe Yes, Maybe No

*D*ecember 24. *A few words about my room. Every piece of furniture in it bears a tin tag with the words* Moscow Hotels *and then the inventory number. The hotels are collectively administered by the state (or the city?). The double windows of my room have been sealed shut for the winter. Only a small flap toward the top can be opened. The small washtable is made of tin, lacquered below and with a very polished top and a mirror in addition. The bottom of the basin has three drain holes that cannot be plugged. A thin stream of water flows from a faucet. The room is heated from the exterior, but given its particular location, the floor is also warm and even when the weather is moderately cold, the heat becomes oppressive as soon as you close the little window. Every morning before nine, when the heat is turned on, an employee knocks at the door to check if the trap window has been shut. This is the only thing that one can rely on here. The hotel has no kitchen, so one can't even get a cup of tea. Once, the evening before we drove out to see Daga, we asked to be awakened the following morning, and a Shakespearian conversation on the theme of "waking" ensued between Reich and the Swiss (which is the Russian name for hotel porter). The man's reply to our request to be awakened: "If we think of it, we'll wake you. But if we don't think of it, we won't. Actually, we usually think of it, in which case we do wake people. But to be sure, we also occasionally forget to when we don't think of it. In which case we don't. We're of course under no obligation, but if we remember in time, then naturally we do. When do you want to be awakened?—At seven. We'll make a note of that. See, I'm putting the message here, let's hope he finds it. Of course if he doesn't, he won't wake you. But usually we in fact do." In the end we were of course not wakened and they explained: "You were already up, what was the point of waking you?"*

Walter Benjamin, Moscow Diary

number can he or she call you directly — either from another room in the hotel or from outside. A red light on the nightstand usually means you owe money. Each spring/summer many hydroelectrical plants shut down a few weeks for spring cleaning, and large sections of the city may be without hot water, including your hotel.

Hotels have a restaurant, a few cafes located on different floors, foreign currency bars and a post office. A brochure is usually provided in each room listing the facilities and phone numbers. Most Intourist hotels are accustomed to catering to groups. Sometimes it is quite impossible for an individual to get a table in a restaurant for lunch or dinner without a reservation or a group. This can get quite frustrating. Make a reservation in the morning at the service desk. Many hotels now offer the "Swedish table", a cafeteria-style restaurant. Check to see if your hotel has one. Here a quick inexpensive smorgasborg-type breakfast, lunch or dinner can be found.

Communications
Communications can be a *bolshoi* problem in the Soviet Union! Be patient. Calls to the States can take days, but those to Europe go through faster. You can order a call for a specific time at the Service Bureau in your hotel. Your call may come through immediately (put through to your room); sometimes your waiting period is two days or more. (Try to reserve a call for the evening. This way, if it is late, you will be in your

room and will not have to miss a tour.) There is also a central number in each city that you can dial directly to place a phone order. The operator usually speaks English. Note that sometimes the operators disconnect if an answering machine comes on so try to forewarn the operator when ordering the call.

Also, be prepared for overseas calls to be quite expensive. To call anywhere in the States at any time costs about $10 per minute. England is $5 per minute. (You can pay in rubles.) Local calls can be made from the hotel room, free of charge. Long-distance calls within the USSR can be made (also from your room) once you know the area code. For example, Moscow is 095 and Leningrad 812. To call Moscow from

Leningrad dial 8 (to get a long-distance line), then 095 and the seven-digit number. To make a local call from the street: pay phones take two kopeks. Use either a two-kopek piece or two one-kopek pieces. A 10-kopek coin also works.

Special "long-distance" phones can also be used for calling other cities within the Soviet Union. Here you must use 15-kopek coins only. Deposit the coins and remember to push the black button at the bottom when the call goes through. You can also go to the city's long-distance telephone center (*peregovorny punkt*). You must preorder and pay for the number of minutes of your call. There is usually a waiting line. The number of the booth you are assigned to is announced by loudspeaker. Some hotels have telex and fax facilities.

The post office sends telegrams and packages, but do not wrap the package. The contents must be inspected before shipping. Mail is slow and erratic. Many travelers arrive home before their postcards! Any mail sent to the USSR takes several weeks to a month. If you are staying for a length of time, mail to each city can be addressed to either "Post Restante" or care of Intourist. The Moscow address is Hotel Intourist (Poste Restante), 3/5 Gorky St., K-600 Moscow, USSR. In Leningrad: Poste Restante, C-400/ 6 Nevsky Prospect, Leningrad. If you know what hotel you will be staying in, have mail addressed to you care of that hotel. Mail will not be delivered to you in your room, nor will you be contacted. You must check at the lobby service counter, which gives you the whole guest-mail stack to sift through.

Money
Soviet currency is the *ruble*. It comes in note denominations of 1, 3, 5, 10, 25, 50 and 100. The ruble is divided into 100 *kopeks*. There are 1, 2, 3, 5, 10, 15, 20, 50 kopek coins and a one-ruble coin.

Shopping Hours
Most local stores open between 8 and 10 a.m. and close between 5 and 8 p.m. They close for an hour sometime between 12 and 3 p.m. for lunch. Restaurants and cafes also close for a few hours during the day. If you are on a tight schedule, try to check operating hours first. Beriozkas are open from 9 a.m. to 8-11 p.m. Some also close an hour for lunch. Check the Practical Information section at the back of the book for holiday and festival dates, when stores are usually closed.

Photography Restrictions
You may photograph anything you wish except for the following: military installations, border areas, airports and from airplanes inside the country, railway stations, bridges, tunnels, power and radar stations, telephone and telegraph centers and industrial enterprises. If you are not sure, inquire before you shoot. Ask permission at factories, state institutions and farms — and of individuals, who may not want their picture taken. Understand that Soviets are sometimes sensitive about foreigners photographing what they perceive as being backward or in poor condition. Always remain courteous.

Travel Restrictions
One cannot venture more than 35 kilometers outside of the city. Only

the cities specified on the visa can be visited. Unless the visa is extended, one must exit the country on the date shown on the visa.

Speculators

Especially in the big cities, you will most likely be approached by people asking, "Do you speak English?" and trying to sell everything from lacquer boxes and caviar to army watches. Some may even want to buy your clothes. The government is trying to discourage speculation, since most want to sell their wares for foreign currency and dealing in foreign currency is illegal. Work out your own bargain, but be discreet. Many will ask to change money; it is best to stay away. One added note: these days, any male may be approached by an attractive lady in a hotel bar or even elevator. Prostitution is becoming a large problem in Moscow and Leningrad. Paying for more than a drink can lead to an arrest. Plainclothes police often patrol the hotel.

Etiquette

Russians on the surface appear very restrained, formal, even somewhat glum. But there is a dichotomy between public and private appearance. In private and informal situations or after friendship is established, their character is suddenly charged with emotional warmth, care and humor. They are intensely loyal and willing to help. Arriving in or leaving the country will merit great displays of affection, usually with flowers, bear hugs, kisses and tears. If invited to someone's home for dinner, expect large preparations. The Russians are some of the most hospitable people in the world. If you cannot handle alcohol, watch out for the endless number of toasts!

The formal use of the "patronymic" (where the father's first name becomes the children's middle name) has been used for centuries. For example, if Ivan names his son Alexander, Alexander's patronymic is Ivanovich. Especially in formal or business dealings, try to remember the person's patronymic: Alexander Ivanovich, or Mariya Pavlova (her father's name is Pavel or Paul). As with Western names, where Robert is shortened to Bob, the same is done with Russian first names, once you have established a friendship. Call your friend Alexander "Sasha", Mikhail "Misha", and Mariya "Masha", or use the diminutive form, "Mashenka".

Complaints

Each restaurant and cafe has a service book (*kniga zhalov*), where you can register complaints. Hotel complaints can be reported to the service desk. Remember that rules, regulations and bureaucracy play a large role in Soviet life — with many uniformed people enforcing them. People here are not always presumed innocent until proven guilty. When dealing with police or other officials, it is best to be courteous while explaining a situation. For example, police in the streets will randomly pull over vehicles to spot-check the registration. If you are pulled over, it does not mean you did anything wrong. If you are kept waiting long, as in restaurants for service, remember that everyone else is waiting too. Be patient and remember you are in a foreign country. Do not lose your temper (humor often works better), mock or laugh when not appropriate.

A few commonly used words are *nyet* and *nelzya*, which mean "no and "it's forbidden." The Russian language uses many negations. If someone tells you that something is forbidden, it may mean that they simply do not know or want to take responsibility for something. Ask elsewhere. The *babushki* are a hearty breed and love to take on the voice of authority!

Food

Russian cooking is both tasty and filling, and in addition to the expected borsch and beef stroganov, it includes many delectable regional dishes from the 15 republics such as Uzbekistan, Georgia or the Ukraine.

The traditions of Russian cooking date back to the simple recipes of the peasantry, who made full use of the abundant supply of potatoes, cabbage, cucumbers, onions and bread to fill their hungry stomachs. For the cold northern winters, they would pickle the few available vegetables, and preserve fruits to make jam. The somewhat bland diet was pepped up with sour cream, parsley, dill and other dried herbs. A popular old Russian saying expressed this: *Shchi da kasha, Pishcha nasha*, "Cabbage soup and porridge are our food". The writer, Nikolai Gogol, painted a picture of the Russian peasant's kitchen: "In the room was the old familiar friend found in every kitchen, namely a *samovar* and a three-cornered cupboard with cups and teapots, painted eggs hanging on red and blue ribbons in front of the icons, with flat cakes, horseradish and sour cream on the table along with bunches of dried fragrant herbs and a jug of *kvas*" (dark beer made from fermented black bread). Russians are still quite proud of these basic ingredients in their diet, which remain the staples of the Russian meal today. They will boast that there is no better bread (*khleb*) in the world than a freshly baked loaf of Russian black bread. Raisa Gorbachev presented Nancy Reagan with a cookbook containing hundreds of potato recipes!

Peter the Great introduced French cooking to his empire in the 18th century. While the peasantry had access only to the land's crops, the nobility hired its own French cooks, who introduced eating as an art, and often prepared up to ten elaborate courses, filled with delicacies. Even-

tually many of the Russian writers ridiculed the monotonous and gluttonous life of the aristocracy, many of whom planned their days around meals. Ivan Goncharov coined the term "Oblomovism" in his novel *Oblomov* (1859) to characterize the sluggish and decadent life of the Russian gentry. In *Dead Souls*, Nikolai Gogol described a typical meal enjoyed by his main character in the home of an aristocrat. "On the table there appeared a white sturgeon, ordinary sturgeon, salmon, pressed caviar, fresh caviar, herrings, smoked tongues and dried sturgeon. Then there was a baked 300-pound sturgeon, a pie stuffed with mushrooms, fried pastries, dumplings cooked in melted butter, and fruit stewed in honey... After drinking glasses of vodka of a dark olive color, the guests had dessert... After the champagne, they uncorked some bottles of cognac, which put still more spirit into them and made the whole party merrier than ever!"

Vodka was (and still is) the indispensable drink of any class or occasion. Neither the Russian peasant nor aristocrat ever drank vodka without making a thorough job of it! Anton Chekhov wrote of a group of Russian peasants who, "on the Feast of the Intercession, seized the chance to drink for three days. They drank their way through fifty rubles of communal funds...one peasant beat his wife and then continued to drink the cap off his head and boots off his feet!"

Most travelers on a group tour will be provided with up to three meals a day. Breakfast (*zavtrak*) consists of coffee or tea, juice, eggs, kasha, cheese, cold meats or sausage and a plentiful supply of bread and butter. Some hotels now offer a Swedish table, providing a better selection. For those who normally do not start the day with a heavy breakfast, bring along a bottle of instant coffee and cream, packaged oatmeal, and the like, plus an electric coil to boil water in your room. Lunch (*obyed*) consists of soup, bread, salad, and usually a choice of meat, chicken or fish with potatoes, a pickled vegetable and a sweet dessert of cakes or *morozhnoye* (ice cream). Over 170 tons of ice cream are consumed in Moscow and Leningrad each day! Salads or vegetables will include cucumbers, tomatoes, cabbage, beets, potatoes and onions but fresh vegetables and fruit are not abundant. Sour cream (*smetana*) is a popular condiment — Russians love sour cream on everything. Some even drink a glass for breakfast! Dinner (*oozhiin*) is much the same as lunch, except vodka, wine, champagne or cognac will usually be served.

Most hotel restaurants do not offer a wide selection; on a group tour you will be served a fixed menu each day with few alternatives. In addition, many selections which appear on the menu do not exist in the kitchen. If the dish is not priced, it is not available. Hotel and foreign currency restaurants usually have better and faster service. Tipping is accepted (5-10 percent), but use your own judgement — waiters are notorious for disappearing just at the moment you have a question. If you do get discouraged with the service, the meal, or even the language problem (though many menus are written in English, German and Russian), remember always that diplomacy and patience are virtues. Find the boss or the Intourist Desk to express a complaint — or ask for the restaurant's *kniga zhalov* (complaint book).

Dining and Drinking

The first point to remember when dining out is that most Soviets consider eating out an expensive luxury and enjoy turning dinner into a leisurely evening-long experience. Many restaurants provide entertainment, so do not expect a quick bite. In the European fashion, different parties are often seated together at the same table — an excellent way to meet the locals.

If you are short of time, try to eat in your hotel. Hotels are set up to accommodate group tours. Many individual travelers experience difficulties in obtaining a simple meal in their hotel restaurant. If the hotel does not have a Swedish Table buffet (*Shvetski Stol*), you can make a dining room reservation earlier in the day at the Intourist Service Desk. To speed up a meal you can even preorder your appetizers, so that they are on the table when you arrive. Check to see how long a dish takes to prepare — a meat dish may take 10-15 minutes, while chicken sometimes takes up to an hour!

If you are going out to a restaurant, it is also advisable to make a reservation. The sign *Mect Het* may appear, meaning No Space Available. Stick your head in the door; often, if the proprietor notices a foreigner, he will miraculously find an empty table!

Most restaurants (in Cyrillic *pectopah*, pronounced "restoran") are open from 11 a.m. to 11 p.m., and close for a few hours in the afternoon. Restaurants with music and dancing can be on the expensive side. Sometimes no liquor is served, but you can bring your own. Many of the newly opened co-op restaurants specialize in a regional cuisine — such as *shashlik*, shish kebab, or other spicy dishes. Others may provide one choice as the "plat du jour." Even though there may not be a wide selection, the food is usually tasty and the meal served quickly in pleasant surroundings.

As an individual traveler it can be hard to find anything to eat other than bread, sweets or Pepsi Cola, though since *perestroika*, more cafes are springing up about town. Even though smaller than restaurants and with limited menus, they offer an adequate and quick meal. Look for the *zakusochnaya*, a snack-type bar serving hot and cold appetizers that often specialize in one dish, which reflects its name: *Blinnaya* serves *blini*; *Pelmennaya, pelmeni*; *Pirozhkovnaya, pirozhki*; *Shashlichnaya, shashlik*; *Chainaya,* tea. Learn the letters of the Russian alphabet so you can recognize these cafes on the street. All cafes serve coffee or tea and some type of bottled soda. Recently, a few Western fast-food chains have opened in Moscow, such as McDonalds and even Baskin Robbins ice cream.

Bars are found in all the major hotels. For *valuta* (foreign currency), they serve a selection of Soviet and Western sodas, spirits, apertifs, snacks, and sometimes a few hot dishes. At ruble bars, you'll get Russian wines, champagne and cognac, along with espresso coffee, sandwiches and pastries. These are usually open to 2 a.m. Many times a hotel will have a small bar or cafe on your floor. Drink only bottled water, though it is salty; there are many types of bottled sodas. Watch out for iced drinks, chilled fruit juices and *kompot* (fruit in sugared water), which are often made from the local water.

If invited to a Russian home, expect a large welcome. The Russians love hospitality and usually prepare a spread. If you can, bring along a bottle of champagne or vodka — since these are harder for Russians to buy. A toast is usually followed by swigging down the entire shot of vodka — and then another toast! Be aware that vodka adds up after an entire evening of toasts—you may want to consider sipping a few (to the chagrin of your host). Some popular toasts are: *Za Mir I Druzhba* (To Peace and Friendship), *Do Dnya*, (Bottoms Up), and the most popular, *Na Zdoroviye* (To Your Health!).

On the Menu

The menu is divided into four sections: *zakuski* (appetizers), *pervoye* (first course), *vtoroye* (second course), and *sladkoe* (dessert). The ordering is done all at once, from appetizer to dessert. *Zakuski* are Russian-style hors d'oeuvres that include fish, cold meats, salads, and marinated vegetables.

Ikra is caviar: *krasnaya* (red from salmon) and *chornaya* (black from sturgeon). The best is *zernistaya*, the fresh unpressed variety. The most expensive is the black *Beluga*; another is *Sevruga*. Caviar is usually

A New World Indeed

And then the Gypsy Restaurant. I know it has another name but I do not know what it is, or where it is. But since it is a night restaurant of sorts—the only place where a little public night gayety is to be found in all Moscow—it will not be hard for any one who knows Moscow to identify it.

I was taken there by Reswick, the representative of the Associated Press, and we timed ourselves to arrive at midnight, previously taking the trouble to telephone for a table. And knowing the economic and social restrictions of the Soviet Empire at the time, I was more cheered than not, for I had expected little. It is so in Russia. You know that all bourgeois gayety is suspect, and certainly a night restaurant of any description is bourgeois—and so likely to be patronized by conniving capitalists, concessionaries, money hoarders or grafters who are not in sympathy with the Communistic ideal, and so not entitled to gayety, or indeed relaxation in any form. Yet such is the nature of man, as well as all Russians, that it is difficult to taboo quite everything. The heart of him is unregenerate. And being so, some bits of compromise must be made here and there. Only then, a resort such as this becomes a kind of Communist trap. For it tends to draw these unregenerate, and eke secretly gilded flies, out into the light, where they can be pounced upon by the virtuous and self-sacrificing. Ha! ha! You will hoard money, will you? You will graft or profiteer and then come to such a place as this to make merry! Very good, come to the Cheka! Come to the office of the G.P.U. We will look into your affairs. Perhaps you have not paid all your dues, accounted for all of your takings.

So, as I say, I was not a little pleased to find a quite cheery room, not badly lighted; the food, as it proved, good; the music consisting of ten genuine gypsies of assorted ages and sizes all sitting on a

platform, tambours or castanets in hand, and indulging at intervals in
various spirited and yet invariably mournful airs, which recited, as I was
told, how love, and spring, come early and are soon over–how follow the
brief, scorching days of passion and then the sad, brown leaves of autumn
and the snows of winter. "Gather ye rosebuds while ye may." And yet, so
different is the Russian temperament from ours that it can dine and
dance to these airs. And again, so different is the Russian temperament
from ours that it finds nothing incongruous in a night restaurant where
the music is furnished by ten none-too-attractive and, in certain in-
stances withered and wrinkled gypsies, their ears dangling bangles, their
brown, clawy hands thrumming tambours or strings, their throats
chanting wistful and yet defiant tunes of the sorrows that befall us all.
Indeed, my friend, who was surely a Russian man of the world, was
enthusiastic in his praise, beating time with his hands and stamping with
his feet and saying how lovely the old sad airs were–how wistful and
tearful and hence wonderful. And all the other diners equally loud in
their approval.

"Yet imagine this in New York or Chicago," I thought! "Imagine
any night club employing such a world-worn and sinister group as this!
Imagine! 'Tis Russia, and none other than Russia."

But I am running ahead of myself. What really interested me at
first, and after, were the patrons themselves. Here we were, now in the
only public night resort of any consequence, and yet see how it was–low-
ceiled and decorated not at all, the furniture of that same mixed and au
contraire character that marked the Restaurant Tolstoi. And apart from
a few men and women in evening dress (how very few, indeed!), an
assortment of garments that left me breathless. Upon my word, this is the
new, free, different world, this Russia of to-day. For here now comes a
strapping young fellow, his plump, pasty-faced girl on his arm, and
while she is in flouncy white and wears high-heeled slippers, he is in the
standardized dark blue blouse and leather belt, his trousers passing into
high polished boots, his oily black hair combed backward in long graceful
lines over his ears. And behind him, at another table, with his girl, as
dark and curly as an Italian Juliet, a blondish youth in a light summer
suit far from new and such as one might wear in July–never in

December–yet as swagger as you please on account of it. For mark you, these western suits of whatever vintage, even with an occasional patch, are not to be had in Russia at all. They do not make such cloth–(too luxurious as yet)–and they cannot afford to import it. The cheaper grades cost plenty here, God knows! And so should a foreigner arrive and sell such a suit or leave it indifferently behind–Presto! a Russian, below the rank of an official, say, in a new and smart outfit! And the wonder of it, English or American! Cut right, and with a distinctive pattern. Ha, ha! And yet, as you say to yourself, the knees bag, and surely the thing doesn't fit as well as it should. But who are you to judge? Are not you the outsider? It is the Russian, the insider, who will be impressed by this. And so...no wonder he is applauding loudly, and the girl, too.

But our evening is young. Wait! Here comes a Kalmuk, with an overcoat that I swear has somehow the look of a corset attached to a hoopskirt–(the skeleton frame, I mean), and with a fur hat that has the dimensions of a very, very, very wide and decidedly truncated dish pan. And with him his girl or wife–small, brown, black-eyed, intense, and even a little savage-looking, and in a combination of things half silk, half linen, that are green, yellow, brown, black, purple. You gaze and are impressed. For after all, if this were a stage–the chorus of some colorful show–it could not be so much better.

And then next, a really portly Russian, of perhaps the trader or bloodsucker type–fat, red-cheeked, double-chinned, puffy-necked, a really beastlike type. And with him two attractive and yet semi-obese girls or women of not over twenty-six or seven, with a heavy, meaty sensuality radiating from every pore. The white flabby double chins and crinkled necks. The small and yet fat and even puffy hands. The little, shrewd, greedy eyes, half concealed by fat lids. And yet they too are moved by those gypsy laments, and sing or beat time with their heavily bejeweled fingers. Surely some Cheka agent or G.P.U. will see these and call our fat friend to an accounting on the morrow. Surely, surely.

But along with these the artist types. And writers. Ho, should they be excluded? And why, pray? The outer door is heard to close and here enters, as brisk and flippant as the chill wind he brings with him, Ivan Ivanovitch, say–painter or sculptor or poet, and looking all three. That flaring chrysanthemum hair. The thin, yellow, downy mustaches. The long, waxy, artistic, and yet vital hands. The swagger and even defiant or tolerant air. You think perhaps that he is to be overawed by poverty, or defeated by the gayety of this place. Go to! Heigh, ho! We artists will show you what art and poverty are like, and genius also! And so, an overcoat! (I am not exaggerating. God forgive me, should I!) And so an overcoat (and in this Moscow weather no less), of nothing other than cretonne or its loom sister–a vari-colored and flaring, posterish thing of quite Chinese exuberances, as who should say the more of this, the better. And to top the thing off–yellow gloves. And worn with what an air! Surely in this case it is the manner and not the clothes that make the man. But with his girl on his arm or preceding him, in a trim English walking suit, which has been come by God knows how! Yet not expensive. No, no. A thing that could be picked up in London for twenty shillings, or in New York on Fourteenth Street for nine or ten dollars. But here in Moscow, heigh, ho!

Indeed I might continue this for pages. For Moscow, and all Russia for that matter, is to-day picturesque if poor–all the more so because it is poor. And patches and rags and makeshift and mixtures of the most amazing character are the veriest commonplaces of the hour. Yet as for being deplored–nonsense! Who is rich? Who can be rich? And as for bourgeois, capitalist, fashions, pouf! Also tush! We will do these things as we wish, devise new ways and means. And so you yourself, fresh from London, or New York, and with all your capitalistic and other class notions still strong upon you are suddenly swept into the newness, the strangeness, the freshness of it all. Heigh ho! Bully for a new day! Bully for a new idea! To hell with fashion plates, with what the west, or the north, or the south, may think! This is Russia. This is the new, shifting, shimmering, changeful, colorful, classless day of a new social order. A new world indeed. A fresh deal. Verily. Selah. And let us hope that no real harm comes to it, lest something fresh and strange and new and of glorious promise pass from the eyes and the minds and the hopes of men.

Theodore Dreiser, Dreiser Looks at Russia, 1928

available at Intourist restaurants and can be bought in the Beriozka shops.

Many varieties of Russian soup are served, more often at lunch than dinner. *Borsch* is the traditional red beet soup made with beef and served with a spoonful of sour cream. *Solyanka* is a tomato-based soup with chunks of fish or meat and topped with diced olives and lemon. *Shchi* is a tasty cabbage soup. A soup made from pickled vegetables is *rasolnik*. *Okroshka* is a cold soup made from a *kvas* base.

Meals consist of meat (*mya'so*), chicken (*kur'iitsa*), or fish (*rii'ba*). *Bifshtek* is a small fried steak with onions and potatoes. Beef Stroganov is cooked in sour cream and served with fried potatoes. *Kutlyeta po Kiyevski* is Chicken Kiev, stuffed with melted butter (cut slowly!); *Kutlyeta po Pajarski* is a chicken cutlet; *Tabak* is a slightly seasoned fried or grilled chicken. The fish served is usually salmon, sturgeon, herring or halibut.

Other dishes include *blini*, small pancakes with different fillings; *pelmeni*, boiled dumplings filled with meat and served with sour cream; and *pirozhki*, fried rolls with a meat filling.

Dessert includes such sweets as *vareniki*, sweet fruit dumplings topped with sugar, *tort* (cake), *ponchiki* (sugared donuts), or *morozhnoye* (ice cream).

Chai (tea) comes with every meal. It is always sweet; ask for *biz sak'hera*, for unsweetened tea. Many Russians stir in a spoonful of jam instead of sugar. Coffee is not served as often. Alcoholic drinks consist of *pivo* (beer); *kvas* (like near-beer); *shampanskoye* (champagne); *vino* (wine) and vodka. Alcoholic drinks are ordered in grams; a small glass is 100 grams and a normal bottle consists of 750 grams or three quarters of a liter. The best wine comes from Georgia and the Crimea. There are both *krasnoye* (red) and *beloye* (white). The champagne is generally sweet. The best brandy comes from Armenia — *Armyanski konyak*. *Nalivka* is a fruit liquer. Vodka is by far the favorite drink and comes in a number of varieties other than Stolichnaya, Moskovskaya or Russkaya. There is *limonnaya* (lemon vodka), *persovka* (with hot peppers), *zubrovka* (flavored with a special grass), *ryabinovka* (made from ash berries), *tminaya* (caraway flavor), *starka* (a smooth dark vodka), *ahotnichaya vodka* (hunter's vodka), and *zveroboy* (animal killer!). One of the strongest and most expensive is *Zolotoye Koltso*, the Golden Ring. Vodka can be most easily found in the Beriozkas, along with beer, champagne, wine and Western alcohols.

Shopping

Most group travelers to the Soviet Union don't have much time, in between excursions, to spend on leisurely shopping. Besides, unlike other countries in the world, the Soviet Union is not a shopper's paradise. Stores don't brim over with speciality goods, and many items are always in short supply. Most goods are set at a fixed (state) price, sales are rare, and bargaining is not widely practiced.

The Beriozka

The best, quickest and most convenient way to shop is at the Beriozka, the foreign currency store, which is usually located right in your hotel. These range from a few counters to large two-story emporiums that resemble a Western department store. Beriozkas *only* accept foreign currency (cash, traveler's checks, credit cards). Bring a supply of small bills and change — the clerk gives change in whatever currency is left in the cash register.

The Beriozkas have the best selection of Soviet goods at the most reasonable prices. Many times the same product is more expensive (in rubles) in local stores, if it can be found at all. Probably the most popular Russian souvenir is the *matryoshka*, the painted set of nested dolls. *Khokhloma* lacquerware comes in the form of trays, cups, spoons, bowls and vases. There are also miniature painted lacquer boxes and brooches from the Golden Ring villages of Palekh and Fedoskino. Other good buys are handicrafts, wood carvings, amber, fur hats, embroidered shawls and linens, lace, filigree jewelry, ceramics, samovars, balalaikas, painted eggs, caviar, tea and tea sets, vodka, books, records, and *znachki* (small pins used for trading). These stores also have a small supply of food, snacks, sodas, liquor, and cigarettes. It's good to pick up a few items for late-night munchies.

Most Beriozkas are open from 9 a.m. to 8 p.m. daily and close an hour for lunch sometime between 12 and 3 p.m. In Moscow, the largest Beriozkas are in the Rossiya, Mezhdunarodnaya and Ukrainia hotels. Your hotel also has small kiosks and post offices that sell foreign newspapers, magazines and books, postcards, stamps, and pins.

The Local Store

If there's time, try to visit a few of the local stores about town. This gives a much better feel for the shopping life of the average Soviet citizen. These stores accept only rubles, no traveler's checks or credit cards. Some of the store designations are: *univermag*, the large department store; *kommissioniye*, commission or second-hand store, *co-op*, cooperative; *rinoks*, the farmers' market; and *kiosks*. Most stores are open daily (except Sundays) from about 10 a.m. to 8 p.m., and close for an hour for lunch.

Shopping Tips

Usually the procedure for purchasing an item in a local store involves several steps. First, locate the desired item and find out its price. Second, go to the *kassa* (cashier's booth) and pay. Third, bring the receipt back to the salesgirl, who will wrap and hand over your purchase. Prices are usually posted, especially in food stores. If things get too mathematical for you to fathom (one kilo of chocolate is three rubles and one kilo of candy is two rubles and you want a quarter kilo of each), ask a salesgirl to give you the total. Most stores still use an abacus to tally. Know your exact bill; if you are even one kopek off, you must return to the cashier to pay the discrepency! Sometimes you'll have to muscle your way toward the counter. If you have to stand in a long line (a way of life for most of the population), take the opportunity to practice your Russian. If you have any questions, don't be afraid to ask — many even know a few words of English and would be glad to help. If you see something you like, buy it! Most likely, it won't be there when you go back. Always bring along a small string or shopping bag; the stores and markets don't provide any, and you may wind up having to put two kilos of strawberries in your pocket or purse.

Some of the interesting stores in Moscow are **GUM** Department Store in Red Square, **Detsky Mir** (Children's World) and **Dom Knigi** (House of Books). Popular shopping districts are along the Arbat, Kuznetsky Most, Gorky, Petrovka and Stoleshnikov streets. Many Western companies are coming to Moscow; Christian Dior and Estee Lauder opened shops on Gorky St. For a more complete listing of Beriozkas, and local stores and their locations, see the Practical Information Section.

Moscow

Introduction

Moscow has, for centuries, been an inseparable part of the life of all Russia. Moscow's history dates back more than 800 years to 1147, when Prince Yuri Dolgoruky established the first small outpost on the banks of the Moscow River. The settlement grew into a large and prosperous town, which eventually became the capital of the principality of Moscovy. By the 15th century, Moscow was Russia's political, cultural and trade center, and during the reign of Ivan the Great, it became the capital of the Russian Empire. Ivan summoned the greatest Russian and European architects to create a capital so wondrous that "reality embodied fantasy on an unearthly scale," and soon the city was hailed as the "New Constantinople". In the next century, Ivan the Terrible was crowned the first Czar of all Russia inside the Kremlin's magnificent Uspensky Cathedral. The words of an old Russian proverb suggested the power within the Kremlin: "There is only God and the center of government, the Kremlin." People from all over the world flocked to witness the splendors in the capital of the largest empire on earth. By the 18th century, a foreign traveler wrote that Moscow, "so irregular, so uncommon, so extraordinary, and so contrasted, had never before claimed such astonishment!"

In 1712, after Peter the Great transferred the capital to St. Petersburg, Moscow remained a symbol of national pride. Many eminent writers, scientists, artists and musicians, such as Pushkin, Tolstoy, Lomonosov, Repin and Tchaikovsky, lived and worked in Moscow, which never relinquished its political significance, artistic merit and nostalgic charm. Even when Napoleon invaded in 1812, he wrote "I had no real conception of the grandeur of the city. It possessed fifty palaces of equal beauty to the Palais d'Elysee furnished in French style with incredible luxuries." After a terrible fire destroyed Moscow during Napoleon's hasty retreat, Tolstoy wrote that "it would be difficult to explain what caused the Russians, after the departure of the French in October 1812, to throng to the place that had been known as Moscow; there was left no government, no churches, shrines, riches or houses — yet, it was still the same Moscow it had been in August. All was destroyed, except something intangible, yet powerful and indestructable...Within a year the population of Moscow exceeded what it had been in 1812!" Moscow symbolized the soul of the empire, and Tolstoy later observed that Moscow remains eternal because "Russians look at Moscow as if she is their own mother."

Moscow also played an important role in the country's political movements. The revolutionary writers, Herzen and Belinksy, began their activities at Moscow University. Student organizations supported many revolutionary ideas, from Chernyshevsky's to Marx's. Moscow workers backed the Bolsheviks during the October 1917 Revolution and went on to capture the Kremlin. After more than two centuries, Moscow once again became Russia's capital. But this time, the city would govern the world's first socialist state. Trotsky, Lenin's main supporter, wrote that when "finally all the opposition was overcome, the capital was transferred back to Moscow on March 12, 1918 ...Driving past Nicholas's palace on the wooden paving, I would occasionally glance over at the Emperor Bell and Emperor Cannon. All the barbarism of Moscow glared at me from the hole in the bell and the mouth of the cannon... The carillon in the Saviour's Tower was now altered. Instead of playing 'God Save the Czar,' the bells played the 'Internationale,' slowly and deliberately, at every quarter hour."

Today Moscow is not only the capital of the Soviet Union, but also the capital of the largest of the 15 republics, the Russian Soviet Federation. The Kremlin remains the seat of the Communist Party and the Soviet Government. The largest city in the USSR, Moscow has a population of over nine million.

Whether the visitor has a few days or several weeks, there is always plenty to do and see. Moscow has over 2,500 monuments, 50 theaters and concert halls, 4,500 libraries, 125 cinemas and 70 museums, visited annually by over 20 million people from 150 countries. Moscow is also rich in history, art and architecture. One of the most memorable experiences of your trip to the Soviet Union will be to stand in **Red Square** and look out on the golden magnificence of the cathedrals and towers of the Moscow **Kremlin** and **St. Basil's Cathedral**.

Other attractions include the **Novodevichy Convent** that dates back to 1514 and the **Andronikov Monastery**, which houses the **Andrei Rublev Museum of Old Russian Art** and the famed iconist's masterpieces. Moscow's museums and galleries host the collections of Russian and foreign masters. There are also the cozy side streets to explore, little changed since the time of Ivan the Terrible. The nighttime reflections of the Kremlin's ancient clock tower and golden onion domes on

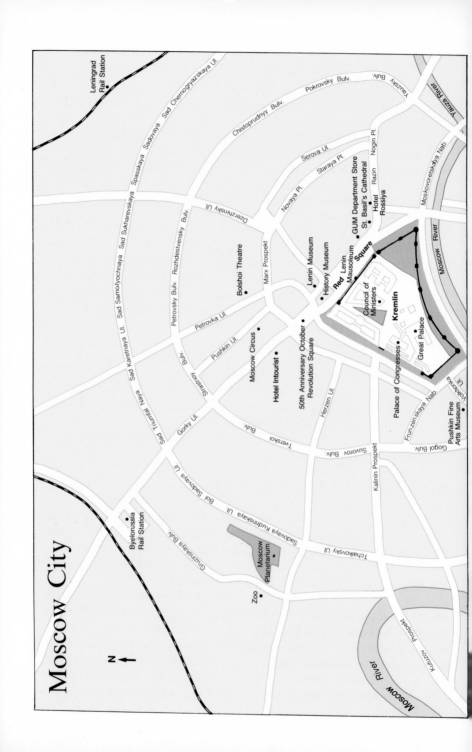

Moscow City

N

Leningrad Rail Station

Byelorussia Rail Station

Pokrovsky Bulv.

Yauzsky Bulv.

Chistoprudnyy Bulv.

Spasskaya

Sadovaya Sad Chernogryazskaya Ul.

Serova Ul.

Yauza River

Staraya Pl.

Sad Sukharevskaya

Novaya Pl.

GUM Department Store

Nogin Pl.

St. Basil's Cathedral

Razin

Hotel Rossiya

Dzerzhinsky Ul.

Sad Samotyochnaya

Rozhdestvensky Bulv.

Marx Prospekt

Lenin Museum

Red Square

Lenin Mausoleum

Moskovoretskaya Nab.

Bolshoi Theatre

History Museum

Petrovsky Bulv.

Council of Ministers

Moscow River

Sad Karetnaya Ul.

Petrovka Ul.

Kremlin

Pushkin Ul.

Moscow Circus

50th Anniversary October Revolution Square

Great Palace

Strastnoi Bulv.

Hotel Intourist

Herzen Ul.

Palace of Congresses

Sad Triumfal Neva

Gorky Ul.

Tverskoi Bulv.

Suvorov Bulv.

Frunzenskaya Nab.

Volkonka Ul.

Gruzinskaya Bulv.

Bol. Sadovaya Ul.

Kalinin Prospekt

Gogol Bulv.

Pushkin Fine Arts Museum

Byelorussia Rail Station

Sadovaya Kudrinskaya Ul.

Tchaikovsky Ul.

Moscow Planetarium

Kutuzov Prospekt

Zoo

Moscow River

Moscow River

Paveletsky
Rail Station

Valovaya Ul.

Zitnaja Ul.

Dmitrova Ul.

Krymsky Val Ul

Kropotkinskaya Nab.

Donskoi Monastery

Gorky Park

Moscow River

Kropotkin Ul

Zubovsky Bulv.

Prospekt

Smolensky Bulv.

Bolshaya Pirogovskaya Ul.

Komsomolsky

Lenin Prospekt

Moscow River

Kiev Rail Station

Novodevichy
Monastery

Lenin Stadium

Lenin Hills Tower

Kosygina Ul.

University

Prospekt

0   200   400   600   800 m

0   200   400   600   800 yards

© The Guidebook Company Ltd

the Moskva River bring to mind the lyrics of one of Russia's most popular songs: "Lazily the river like a silvery stream, ripples gently in the moonlight; and a song fades as in a dream, in the spell of this Moscow night."

Moscow has an eternal enchantment that can be felt in the early light of dawn, in the deepening twilight, on a warm summer's day or in the swirling snow of winter.

Arrival

The route from the international airport into the town center winds along the Leningradsky Highway, linking Moscow with Leningrad. About 14 miles (23 km) from the airport are large anti-tank obstacles, **The Memorial to the Heroes** who defended the city against the Nazi invasion in 1941; notice how close the Germans came to entering the city. The highway turns into Leningradsky Prospekt at a place that used to mark the outer border of the city. Here the street was lined with summer cottages. The **Church of All Saints** (1683) stands at the beginning of the prospekt. Other sights along the route are Peter the Great's Moorish Gothic style **Petrovsky Palace**, built in 1775, and the 60,000-seat Dynamo Stadium. At no. 33 is the **Palace of Newlyweds**, where marriage ceremonies are performed. As you approach the center of Moscow, the Byelorussky Railway Station is on your right. Trains run from here to destinations in Western and Eastern Europe. This station marks the beginning of one of Moscow's main thoroughfares, Ulitsa Gorgovo (Gorky Street).

Before setting out on your first tour, take a minute and study a map of Moscow. Notice that it is made up of a system of rings. The Kremlin and Red Square lie at the center. A series of thoroughfares jut out from the square. Five concentric rings circle Red Square, each historically marking an old boundary of the city, showing its age like a cross-section of a tree.

Centuries ago, each ring was fortified by stone, wooden or earthen ramparts, which one could only enter through a special gate. The area around the Kremlin, once known as *Kitai-gorod*, formed the original border of the city in the 15th and 16th centuries. Many of the streets and squares in this area carry their original names: Petrovskaya Vorota (Peter's Gate), Kitaisky Proyezd (Kitai Passage), Ulitsa Razina (Razin Street), and Valovaya Ulitsa (Rampart Street).

The second ring is known as Bulvarnoye Koltso (Boulevard Ring). The city's suburbs were placed beyond this ring in the 17th century. The Sadovoye Koltso (Garden Ring) is the third ring that runs for ten miles (16 km) around the city. This is also connected by the Koltso Metro line that stops at various points around the ring. The fourth ring, that stretched 25 miles (40 km) around the city, was known as the Kamer-Kollezhsky Rampart; it served as a customs boundary in the 18th and 19th centuries. The fifth ring is the Moscow Circular Road, which marks the present boundary of Moscow. The area past this ring is known as the Green Belt, a protected forested area where many Moscovites have country and summer houses, known as *dachas*.

Metro

One of the quickest and easiest ways of getting around Moscow is by Metro. Construction began in 1931, under Stalin. Many Soviet and foreign architects and engineers spent four years building the deep stations, which served as bomb shelters during WW II. The first line was opened on May 15, 1935. Today, nine lines and over 100 stations connect all points of the city. The Metro (with over 125 miles/200 km of track) operates daily from 6 a.m. to 1 a.m. and the trains are frequent, arriving every 50 seconds during rush hour. Many of the older stations are beautifully decorated with mosaics, marble, stained glass, statues and chandeliers, and are absolutely immaculate. Some of the more interesting ones are: Prospekt Marxa, Mayakovskaya, Byelorusskaya, Komsomolskaya, Kievskaya and Ploshchad Sverdlova.

The Metro is easy to use by looking at a map. All the color-coded lines branch out from a central point, and are intersected by the brown Koltso (Circle) line. Entrances above ground are marked by a large "M." Take the sometimes long and fast escalator down to the station. Maps are located before the turnstiles. It costs five kopeks to any destination. If you do not have a five-kopek coin, automatic machines give change in each station. (Change for ruble notes or 10-day and monthly passes can be purchased at the cashier window.) Since station names are written only in Russian, ask someone to write down the name of your destination. If you have trouble finding your way, show it to the attendant, who usually stands at the entrance — or ask: people are very helpful to strangers and many understand some English. At times, the trains can be crowded and commuters push to get where they're going. Stand near a door as your stop approaches. The names of stops are announced in each

car. Maps of the route are also posted inside each train car (in Russian). Metro tours can be booked through Intourist.

Red Square

Most visitors begin their acquaintance with Moscow in **Red Square**, *Krasnaya Ploshchad*, the heart of the city. It was first mentioned in 15th-century chronicles as the *Torg*, the Great Marketplace and main trading center of the town. From the time of Ivan the Great, the square was used as a huge gathering place for public events, markets, fairs and festivals. Many religious processions came through the square led by the Czar and Patriarch of the Orthodox Church. It was also the scene of political demonstrations and revolts, and the site of public executions.

The magnificent square, which encompasses an area of over 70,000 square meters is bounded by the **Kremlin** walls, **St. Basil's Cathedral**, **Lenin Mausoleum**, the **Historical Museum** and **GUM Department Store**.

Today, national celebrations are held here; on May Day and Revolution Day (November 7), huge parades and festivities fill Red Square. The closest metro stop is Prospekt Marxa.

St. Basil's Cathedral

The square's most famous and eye-catching structure is **St. Basil's Cathedral**. This extraordinary creation was erected by Ivan IV (the Terrible) in 1555-61, to commemorate the annexation to Russia of the Mongol states of Kazan and Astrakhan. Since this occurred on the festival of the Intercession of the Virgin, Ivan the Terrible named it the Cathedral of the Intercession. The names of the architects were unknown until 1896, when old manuscripts mentioning its construction were found. According to legend, Ivan the Terrible had the two architects, Posnik and Barma, blinded so they could never again create such a beautiful church. However, records from 1588, a quarter century after the cathedral's completion, indicate that Posnik and Barma built the chapel at the northeast corner of the Cathedral, where the holy prophet, Basil (Vasily), was buried. Cannonized after his death, Basil the Blessed died the same year (1552) that many of the Mongol Khannates were captured. Basil had opposed the cruelties of Ivan the Terrible; since most of the population also despised the Czar, the Cathedral took on the name of St. Basil's after Ivan's death.

The Cathedral is built of brick in traditional Russian style with colorful, asymmetrical, tent-shaped, helmet and onion domes situated over nine chapels. The interior is filled with 16th- and 17th-century icons and frescoes, and the gallery contains bright wall and ceiling paintings of red, turquoise and yellow flower patterns. Locals often refer to the cathedral as the "stone flower in Red Square". The French stabled their horses here in 1812 and Napoleon wanted to blow it up. Luckily, his order was never carried out.

The interior, now open to the public, has undergone much restoration. Inside is a branch of the Historical Museum that traces the history of the Cathedral and Ivan IV's campaigns. Under the belltower (added in the 17th century), an exhibition room traces the architectural history of St. Basil's with old sketches and plans. The museum is open daily from 9:30 a.m. to 5:30 p.m. except Tuesday and the first Monday of each month.

In front of the cathedral stands the bronze **Monument to Minin and Pozharsky**, the first patriotic monument in Moscow built from public funding; it originally stood in the middle of the square. Sculpted by Ivan Martos in 1818, the monument depicts Kozma Minin and Prince Dmitri Pozharsky, whose leadership drove the Polish invaders out of Moscow in 1612. The pedestal inscription reads "To Citizen Minin and Prince Pozharsky from a grateful Russia 1818."

Near the monument is **Lobnoye Mesto**, the "Place of Skulls". A platform of white stone stood here for more than four centuries, on which public executions were carried out. Church clergymen blessed the crowds and the Czar's orders and edicts were also announced from here.

The Lenin Mausoleum

By the Kremlin wall on the southwest side of the square stands the **Lenin Mausoleum**. Inside, in a glass sarcophagus, lies Vladimir Ilyich Lenin, who died on January 21, 1924. Three days after his death, a wooden structure was erected on this spot. Four months later, it was rebuilt and then replaced in 1930 by the granite, marble and black labradorite mausoleum, designed by Alexei Shchusev. "Lenin" is inscribed in red porphyry. For more than 65 years, Soviets and foreigners have stood in the line that stretches from the end of Red Square to the Mausoleum to view the idolized revolutionary leader and "Father of the Soviet Union". Two guards man the entrance, and at every hour on the hour, as the Kremlin clock chimes, the ceremonial changing of the guard takes place. Exactly two minutes and 45 seconds before the hour,

two armed sentries march toward the entrance of the Mausoleum to relieve the stationed guards.

Photography is prohibited and cameras should be placed out of sight in a bag. Even the slightest impolite gesture, such as placing hands in pockets, will draw a reprimand from the security guards. Once inside, visitors are not allowed to pause and hold up the line. If you are with a group, the tour will usually be brought to the front of the line. If you are not with a tour group, foreign tourists can wait at the corner of the Historical Museum (facing 50th Anniversary of October Square), where officers organize a separate, much shorter line and lead you right in on Tues., Wed., Thurs., and Sat. from noon to 1 p.m. and on Sundays from 1 to 2 p.m. The Mausoleum is open in summer on the same days as above from 9 a.m. to 1 p.m. (in winter 11 a.m. to 2 p.m.) and on Sundays from 9 a.m. to 2 p.m. (in winter from 11 a.m. to 4 p.m.).

Marble reviewing stands on both sides of the Mausoleum hold up to

10,000 spectators on national holidays. Atop the Mausoleum is a tribune, where the heads of the Soviet government and Communist Party stand on May Day and Revolution Day.

Behind the Mausoleum, separated by a row of silver fir trees, are the remains of many of the country's most honored figures in politics, culture and science, whose ashes lie in urns within the Kremlin wall. They include Lenin's sister, his wife, Sergei Kirov, Maxim Gorky, A.K. Lunacharsky, the physicist Sergei Korolyov and the cosmonaut Yuri Gagarin. Foreigners include John Reed and William Hayword (USA), Arthur McManus (England), Clara Zetkin and Fritz Heckert (Germany) and Sen Katayama (Japan). There are also the tomb- stones of previous leaders of the Communist party: Sverdlov, Dzerzhinsky, Frunze, Kalinin, Voroshilov, Suslov and Stalin, who was once buried next to Lenin in the Mausoleum. Nearby are the granite-framed common graves of 500 people who died during the October 1917 Revolution.

The Historical Museum

At the opposite end of the square from St. Basil's is a red-brick building, decorated with numerous spires and *kokoshnik* gables. This houses the **Historical Museum**. It was constructed by Vladimir Sherwood between 1878 and 1883 on the original site where Moscow University was founded in 1755 by the Russian scientist, Mikhail Lomonosov. When opened in 1883, the museum had over 300,000 objects and was supported by private donations. Today, the government museum contains over four million items in 48 halls that house the country's largest archaeological collection, along with manuscripts, books, coins, ornaments and works of art from the Stone Age to the present day. These include birch-bark letters, clothing of Ivan the Terrible, Peter the Great's sleigh, Napoleon's sabre and the "Decree on Peace," written by Lenin. The museum is open Wed. 11 a.m. to 7 p.m., other days 10 a.m. to 6 p.m. It is closed on Tuesday and the last day of each month.

GUM

Next to the Historical Museum, stretching across the entire northeast side of Red Square, is the three-story State Universal Store, known as **GUM**. It is the largest shopping center in the Soviet Union, with a total length of 1.5 miles (2.5 km). It was designed by Alexander Pomerantsev in 1895, when it was known as the Upper Trading Stalls and contained 200 shops. In 1953, the building was reconstructed and now handles almost half a million shoppers a day! It is worth a visit to see the interior of old Russian shops, ornate bridges, ornamental stucco designs and the large glass roof. Souvenir shops are on the ground floor. Open daily 8 a.m. to 9 p.m. and closed on Sunday.

The Kremlin

"The earth as we all know, begins at the Kremlin. It is the central point." (Poet Mayakovsky).

The Moscow **Kremlin**, an outstanding monument of Russian history, winds around a steep slope high above the Moskva River, enclosing an area of over 70 acres next to Red Square. The Russian word *kreml* (that now represents the seat of Soviet government) was once used to de-

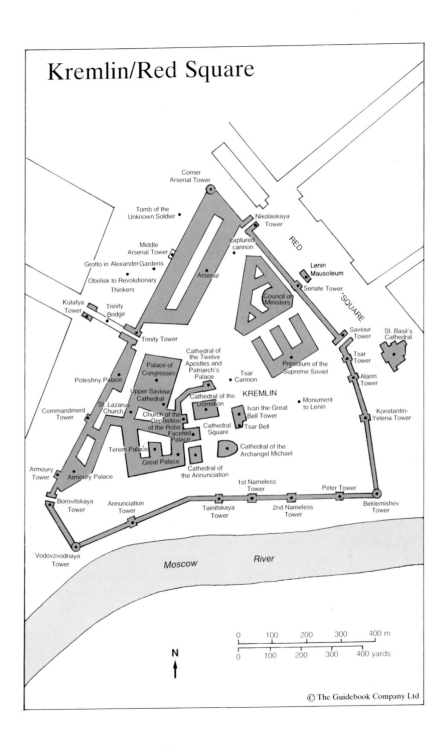

Kremlin/Red Square

Corner Arsenal Tower

Tomb of the Unknown Soldier

Nikolaskaya Tower

RED

Middle Arsenal Tower

captured cannon

Grotto in Alexander Gardens

Obelisk to Revolutionary Thinkers

Arsenal

Lenin Mausoleum

Senate Tower

Council of Ministers

Kutafya Tower

Trinity Bridge

SQUARE

Trinity Tower

Saviour Tower

St. Basil's Cathedral

Cathedral of the Twelve Apostles and Patriarch's Palace

Tsar Tower

Palace of Congresses

Presidium of the Supreme Soviet

Alarm Tower

Poteshny Palace

Tsar Cannon

KREMLIN

Upper Saviour Cathedral

Cathedral of the Dormition

Commandment Tower

St. Lazarus Church

Church of the Deposition of the Robe

Ivan the Great Bell Tower

Monument to Lenin

Konstantin-Yelena Tower

Faceted Palace

Cathedral Square

Tsar Bell

Terem Palace

Cathedral of the Archangel Michael

Armoury Tower

Great Palace

Armoury Palace

Cathedral of the Annunciation

1st Nameless Tower

Peter Tower

Borovitskaya Tower

Annunciation Tower

Tainitskaya Tower

2nd Nameless Tower

Beklemishev Tower

Vodovzvodnaya Tower

Moscow   River

N

| 0 | 100 | 200 | 300 | 400 m |

| 0 | 100 | 200 | 300 | 400 yards |

© The Guidebook Company Ltd

scribe a fortified stronghold that encased a small town. A Russian town was usually built on a high embankment, surrounded by a river and moat, to protect against invasions. The word *kreml* may originate from the Greek *kremnos* meaning "steep escarpment." The medieval kremlin acted as a fortress around a town filled with palaces, churches, monasteries, wooden peasant houses and markets. The Moscow Kremlin was built between the Moskva River and Neglinnaya River, which now flows underground. It is about a half mile (one km) long and up to 62 feet (19 meters) high and 21 feet (6.5 meters) thick. Twenty towers and gates, and over ten churches and palaces lie inside its walls. The Moscow Kremlin has a fascinating eighth-century history. The closest Metro stops are Prospekt Marxa and Biblioteka Imena Lenina.

History

The Kremlin is the oldest historical and architectural feature of Moscow. The first written account of Moscow comes to us from an old chronicle that describes Prince Yuri Dolgoruky of Suzdal receiving Prince Svyatoslav on Borovitsky (now Kremlin) Hill, in 1147. Nine years later, Dolgoruky ordered a fort built on this same hill, which later became his residence. In 1238, the invading Mongols burned the fortress to the ground. By 1326, the Kremlin was encased by thick oak walls, and Grand-Prince Ivan I added two stone churches to the existing wooden ones. During this time, the Metropolitan of Kiev moved the seat of the Orthodox Church from Vladimir to Moscow. In 1367, Prince Dmitri Donskoi replaced the wooden walls with limestone to fortify them against cannon attack. Moscow was referred to as *Beli Gorod*, the "White Town". The Mongols invaded once again in 1382; they razed everything and killed half the population. Within 15 years, the Kremlin walls were rebuilt and the iconists Theophanes the Greek and Andrei Rublev painted the interior frescos of the new Cathedral of the Annunciation.

Ivan III (1460-1505) and his son, Vasily III, were responsible for shaping the Kremlin into its present appearance. Once the Mongols no longer posed a threat to the city, the leaders concentrated more on aesthetic than defensive designs. Ivan the Great commissioned well-known Russian and Italian architects to create a magnificent city to reflect the beauty of the "Third Rome" and the power of the Grand Prince and Metropolitan. The white stone of the Kremlin was replaced by red-brick walls and towers, and the Assumption and Annunciation

cathedrals were rebuilt on a grander scale. During the reign of Ivan IV, the architecture took on more fanciful elements and asymmetrical designs with colorful onion domes and tall pyramidal tent roofs, as embodied in St. Basil's — a style now termed "Old Russian". The Patriarch Nikon barred all tent roofs and ornamental decorations from churches when he took office in 1652, terming the external frills sacrilegious. By 1660, though, the reforms of Nikon had created such schisms in the church that he was forced to step down. Immediately, the old decorative details were again applied to architecture.

Catherine the Great drew up plans to redesign the Kremlin in the new Neo-Classicism, but they were never carried out. During the War of 1812, Napoleon quartered his troops inside the Kremlin for 35 days. Retreating, he tried to blow it up, but townspeople extinguished the burning fuses, though three towers were destroyed. In the mid-1800s, the Kremlin Palace and Armory were built. In 1918, the Soviet government moved the capital back to Moscow and made the Kremlin its permanent seat. Lenin signed a decree to protect the works of art and historical monuments and ordered the buildings restored and turned into museums.

View From Red Square

Red-ruby stars were mounted on the five tallest towers in 1937, replacing the double-headed eagle. The towers of the Kremlin were named after the icons that used to hang above their gates. The most recognizable tower, the **Spasskaya (Saviour) Clock Tower**, stands to the right of St. Basil's. It is 201 feet (67 meters) high and served as the official entrance for the czars, who had to cross a moat over an arched stone bridge to reach the gate. It is now the main entrance used by government officials, who pull up in black limousines. The Saviour Icon once hung above the Spasskaya gate. Inscriptions in Latin and Old Russian name the Italian Solario as the builder in 1491. Later, the Scottish architect Christopher Galloway mounted a clock on its face in the mid-17th century, which was replaced in 1918. It plays the anthem "Internationale", and like Big Ben in London, the chimes of the Spasskaya Tower are broadcast over the radio to mark the hour.

The tower behind Lenin's Mausoleum is known as the **Senate Tower**; it stands in front of the Senate building. To the right of the Mausoleum stands the **Nikolskaya Tower**, where the Icon of St. Nicholas was kept. In 1492, Solario built a corner tower next to a courtyard used by Sobakin Boyars. The **Sobakin Tower** is now called the **Corner Arsenal Tower**, where munitions were stored.

Entering the Kremlin

The two main entrances to the Kremlin are through the Kutafya and Borovitskaya Towers. All group tours are taken through the latter gate on the west side, which is closest to the Kremlin Armory. If you are near the Alexandrov Gardens, go through the **Kutafya Tower** (which runs through the middle of the gardens) from Revolution Square and turn right next to the Metro stop Biblioteka Imeni Lenina. The Kutafya watchtower, built in the early 16th century, was approached by a drawbridge that spanned a moat. The tower was connected by a stone bridge, under which the Neglinnaya River once ran, to the **Troitskaya** (Trinity) **Tower**. Built in 1495, it was named after the Trinity-Sergius Monastery.

Palace of Congresses

As you enter the Kremlin through the Kutafya/Trinity Towers, the modern **Palace of Congresses** is on your right. Khrushchev approved the plans for this large steel, glass and marble structure. Built by Mikhail Posokhin, it was completed in 1961 for the 22nd Congress of the Communist Party. When no state congresses or international meetings are in session, the palace is used for ballet and opera performances. Sunk 45 feet (15 meters) into the ground so as not to tower over the Kremlin, the Palace contains 800 rooms and the auditorium seats 6,000.

The Arsenal

The yellow two-story building to the left of the entrance tower was once used as the **Arsenal**. Peter the Great ordered it built in 1702 (completed in 1736), but later turned it into a Trophy Museum. Along the front of the arsenal are 875 cannons and other trophies captured from Napoleon's armies in 1812. Plaques on the wall list the names of men killed defending the arsenal during the Revolution and WW II.

Council of Ministers Building

As you walk through the square, the three-story triangular building of the former Senate is directly in front. Catherine the Great had it built in classical style by Matvei Kazakov in 1787. It is now used by the Soviet **Council of Ministers**. The large green dome is topped by the national flag. The front wall plaque is marked by Lenin's portrait and the inscrip-

The Man in the Window

*T*he building stands behind the high red-brick wall known to the entire world. There are many windows in that building, but one was distinguished from all the others because it was lit twenty-four hours a day. Those who gathered in the evening on the broad square in front of the red-brick wall would crane their necks, strain their eyes to the point of tears, and say excitedly to one another: "Look, over there, the window's lit. He's not sleeping. He's working. He's thinking about us."

If someone came from the provinces to this city or had to stop over while in transit, he'd be informed that it was obligatory to visit that famous square and look and see whether that window was lit. Upon returning home, the fortunate provincial would deliver authoritative reports, both at closed meetings and at those open to the public, that yes, the window was lit, and judging by all appearances, he truly never slept and was continually thinking about them.

Naturally, even back then, there were certain people who abused the trust of their collectives. Instead of going to look at that window, they'd race around to all the stores, wherever there was anything for sale. But, upon their return, they, too, would report that the window was lit, and just try and tell them otherwise.

The window, of course, was lit. But the person who was said never to sleep was never at that window. A dummy made of gutta-percha, built by the finest craftsmen, stood in for him. That dummy had been so skillfully constructed that unless you actually touched it there was nothing to indicate that it wasn't alive. The dummy duplicated all the basic features of the original. Its hand held a curved pipe of English manufacture, which had a special mechanism that puffed out tobacco smoke at pre-determined intervals. As far as the original himself was concerned, he only smoked his pipe when there were people around, and his moustache was of the paste-on variety. He lived in another room, in which there were not only no windows but not even any doors. That room could only be reached through a crawl-hole in his *safe, which had doors both in the front and in the rear and which stood in the room that was officially his.*

He loved this secret room where he could be himself and not smoke a pipe or wear that moustache; where he could live simply and modestly, in keeping with the room's furnishings—an iron bed, a striped mattress stuffed with straw, a washbasin containing warm water, and an old gramophone, together with a collection of records which he personally had marked—good, average, remarkable, trash.

There in that room he spent the finest hours of his life in peace and quiet; there, hidden from everyone, he would sometimes sleep with the old cleaning woman who crawled in every morning through the safe with her bucket and broom. He would call her over to him, she would set her broom in the corner in business-like fashion, give herself to him, and then return to her cleaning. In all the years, he had not exchanged a single word with her and was not even absolutely certain whether it was the same old woman or a different one every time.

One time a strange incident occurred. The old woman began rolling her eyes and moving her lips soundlessly.

"What's the matter with you?"

"I was just thinking," the old woman said with a serene smile. "My niece is coming to visit, my brother's daughter. I've got to fix some eats for her, but all I've got is three roubles. So it's either spend two roubles on millet and one on butter, or two on butter and one on millet."

This peasant sagacity touched him deeply. He wrote a note to the storehouse ordering that the old woman be issued as much millet and butter as she needed. The old woman, no fool, did not take the note to the storehouse but to the Museum of the Revolution, where she sold it for enough money to buy herself a little house near Moscow and a cow; she quit her job, and rumor has it that to this day she's still bringing in milk to sell at Tishinsky market.

Vladimir Voinovich, A Circle of Friends

tion, "Lenin lived and worked in this building from March 1918 to May 1923". The Central Committee of the Communist Party meets in **Sverdlov Hall**. The hall's 18 Corinthian columns are decorated with copies (originals in the Armory) of bas-reliefs portraying czars and princes. Lenin's study and flat are in the east wing. Special objects stand on his desk, such as the Monkey Statue presented to him by Armand Hammer in 1921. The study leads to a small four-room apartment that Lenin shared with his wife and younger sister. Across from the Council of Ministers, near the Spasskaya Tower, is the **Presidium of the Supreme Soviet** and the **Kremlin Theater**, which was built between 1932 and 1934. The theater seats 1,200. These buildings can only be visited with special permission.

Patriarch's Palace

Opposite the former Senate is the four-story **Patriarch's Palace** and his private chapel, the **Church of the Twelve Apostles**, which now house the **Museum of 17th-Century Life and Applied Art**, with over 1,000 exhibits. Patriarch Nikon commissioned the palace for himself in 1635. After Nikon banned elaborate decorations on church buildings, he had the architects Konstantinov and Okhlebinin design the structure in simple white Byzantine fashion. The palace was placed near the main cathedral and the Trinity Gate, where clergy formally entered the Kremlin. The vaulted **Krestovskaya Chamber** (Hall of the Cross), built without a single support beam, was used as a formal reception hall. Every three years, the chamber was used for making consecrated oil for the Russian churches. In 1721, Peter the Great gave the palace to the Church Council of the Holy Synod. The museum has an interesting collection of rare manuscripts, coins, jewelry, furniture, fabrics, embroidery and table games. Books include an ABC primer written for the son of Peter the Great. Two of the halls are decorated to look like a 17th-century house. Some of the displays in the Church of the Twelve Apostles are wine coffers and ladles, on which Bacchus is carved. These objects belonged to the society of the "Highest and Most Jolly and Drunken Council," founded by Peter the Great to make fun of all the (non-progressive) church rituals. The museum is closed on Thursdays.

Emperor Cannon

Right next to the Palace is the 40-ton **Emperor Cannon**. Its 890mm-bore makes it the largest cannon in the world. It was cast in 1586 by

Andrei Shchokhov and never fired. A likeness of Fedor I is on the barrel. The decorative iron cannon balls (weighing one ton each) were cast in the l9th century.

Across from the cannon in the southeast corner of the Kremlin lie the **Tainitsky** (Secret) **Gardens**. Winter fairs are held here for children during New Year celebrations. A statue of Lenin rests on the highest spot, known as **Kremlin Hill**. To the left of the statue is the **Cosmos Oak**, which cosmonaut Yuri Gagarin planted on April 14, l961. This vantage point affords a good view of the Kremlin and Spasskaya Tower. The **Czar's Tower** stands to the right of it and is decorated with white-stone designs and a weathervane. A wooden deck used to stand on top of the tower, from which Ivan the Terrible supposedly watched executions on Red Square. The tower directly behind Lenin is the **Nabatnaya** (Alarm) **Tower**; the bell that used to hang here is on display in the Armory Museum. Farther to the right is the **Konstantino-Yeleninskaya Tower**, which honors St. Constantine and St. Helen. The corner tower is called **Moskvoretskaya**, built in 1487 by Marco Ruffo. It was known as Beklemischevskaya, named after Ivan Beklemisch, whose home stood next to the tower in the l6th century; his spirit is said to have haunted it. The Mongols broke through this tower to enter the Kremlin in the l7th century.

Emperor Bell

The largest bell in the world stands on a stone pedestal by the Secret Gardens. The bell, 18 feet (six meters) high, weighs 210 tons. The surface bears portraits of czars and icons. It was first designed in l733 by Ivan Matorin and his son Mikhail and took two years to cast. A 11.5-ton fragment broke off during the fire of 1737, when water was thrown on it. After the fire, the bell was returned to its casting pit, where it lay for a century. The architect Montferrand raised the bell in l836.

The square between the Spasskaya Tower and the bell was known as **Ivan's Square**, along which government offices were located. Officials read the Czar's new decrees and criminals were flogged here.

Bell Tower

Behind the Emperor Bell stands the three-tiered **Bell Tower of Ivan the Great**. Built betweem 1505 and 1508, the tower contains 21 bells that hang in the arches of each section, the largest of which is the Uspensky (Assumption) Bell, weighing 70 tons. The Old Slavonic inscription around the gilded dome notes that it was added to the belfry in 1600 by Boris Godunov. This was once the tallest structure (243 feet/81 meters) in Moscow and was used as a belfry, church and watchtower. When the enemy was sighted, the bells signaled a warning. A small exhibition hall is on the ground floor of the belfry.

Cathedral of the Assumption

In front of the belltower stands the Kremlin's main church, the **Assumption Cathedral** or **Uspensky Sobor**. It faces the center of Cathedral Square, the oldest square in Moscow, built in the early 14th century. In 1475, Ivan the Great chose the Italian architect Aristotile Fioravante to design the church. He modeled it after the Cathedral of the Assumption in Vladimir.

This church, also known as the Cathedral of the Dormition of the Virgin, was built on the site of a stone church by the same name, first constructed by Ivan I. For two centuries, this national shrine stood as a model for all Russian church architecture. Within its walls, czars were coronated and patriarchs crowned. It also served as the burial place for Moscow metropolitans and patriarchs.

Combining Italian Renaissance and Byzantine traditions, the cathedral is built from white limestone and brick with *zakomara* rounded arches, narrow-windowed drums and five gilded onion domes. The ornamental doorways are covered with frescos painted on sheet copper; the southern entrance is especially interesting, decorated with 20 biblical scenes in gold and black lacquer.

The spacious interior, lit by 12 chandeliers, is covered with exquisite frescos and icons that date back to 1481. The artists, Dionysius, Timofei, Yarets and Kon, wove together the themes of heaven and the unity of Russia's principalities, symbolizing the "Third Rome". Some of these can still be seen over the altar screen. The northern and southern walls depict the life of the Blessed Virgin. In 1642, more than 100 masters spent a year repainting the church, following the designs of the older wall paintings. These 17th-century frescos were restored after the revolution. The elaborate **iconostasis** (altar screen) dates from 1652. Its upper rows were painted by monks from the Trinity-Sergius Monastery in Zagorsk in the late 1600s. The silver frames were added in 1881. To the right of the royal gates are two 12th-century icons from Novgorod, St. George and the Saviour Enthroned. A 15th-century copy of the country's protectress, the Virgin of Vladimir also lies to the left. The

original (in the Tretyakov Gallery) was brought to Moscow from Vladimir in 1395 by Vasily I. The icons, Saviour of the Fiery Eye, the Trinity, and the Dormition of the Virgin, were specially commissioned for the cathedral in the 14th and 15th centuries. Napoleon's armies used some of the icons as firewood and tried to carry off tons of gold and silver. Most of it was recovered, and the central chandelier, Harvest, was cast from silver recaptured from the retreating troops.

The Metropolitan, Peter (co-founder of the cathedral), and his successor are buried in the southern chapel. The 15th-century fresco, *Forty Martyrs of Sebaste,* separates the chapel from the main altar. Other metropolitans and patriarchs are buried along the northern and southern walls and in underground crypts. Metropolitan Iov is buried in a special mausoleum, above which hangs the icon of Metropolitan Peter, the first Moscow metropolitan. The gilded sarcophagus (1606–12) of Patriarch Hermogenes (1606-12) stands in the southwest corner covered by a small canopy. During the Polish invasion, imprisoned by the Poles, he starved to death. After Patriarch Adrian, Peter the Great abolished the position and established the Holy Synod. The Patriarch seat remained vacant until 1917.

Ivan the Terrible's carved wooden throne stands to the left of the southern entrance. Made in 1551, it is known as the Throne of the Monomakhs. It is elaborately decorated with carvings representing the transfer of imperial power from the Byzantine Emperor Monomakus to the Grand-Prince Vladimir Monomakh (1113-1125), who married the emperor's sister. The Patriarch's throne can be found by the southeast pier; the clergy sat upon the elevated stone that is decorated with carved flowers. The *Last Judgement* is painted over the western portal. Traditionally, the congregation exited through the church's western door. The last theme portrayed was the Last Judgement — a reminder for the people to work on salvation in the outside world. Closed on Thursdays.

Church of the Deposition of the Robe
Next to the Assumption Cathedral is the smaller single-domed **Church of the Deposition of the Virgin's Robe**, built by Pskov craftsmen in 1484-85. It once served as the private chapel of the patriarchs and was linked by a small bridge to his palace. It later became a court chapel in 1653. The iconostasis was done by Nazari Istomin in 1627. The interior wall paintings are devoted to the Blessed Virgin. The northern gallery displays an exhibit of wooden handicrafts. Closed on Thursdays.

Terem Palace

In the small courtyard next to the church is the **Terem Palace** and the **Golden Palace of the Czarina**, which served as the reception place for czarinas in the l6th century. The Terem Palace resembles a fairy-tale creation with its checkerboard roof and 11 golden turrets. It housed the children and female relatives of noblewomen, and was built for Czar Mikhail Romanov, whose private chambers on the fourth floor were later occupied by his son, Alexei. Many state functions took place here and in the Hall of the Cross. The Czar received petitions from the population in the Golden Throne Room. Only the Czar's wife, personal confessor and blind storytellers were allowed into the private chapel and Royal Bedchamber, which looks like a scene out of the Arabian Nights. All the chapels of the Terem were united under one roof in 1681, which included the Churches of the Resurrection, Crucification, Saviour and St. Catherine. The adjoining Golden Palace of the Czarina was built in 1526 by Boris Godunov for his sister Irina, who was married to Czar Fedor I. This was her own private reception hall. When Fedor died, Irina refused the throne (the last son of Ivan the Terrible had died earlier in an epileptic attack); her brother, Boris Godunov, became the first elected czar. Admission to the Terem is only with special permission.

Palace of Facets

Facing the bell tower is the two-story Renaissance-style **Palace of Facets**, one of Moscow's oldest civil buildings, constructed by Ruffo and Solario between 1487 and 1491. It took its name from the elaborate stone facets decorating the exterior. State assemblies and receptions were held here — Ivan the Terrible celebrated the victory over Kazan in 1532 in this palace, as did Peter the Great after defeating the Swedes at Poltava in 1709. After Ivan III, all wives, including the crowned czarinas, were barred from attending state ceremonies and receptions in the Hall of Facets; a small look-out room was built above the western wall, from which the women could secretly watch the proceedings. Today the Hall is used for State occasions. Entrance to the Palace of Facets is by special permission only.

Cathedral of the Annunciation

This white-stone Cathedral, with its nine gilded domes, stands next to the palace and was built from 1485 to 1489 by Pskov craftsmen as the private chapel of the czars. After a fire in 1547, Ivan the Terrible rebuilt

the cathedral with four additional chapels. Inside, frescos that date back to 1508 were painted by Theodosius; many were restored in the l960s. The iconostasis contains icons by Andrei Rublev, Theophanes the Greek and Prokhor of Gorodets, painted in 1405. Portraits of princes, Greek philosophers and poets, such as Plato, Aristotle and Virgil, can be found on the pillars and in the galleries. Closed on Thursdays.

Archangel Cathedral

The third main cathedral of the Kremlin is the five-domed **Cathedral of the Archangel** (l505-08), which served as the burial place of the czars. It stands directly across from the Annunciation Cathedral. Ivan the Great commissioned the Italian architect Alevisio Novi to rebuild the church. He combined the styles of Old Russian and Italian Renaissance; notice the traits of a Venetian palazzo. The surviving frescos date back to 1652 and depict aspects of Russian life. A large iconostasis (l680) is filled with 15th- to 17th-century icons, including the *Archangel Michael*, by Rublev. Nearly 50 sarcophagi line the walls of the cathedral, containing grand-princes and czars and some of their sons. White tombstones give their names in Old Slavonic. The first grand-prince to be buried here was Ivan I in l341, who built the original church. After Peter the Great moved the capital to St. Petersburg, the czars were buried in the Peter and Paul Fortress, except for Peter II, who died in Moscow. Closed on Thursdays.

Behind the cathedral stands **Peter's Tower**, named after the first Moscow Metropolitan. The fourth unadorned tower from the corner is the **Tainitskaya** (Secret) **Tower**, which had an underground passage to the Moskva River. The next one over is the **Annunciation Tower**, which contained the Annunciation Icon. The round corner tower is called the **Vodovzvodnaya** or Water-Drawing Tower, in which water was raised from the river to an aqueduct that led to the gardens.

Grand Kremlin Palace

Built in 1838-49, the **Grand Palace**, behind the Archangel Cathedral, was the Moscow residence of the Imperial family. Nicholas I commissiioned Konstantin Thon to erect it on the site of the Grand-Prince Palace in l838-49. There are 700 rooms and five elaborate reception halls; two of these, along the southern wall overlooking the river, were combined to form the Meeting Hall of the Supreme Soviet and Russian Federation. The long gold and white St. George Hall has 18 columns decorated with statues of victory. The walls are lined with marble plaques with the names of heroes awarded the Order of St. George (introduced by Catherine the Great) for service and courage. The six bronze chandeliers hold over 3,000 light bulbs. This hall is now used for special state receptions and ceremonies; cosmonaut Yuri Gagarin received the Golden Star Hero Award here in 1961. The Hall of St. Catherine served as the Empress' Throne Room. The Hall of Vladimir connected the Palace of Facets, Golden Palace of the Czarina and Terem Palace. The ground floor rooms used to contain the Imperial family's bedchambers. Entrance is gained only by special permission.

Amusement Palace
The **Poteshny** (Amusement) **Palace**, situated behind the Grand Palace and the Commandent's Tower, was built in 1652 by Czar Alexis as the residence for his father-in-law. After he died, Alexis turned the palace into a theater.

Armory Palace
The **Oruzheinaya Palata** (Armory Palace) is the oldest museum in the Soviet Union. In 1485, Grand-Prince Vasily III, son of Ivan the Great, constructed a special stone building on the edge of the Kremlin grounds to house the growing collection of the royal family's valuables. It also contained the czar's workshops and a place where armor and weapons were stored. In the late 1600s, Peter the Great converted it into a museum to house the art treasures of the Kremlin. The present building, designed in 1651 by Konstantin Thon, has nine exhibit halls that trace the history of the Kremlin and the Russian state. It also houses a magnificent collection of West European decorative and applied art from the 12th to 19th centuries.

   Hall I (Halls I-IV are on the first floor) exhibits armor and weaponry from the 13th to 18th centuries. Hall II has displays of gold and silver from the 12th to 17th centuries, including jewelry, chalices (one belonging to Yuri Dolgoruky), bowls and watches. Hall III contains gold and silver jewelry from the 18th to 20th centuries, that includes snuff boxes and the fabulous Fabergé eggs. Hall IV has a collection of vestments, including a robe of the first Metropolitan Peter, Peter the Great, and a coronation robe of Catherine the Great. One robe presented to the Metropolitan by Catherine contains over 150,000 semi-precious stones.

Fabergé

In 1842, during the reign of Nicholas I, Gustav Fabergé founded the first Fabergé workshop in St. Petersburg. His son, Peter Carl, later extended the French family business to the cities of Moscow, Kiev, Odessa and London. These workshops produced a wealth of exquisite jewelry, clocks, cut glass, and other decorative objects made from gold, silver and semi-precious stones.

For over a century, Fabergé crafted unique art objects for the Imperial Court. Master craftsmen like Mikhail Perkhin, Erik Kollin, Henrik Wigström and Julius Rappoport had their own Fabergé workshops and sometimes spent years designing and crafting a single piece of art.

The fabulous Fabergé eggs were a favorite gift presented by the Romanov family and other members of the aristocracy. The first Fabergé Easter egg was commissioned in 1885 by Alexander III. When Carl Fabergé proposed to create an Easter gift for the Empress Maria Feodorovna, the Czar ordered an egg containing a special surprise. On Easter morning, the Empress broke open what appeared to be an ordinary egg; but inside, a solid gold yolk contained a solid gold chicken with a replica of the Imperial Crown. The Empress was so delighted by the egg that the Czar ordered one to be delivered to the Court each Easter. Alexander's son, Nicholas II, continued the Fabergé tradition and ordered two eggs each Easter, for his wife and mother.

On Easter morning 1895, Nicholas gave his mother a Fabergé Egg decorated with diamonds, emeralds and a star sapphire. Hand painted miniatures depicting Danish scenes, known by the Dowager Empress (the former Princess Dagmar of Denmark), were hidden inside what became known as the Danish Egg. In 1900 Fabergé presented the Imperial Family with an egg that contained a golden replica of the Trans-Siberian railroad; the train actually moved and could be wound up by a tiny golden key. The 1908 Easter egg had a portrait of Nicholas II on its surface with a model of Alexander I's Palace inside. Other eggs contained flowers (that bloomed by pressing a tiny button) and a model boat.

By the time of the Revolution, Fabergé had created over 50 eggs. When the Russian Exhibition was held in Moscow in 1882, Carl Fabergé received the Gold Medal; later in 1900 at the Exposition Universelle in Paris, he won the Grand Prix award along with the Legion of Honor. Today one of the most extensive Fabergé collections in the world can be seen at the Armory Museum in the Moscow Kremlin.

Hall V (Halls V-IX are on the ground floor) exhibits many of the foreign gifts of silver and gold from the 13th to 19th centuries from England, France, Sweden, Holland and Poland. Hall VI is known as the Throne and Crown Room. The oldest throne belonged to Ivan the Terrible. A Persian Shah presented Boris Godunov with a throne encrusted with 2,000 precious stones in 1604, and the throne of Czar Alexei Romanov contains over 1,000 diamonds. The most interesting is the Double Throne used by Peter the Great and his half-brother Ivan, when they were proclaimed joint czars. Peter's older half-sister, Sophia, acted as Regent and used to sit in a secret compartment in the throne behind Peter to advise him. The Crown of Monomakh (first worn by Grand Prince Vladimir Monomakh in 1113) was used by all grandprinces and czars until Peter the Great. The room also contains gowns and jewelry. Halls VII and VIII contain saddles, bridles and sleigh covers. Hall IX is the Carriage Room, with the world's largest collection of carriages, dating back to Boris Godunov. The most elaborate is the coronation coach made for the Empress Elizabeth. The Diamond Fund Exhibit is a collection of the crown jewels and precious gems. These include the Orlov Diamond (189 carats) that Count Orlov bought for his mistress, Catherine the Great. Catherine the Great's coronation crown is covered with pearls and 4,936 diamonds. (This section is opened with special permission.) A new section of the Armory displays gifts to the USSR from foreign countries.

The State Armory is one of the most interesting museums in Moscow and should definitely be visited. The Intourist Service Desk can book a tour. Only group tours are permitted. These are usually conducted daily, except Fridays, at 9:30 and 11:30 a.m., 2:30 and 4:30 p.m. in English.

The Armory Tower is behind the Armory Palace. One can exit through the Borovitskaya Tower (1490). (Kremlin Hill was originally called Borovitskaya. *Bor* in Old Russian means a "thick forest".) This gate used to be the service entrance to the Kremlin.

Old Moscow

The area to the east of the Kremlin was once known as **Kitai-gorod**. *Kitai* is derived from either the Mongolian for "central" or the Old Russian, *kiti*, meaning "palisade." *Gorod* is the Russian word for town. (In modern Russian, *Kitai* means China. Foreign settlements were later established in this area.) In the 14th century, the central town was surrounded by a protective earthen rampart and served as the central market and trade area, where merchants and townspeople lived. Beyond the rampart lay the forest. Later, Ivan the Terrible constructed a larger fortified wall. The original area of Kitai-gorod stretched from the History Museum on Red Square, along the back of GUM Department Store, and east down to what is now the Hotel Rossiya and the banks of the Moskva River. On each side of GUM are the small streets of 25th October and Kuibyshev. The Rossiya Hotel (behind St. Basil's) is bordered by Razin Street and Kitaisky Prospect.

25th October Street

This street begins at the northeast corner of Red Square and runs along the left side of GUM Department Store. Its former name was Nikolskaya, after the nearby Nikolsky Monastery. It now commemorates the first day of the 1917 Revolution. In the 17th century, the area was nicknamed the "Street of Enlightenment;" Moscow's first learning academy, printing yard and bookshops lined the passage.

The first corner building, as you leave the square, was the **Governor's Office**, where the writer Alexander Radishchev was held before his exile to Siberia (by Catherine the Great) in 1790. His book, *A Journey from St. Petersburg to Moscow*, described the terrible conditions of serfdom. The **Old Royal Mint** stands inside the small courtyard. An inscription on the gates show that Peter the Great built the mint in 1697. When he later moved it to St. Petersburg, the Vice-Governor had his office here.

Across the street by house no. 7 are several buildings that remain from the **Zaikonospassky Monastery**, founded by Boris Godunov in the early 1600s. The name means "Icon of our Saviour"; the monastery used to make and sell icons. The red and white **Saviour's Church** was built in 1661. The church and adjoining buildings housed the Slavic-Greek-Latin Academy, Moscow's first and largest academy for higher education, which operated from 1687 to 1814. Among the first students were the poet Kantemir, the architect Bazhenov and Mikhail Lomonsov (1711-65), who became a renowned poet, historian and educator. Known as the "Father of Russian Science," Lomonsov established Moscow University under Empress Elizabeth in 1755.

At no. 15 was the first Printing Yard, now the **History and Archives Institute**. Ivan the Terrible brought the first printing press to Russia in 1553. On the green building still hang the emblems of the old printing yard, a lion and unicorn, together with a sundial, mounted in 1814. The thick black gates lead to the colorfully tiled **building of the Old Proof-reader**, where Ivan Fedorov spent a year printing Russia's first book. Ivan the Terrible visited Fedorov daily until *The Acts of the Apostles* (now in the Lenin Library) was completed on March 1, 1564. The first Russian newspaper,*Vedomosti*, was printed here in 1703. The present building went up in 1814 and was used as the printing center for the Holy Synod, the council established by Peter the Great that regulated church affairs.

At no. 19 is the **Slavyansky Bazaar**, one of Moscow's oldest, and still most popular, restaurants. When it opened in the 1870s, it became a popular meeting spot for Moscow merchants who negotiated deals over the delicious *blini* pancakes. On June 21, 1877, stage directors Konstantin Stanislavsky and Vladimir Nemirovich-Danchencko worked out the details for the formation of the Moscow Art Theater, over an 18-hour lunch.

Opposite the Printing House is the former **Chizhov Coach Exchange**. The Chizhov family hired out horse-drawn carriages and carts as taxis. The Coach Exchange was popular year round, when Moscow streets were either muddy or frozen. In winter, one could hire a Chizhov *troika* (sled). Next door is the one-domed **Church of the Dormition**.

The small passage known as **Tretyakov Proezd** links **25th October Street** with **Prospekt Marxa**. The wealthy merchant Sergei Tretyakov knocked a passage through the Katai-gorod wall in 1871 to gain quick access to the banks along Prospekt Marxa.

25th October Street leads to Dzerzhinsky Square where it turns into Kirov Street, which runs east to the Leningradsky and Yaroslavky train stations and Sokolniki Park.

Halfway down 25th October Street, make a right on **Kuibyshev Proyezd**. Near the corner stands the red baroque 17th-century **Cathedral of Bogoyavlensky** (Epiphany), once part of a monastery established in the 13th century by Prince Daniil. The cathedral was created over the site of Moscow's first stone church, built by Ivan I. Many of the sculptures that were in the church are now on display in the Donskoi Monastery. The wealthy Boyar Golitsyn family had their burial vaults here until the mid-18th century; they were switched to the Donskoi Monastery outside of town when a cholera epidemic prohibited burial in the city's center.

The Pharmacy Shop at no. 21 is over a century old. The first pharmacy was set up in the Kremlin by Ivan the Terrible in 1581. Beginning in the 1600s, pharmacies sold medicinal herbs in Moscow. The herbs

were grown in the area of what is now the Alexandrov Gardens near the Kremlin.

In the small park stands the **Monument to Ivan Fedorov** (1510-83), the first Russian printer. The passage is still lined with small bookshops; a popular one is Knizhnaya Nakhodka.

Kuibyshev Street

Kuibyshev Passage leads into this street, which begins off the Square and continues past the right side of GUM. It was once the main thoroughfare of Kitai-gorod. In 1497, Ivan the Great gave a parcel of land on this street to 500 Novgorod merchant families to establish the Moscow-Novgorod Trade Exchange, at a time when Novgorod was still independent of Moscovy. The wealthy merchants erected St. Ilyia Church, recognized by its single-dome and *zakomara* gabled arches. Up to 1935 (after which the street was named after a popular revolutionary figure), this passage was known as Ilyinka Street, once the busy thoroughfare of Moscow's bank and financial district. The classical building of the **Moscow Stock Exchange** (1875), with its large Ionic columns, now houses the Chamber of Commerce.

The wealthy merchant Pavel Riabushinsky had Fedor Shekhtel build the Riabushinsky Bank in 1904. Shekhtel also designed the nearby Moscow Merchants Building in 1909. Riabushinsky was a well-respected spokesman for the merchant class and chairman of the Moscow Stock Exchange.

As Kuibyshev Passage continues past the street of the same name, it turns into Ribny Pereulok (Fish Lane), where many food stalls were set up. Later, in 1805, the Italian architect Quarenghi built the **Old Merchant Arcade** that occupied an entire block. The white structure with its Corinthian columns, once filled with boutiques, is now an office building.

Razin Street

Ribny Pereulok leads into **Ulitsa Razina**, which starts near St. Basil's and continues on past the Rossiya Hotel. Near the hotel are the remains of the 16th-century brick rampart walls that surrounded Kitai-gorod; this wall was over 2,500 meters long and six meters high. The street, once known as Varvara, was renamed after Stenka Razin, a popular Cossack rebel who was executed in Red Square in 1671.

The immense structure behind St. Basil's is the **Rossiya Hotel**, completed in 1967 by the architect Chechulin. The hotel is the largest in the world, with rooms for 6,000 people and a superb view of the Kremlin. One of Moscow's largest Beriozka shops is located at the back of the hotel. It also has many cafes and restaurants, the large Central Concert Hall and the Zariadi Cinema. In old Russian, *zariadi* meant "beyond the trading stalls". This area used to lie beyond the old marketplace on the outer fringes of Red Square.

The salmon and white **Church of St. Varvara** (Barbara) stands at the beginning of the street, once named after this saint. This passage once stretched from the Kremlin, along the old trade route, to the town of Vladimir. Prince Dmitri Donskoi used this route on his way to fight the Mongols in the Battle of Kulikovo in 1380.

The small cube-shaped and five-domed **Church of St. Maximus** stands nearby. Built in 1698 by Novgorod merchants, it held the remains of St. Maximus, an ascetic prophet who died in 1433. It now houses a branch of the Society for Environmental Protection.

Between the two, at no. 4 Razin, is the **Old English Inn**, a white-washed house with tiny irregular-placed windows. It originally belonged to a wealthy Russian merchant until, in 1556, Ivan the Terrible presented it to Sir Richard Chancellor, an English merchant who began trade relationships with Russia. Ivan even proposed marriage to Queen Elizabeth, but she declined and instead offered Ivan asylum in England whenever he might need it. Later, the inn was used by English merchants for their stores and living quarters, and English diplomats also stayed here. It has recently been restored and houses findings from local archaeological digs.

Next to the Inn is the **House of Boyars Romanov**, now a branch of the State History Museum that has displays of life from 17th-century Boyardom. The rich Boyar, Nikita Romanov, had his home in the center of Kitai-gorod. Nikita's sister, Anatasia, was married to Ivan the Terrible. Nikita's grandson, Mikhail, who was born in the house, was later elected to the throne in 1613 and began the reign of the Romanov Dynasty. The house was restored in the 19th century and is furnished to look like an early noble household. Open on Wednesday 11 a.m. to 7 p.m. and other days 10 a.m. to 6 p.m. Closed on Tuesdays and the first Monday of the month.

At the back of the Rossiya Hotel is the **Church of St. George on Pskov Hill**. The colorful church, with red walls and a blue belfry (1818), was erected by Pskov merchants in 1657.

On the other side of the Rossiya Hotel, on Kitaisky Proezd by the Moskva River, is the **Church of the Conception of St. Anne in the Corner**. The church stood at the corner of the Kitai-gorod wall and was named after the Virgin's mother, St. Anne. The barren wife of Prince Vasily III, Solomonia (whom he later divorced), often prayed here.

Nogin Square

Razin Street leads north into **Ploshchad Nogina** (with a Metro stop), both named after the revolutionary, Viktor Nogin. On Nogin Square stands the **Church of All Saints on Kulishki**. After Prince Dmitri Donskoi defeated the Mongols at Kulikovo in 1380, he erected a wooden church on the *kulishki* (marshy land). It was replaced by a stone church in the 16th century, which has since been restored.

To the left of the church are the gray buildings of the **Delovoy Dvor**, the business chambers. Built in 1913, they were used for the business operations of the city.

Near the square are the **Ilyinsky Gardens**, with a Monument to the Russian Grenadiers who died in the Battle of Plevna against Turkey in 1877. Along the small side street called Staraya (Old) Prospekt, are the buildings of the Central Committee of the Communist Party. A few-

minute's walk away is a "jewel of merchant architecture," the five-domed **Church of the Holy Trinity in Nikitniki**. In 1620, Mikhail Romanov hired a wealthy merchant from Yaroslavl, Grigory Nikinikov, to work in the financial administration. Nikinikov named his street after himself and later built this church on the site of the wooden Church of St. Nikita (his family saint), which burned down. The oldest icon is St. Nikita, which Nikinikov supposedly rescued from the burning church. The icon of the Trinity can be found on the iconostasis, carved in 1640. The burial chapel of the Nikinikovs lies to the right of the altar.

To the left, Staraya Prospekt turns into Novaya (New) Prospekt. In the other direction, Staraya Prospekt becomes Solyanka Street. *Sol* means salt in Russian, and the old saltyards were along this street in the 17th century. Farther up the street is the **Church of St. Vladimir in the Old Gardens**. At the time, this area was considered the countryside of Moscow; Ivan the Great had a summer palace near the Convent of St. John. Solyanka intersects with Arkhipov Street, named after the artist, who lived here in 1900. Many middle-class artisans lived in this part of the city. On this street, at no. 8, is the **Moscow Synagogue**.

Marx Prospekt

Prospekt Marxa, the city's busiest avenue, sweeps through the center of the city, stretching northeast along the Kremlin wall to Sverdlov and Dzerzhinsky squares.

Dzerzhinsky Square

Marx Prospekt begins at this square with a bronze statue of Feliz Dzerzhinsky (1877-1926), a prominent revolutionary leader, marking its center. The Metro station Dzerzhinskaya exits on to the square. The large department store on one corner is **Detsky Mir** (Children's World), the largest children's store in the USSR. More than half a million shoppers visit daily. Behind it is the Savoy Hotel, and in front, the KGB Headquarters.

Three interesting museums are also along the square. The **Mayakovsky Museum** is on the corner of Kirov Street and Serov Passage. The poet lived here for over a decade; many of his works and personal items are on display. The museum is open Mon. and Thurs. 12-8 and other days 10 a.m. to 6 p.m.; closed on Wednesdays. On Novaya (New) Square Street is the **Museum of the History and Reconstruction of**

Moscow, open Wed. and Fri. 12 to 8 p.m., other days 10 a.m. to 6 p.m., closed Mon. and the last day of the month. Next to it is the **Polytechnical Museum**; opened in 1872, the two house more than 30,000 items that trace the history of Russian science and technology. The library has over 3 million volumes. It is open Tues. and Thurs. 12 to 8 p.m., other days 10 a.m. to 6 p.m., closed same as above. The Statue of Ivan Fyodorov, the first Russian printer, stands a few minutes walk down the prospekt.

Sverdlov Square
The next section of Prospekt Marxa opens on **Ploshchad Sverdlova**, named after the first President of Soviet Russia, Yakov Sverdlov (1885-

---

Banyas

Nothing gives a better glimpse into the Russian character than a few hours in a Russian banya. This enjoyable sauna tradition has been a part of Russian culture for centuries. Traditionally, each village had its own communal bathhouse where, at different times, males or females would stoke wood-burning stoves and spend hours sitting, sweating and scrubbing. The Greek historian Herodotus reported from Russia in the fifth century B.C.: "They make a booth by fixing in the ground three sticks inclined toward one another, and stretching around them wooden felts, which they arrange so as to fit as close as possible; inside the booth a dish is placed upon the ground, into which they put a number of red hot stones; then they take some hemp seed and throw it upon the stones; immediately it smokes, and gives out such a vapor that no Grecian vapor can exceed; they are immediately delighted and shout for joy, and this vapor serves them instead of a water bath." Later, many homes even had their own private banyas and during winter, naked bodies could be seen rolling out in the snow after a vigorous sweat. Today the banya is still a much favored pastime.

Banya complexes are located throughout Moscow. For less than a ruble, the bather can spend many a pleasurable hour in the company of fellow hedonists. No banya is complete without a bundle of dried birch branches, usually sold outside. Birch has always been a popular symbol of Russia, which claims more birch than any other country in the world. (Foreign currency shops throughout the country are called Beriozka, after the birch tree.)

1919). The statue of Karl Marx, inscribed with the words, "Workers of All Countries Unite!", marks its center. The Metro stop is Ploshchad Sverdlova/Revolutsii.

On one corner is the Metropole Hotel, built in 1903 and recently renovated. The mosaic panels on the front were designed by the Russian artist, Mikhail Vrubel. Entrance plaques honor events of the Revolution. Facing the hotel to the right are walls of the 16th-century Kitai-gorod.

Up until 1919, the area was known as Theater Square, for two of Moscow's most prominent theaters were built here, the Bolshoi (Big) and the Maly (Small). One of the world's most famous theaters, the **Bolshoi** was built in 1824 by Osip Bovet and Alexander Mikhailov to

Many older banyas are housed in splendid pre-revolutionary buildings; marble staircases, mirrored walls and gilded rooms, though somewhat faded, are filled with steam and cold pools.

There are three main parts of the banya: the sitting and changing room, the bathing area, and the sauna itself. The bathing area is usually one immense room filled with large benches. Buckets are filled with warm water and birch branches. Here you scrub and rinse, and then carry the wet branches into the hot sauna. The custom is to hit the body lightly with the birch branches; this is believed to draw out toxins and circulate the blood. It's also traditional to hit each other with the branches; since you'll easily blend in like a native, you may find your banya buddy asking if you'd like your back lightly swatted! An old Russian folk-saying claims that "the birch tree can give life, muffle groans, cure the sick and keep the body clean." Cries of "oy oy, tak khorosho" ("how wonderful") and "lyokiim parom" ("have an enjoyable sweat") emanate from every corner. When someone, usually one of the *babushki* (grandmothers) or *dedushki* (grandfathers), gets carried away with flinging water on the heated stones, moans of *khvatit* ("enough") resound from the depths and bodies come racing out of the red-hot steamy interior. Back in the washroom, the bather rinses alternately in warm and cold water and uses a loofa for a vigorous rubdown. Wrapped in a crisp, white towel, the refreshed figure returns to the sitting room to relax and sip tea, water, or even beer or vodka. With the skin glowing and rejuvenated, it's time to take an invigorating walk about the city!

stage performances of ballet and opera. After a fire in 1856, it was
rebuilt by Albert Kavos. The stately building, with its large fountain in
front, is crowned by the famous four bronze horses pulling the chariot of
Apollo, patron of the arts. This is the work of sculptor Pyotr Klodt. The
gorgeous interior consists of five tiers of gilded boxes, whose chairs are
covered with plush red velvet. The chandelier is made from 13,000
pieces of cut glass. The theater premiered compositions by Tchaikovsky,
Glinka, Mussorgsky and Rimsky-Korsakov. The Intourist Service
Bureau at your hotel sells tickets for Bolshoi performances.

Across from the Bolshoi is the light yellow building of the **Maly
Drama Theater**. At its entrance stands the statue of Alexander Ostrovsky (1823-86), the outstanding Russian playwright. The theater is
nicknamed the "Ostrovsky House". Many classic Russian plays are
staged here. On the other side of the Bolshoi is the Central Children's
Theater.

The other end of the square is flanked by the three-story ornamented
brick building of the **Central Lenin Museum** (closed on Mondays and
the last Tuesday of each month) that marks the entrance to Revolution
Square. This building, erected in 1892, once housed the Duma (City
Hall) of Moscow. In 1937, its 34 halls were converted into the country's

largest Lenin museum. Across from the museum is the Moskva Hotel. Before continuing down the avenue to Revolution Square, some old and interesting side streets off Sverdlov Square merit a few minutes of exploration.

Petrovka Street

Ulitsa Petrovka is a small side street that begins in front of the Maly Theater. Three centuries ago, the passage was named after the Petrovsky (St. Peter) Monastery, which also served as a protective stronghold and entrance to the town. The monastery was built by Prince Dmitri Donskoi to honor the Mongol defeat in the Battle of Kulikovo in 1380. Much of this monastery has been restored. The **Museum of Literature** (open Wed. and Fri. 2-9 p.m., other days 11 a.m. to 6 p.m., closed on Mondays and the last day of month), now located at no. 28, traces the history of Russian literature. This neighborhood was the residence of Moscow's coachmakers. The area was nicknamed Karetny Ryad (Carriage Row).

For a long time, the street has been a popular shopping district with stores selling *podarki* (gifts), *bukinisti* (second-hand books) and *almazi* (diamonds). Next to the Maly is the large central department store, TsUM. The Russikiye Uzory sells handicrafts, and at no. 8 is Chasy, one

of Moscow's best watch stores. The Society of World Art had its first exhibition at no. 15, displaying the work of Alexander Benois. The writer Anton Chekhov lived for many years at no. 19. The Hermitage Gardens have been here for over a century.

Kuznetsky Most

The poet Vladimir Mayakovsky wrote, "I love Kuznetsky Most...and then Petrovka." Petrovka Street leads to Kuznetsky Most, a small lane branching to the right. As far back as the 15th century, the area was the popular residence of Moscow's blacksmiths, who lived along the banks of the Neglinnaya River, which, at the time, flowed through here. (In the 19th century, the river was diverted to an underground aqueduct.) Kuznetsky Most, in Russian, means "Blacksmith's Bridge".

Almost every building along this passage has a fascinating story behind it. The steep passage became a highly respected shopping district in the 19th century; items were stamped with "Bought in Kuznetsky Most". At no. 9 was a restaurant called Yar, which Pushkin and Tolstoy mention in their writings. The Artist Unions have their exhibition halls at no. 11. Tolstoy listened to one of the world's first phonographs in the musical shop that was at no. 12, and he wrote of Anna Karenina shopping at Gautier's, at no. 20. The House of Fashion and many airline agencies are also located along the narrow street. At the end is Metro stop Kuznetsky Most.

Neglinnaya Street

Kuznetsky Most connects to Ulitsa Neglinnaya, which runs from Marx Prospekt to Trubnaya Square on the Boulevard Ring. This street also sprang up alongside the banks of the Neglinnaya River, where many popular shops were located. The revolutionary Nikolai Schmit had his furniture store at the corner of Kuznetsky Most. The Moorish-style building of the **Sandunovsky Baths** at no. 14 were frequented by Chekhov. This is still a popular *banya*. The building was bought by the actor Sila Sandunov, who turned them into sauna-baths in the 18th century. On the street is also Moscow's oldest sheet music shop and the State Bank of the USSR. At no. 29 is the popular Uzbekistan Restaurant.

The continuation of Marx Prospekt from Sverdlov Square leads to Revolution Square (50th Anniversary of the October Revolution Square). This area was once known as Okhotny Ryad (Hunter's Lane). The main markets of Moscow spread from here to Red Square. Across from the Moskva Hotel is Dom Soyuzov (House of Trade Unions) on the corner of Pushkin and Tverskaya streets. Built in 1784 by Matvei Kazakov, it used to be the Noble's Club.

Crossing the prospekt via the underpass brings you out in front of the National Hotel. Built in 1903, it is still one of Moscow's finest hotels. Lenin stayed in Suite 107, marked by a plaque. One door down is the Intourist Board of Foreign Tourism. Next comes one of the oldest buildings of Moscow University, built between 1786 and 1793 by Kazakov. In the courtyard are two statues of graduates, Nikolai Ogarev and Alexander Herzen.

In the center of the avenue in Manezhnaya Square stands the Central Exhibition Hall, which used to be the czar's riding school. It was built in classical style in 1817 by Augustin Betancourt. Moscow's largest art exhibitions are now shown here. At no. 21 is the **Kalinin Museum** (closed on Mondays), tracing the life of the party leader, Mikhail Kalinin. Prospekt Marxa ends a few minutes' walk farther down by the Lenin Library and Ulitsa Volkhonka. The closest Metro stop is Biblioteka Imeni Lenina. Open 12 to 8 p.m. Tues. and Wed., other days 10 a.m. to 6 p.m., and closed on Mondays.

Kropotkin Street

Volkhanka Street begins at the Kremlin's Borovuitsky Tower and turns into Kropotkin Street. The **Pushkin Museum of Fine Arts** is at no. 12. The Greek-style building was constructed in 1898 by Roman Klein to house a collection of fine art that had over 20,000 items on display at the 1912 opening. Today, the museum boasts one of the world's largest collections of ancient classical, Oriental and Western European art, with over half a million works. It is open daily 10 a.m. to 8 p.m., Sun. till 6. Directly behind the Pushkin is the **Marx and Engels Museum** at no. 5 Marx and Engels Street, open Tues., Wed., and Fri, 12 to 7 p.m., other days 11 a.m. to 6 p.m. Both are closed on Mondays and the last day of each month.

Across from Metro stop Kropotkinskaya, is the heated **Moskva Open-Air Swimming Pool**, open year round. Tickets are bought at the small *kassa* desk next to the main building. Bathing suits, caps and towels can also be rented. One enters the heated pool through a passage from inside the complex.

Ulitsa Kropotkinskaya was named after the revolutionary scholar, Pyotr Kropotkin (1842-1921). For centuries, the street was known as

Prechistenka (Holy), after the Icon of the Holy Virgin kept in a nearby monastery. Many aristocratic families built their residences along this street. At no. 10 lived Count Orlov, a friend of Pushkin's. The mansion now houses the Soviet Peace Commission. The writer, Turgenev, and the poet, Zhukovsky, also lived on the street. The mansion at no. 12 was built by Afanasy Grigorev. It now houses the **Alexander Pushkin Museum**, with over 80,000 items connected with the poet. It is open Saturday and Sunday from 10 a.m. to 6 p.m., other days 12 to 8 p.m., closed on Mondays and the last Friday of the month. Across the street at no. 11 is the **Leo Tolstoy Museum**. This museum is open from 12 to 7 p.m. and closed on Mondays and the last Friday of the month. The poet, Denis Davydov, lived at no. 17, and Prince Dolgorukov (related to Prince Dolgoruky) once lived at no. 21. The Palace of Fine Arts, at no. 21, hosts art shows. Kropotkin Street ends at the Garden Ring by a statue of Tolstoy.

Across the river at no. 10 Lavrushinsky (near Metro Novokuznetskaya) is the **Tretyakov Art Gallery**. In 1856, the brothers, Sergei and Pavel Tretyakov, avid art patrons, began to collect the works of Russian artists. In 1892, they founded the museum and donated their collection to the city. Today the gallery houses one of the world's largest Russian and Soviet art collections from the tenth to the 20th centuries. It is open daily 10 a.m. to 7 p.m. and closed on Mondays, but check first; the museum is closed occasionally for restoration. A new branch of the Tretyakov (also closed on Mondays) has opened at no. 10 Krymsky Val. This is across from Tverskaya Park near Metro stop Oktyabrskaya.

Kutuzovsky Prospekt

After crossing the Kalinin Bridge, Kalinin St. turns into **Kutuzovsky Prospekt**, named after the Russian General, Mikhail Kutuzov (1745-1813), who fought against Napoleon. The building on the right, with the star-spire, is the Hotel Ukrainia, which has a Beriozka and Ukrainian restaurant. A statue to the Ukrainian poet, Taras Shevchenko, stands in front. Nearby is the House of Toys. Across the street, at no. 6, is the Central Art Fund, selling local handicrafts and artwork. At the next corner is the **Hero City of Moscow Obelisk**. Troops left from here to fight the Germans in 1941. At no. 26, a plaque marks the 30-year residence of Leonid Brezhnev.

The obelisk stands at the entrance of Bolshaya Dorogomilovskaya

St., along which are the Kievskaya Railway Station (with a Metro stop), and a foreign-currency food Beriozka.

The prospekt ends at the **Triumphal Arch** in Victory Square, designed by Osip Bovet in 1829-34 to honor Russia's victory in the War of 1812. It originally stood in front of the Byelorusskaya Train Station, and was moved to this spot in 1968, when Tverskaya Street was widened. Here on Poklonnaya Hill, Napoleon waited for Moscow's citizens to relinquish the keys to the city. *Poklon* means "bow". It was once the custom for people entering or leaving Moscow to stop and bow to the city. From the hill is a magnificent view of Moscow; the writer Anton Chekhov once said "those who want to understand Russia should look at Moscow from Poklonnaya."

In between the Metro station Kutuzovskaya and the arch is the Statue of Mikhail Kutuzov, by Nikolas Tomsky, and the Obelisk that marks the common graves of 300 men who died in the War of 1812.

The large circular building at no. 3 is the **Battle of Borodino Panorama Museum**. The 68 cannons in front were captured from Napoleon. In 1912, to commemorate the 100th Anniversary of the war, Franz Rouband was commissioned to paint scenes of the Battle of Borodino, which occurred on August 12, 1812. The building that holds the large murals was constructed in 1962 to honor the 150th anniversary. Behind the museum is the **Kutuzov Hut**. Here on September 1, 1812, as the French invaded Moscow, Kutuzov and the Military Council decided to abandon the city. The museum and hut are open 10:30 a.m. to 4 p.m. and closed on Fridays.

From here, Kutuzovsky Prospekt turns into Mozhaiskoye Chausee (Minsk Highway), along which is the Mozhaisky Hotel and campgrounds.

Gorky Street

In the 18th century, **Ulitsa Gorkovo** was the main street of the city; today, it is still one of the busiest in Moscow. The long thoroughfare stretches from Red Square past Pushkin and Mayakovsky Squares to Belorusskaya Train Station, where it turns into Leningradsky Prospekt.

The passage was once known as Tverskaya, since it led to the old Russian town of Tver (now Kalinin) 160 miles (256 km) north, and on to St. Petersburg. In pre-revolutionary days, the street, once twisting and narrow, was known for its fashionable shops, luxurious hotels and grandiose aristocratic mansions. Installed here were the city's first electric lamps. The first trams ran along the street, and the first movie theater opened here. In l932, the street was renamed after the Russian writer Maxim Gorky, a favorite of Lenin and Stalin. At this time, it was also reshaped and widened and now retains little of its former appearance. The street continued to be known as Gorky up until 1990, when the Moscow City Council voted to restore the street's old name of Tverskaya.

It takes about an hour and a half to stroll up Tverskaya Street. One can also ride the Metro to various stops along Tverskaya—Pushkinskaya, Mayakovskaya and Belorusskaya—to cut short the time.

Tverskaya Street begins in front of Red Square at the **50th Anniversary of the October Revolution Square**, known as Manezhnaya before l967. The Metro stop, Prospekt Marxa, is at the beginning of the street. On the corner is the elegant old National Hotel with a splendid view of Red Square. A small Beriozka shop is inside to the left. The 22-story structure next door is the modern Intourist Hotel, opened in l971. Inside, toward the back, are slot machines, Beriozkas and a hard-currency cafe. Stop in the cafeteria for a quick lunch. Next to the hotel there is a cooperative restaurant. In between the two hotels is an Intourist Booking Office and a foreign-currency Exchange Bank. Across the street are a number of shops, including the Podarki Souvenir Shop.

Continuing up the street leads past the Yermolova Drama Theater, named after a famous actress, to the Central Telegraph Building, with its globe and digital clock, on the corner of Ogareva Street. The building, designed by Ilya Rerberg in 1927, is open round-the-clock. Telegrams and long-distance calls can be made here.

Across the street at no. 3 Proyezd Khudozhestvennovo Teatra, (Arts Passage Street) is the **Moscow Arts Theater**, established by Stanislavsky and Nemirovich-Danchenko in l896. Here Stanislavsky practiced his "method-acting" and staged many plays by Tverskaya and Chekhov. After *The Seagull*, the bird became the emblem on the outside of the theater. The new building of the Moscow Arts Theater is at no. 22 Tsverkoi Boulevard, off Gorky Street.

The Aragvi Restaurant, specializing in Georgian cuisine, is on the next corner of Stoleshnikov Lane (a right off Gorky). Craftsmen embroidered tablecloths for the czar's court in this lane over 300 years ago. The Stoleshnik Cafe, at no. 6, is decorated in old-Russian style. At no. 11, the pastry shop still uses old-fashioned ovens built into the walls, and has some of the best cakes in the city. The Russian writer, Vladimir

Moscow Burning

arychkine invited a guest to meet me at lunch next day—the Moscow Chief of Police, Schetchinsky by name. Before we had been more than 10 minutes at table a wild-looking police officer rushed in unannounced and uttered one word—"Pajare!"—"Quick!" The Chief of Police sprang from his seat while Narychkine and Jenny, with one voice, exclaimed: "A fire! Where?" A fire is no rare event in Moscow and is always a serious matter, for of the 11,000 houses in the centre of Moscow only 3,500 are of stone, the rest are of wood. Just as St. Petersburg counts its disasters in floods, Moscow numbers the fires that have reduced great stretches of the city to ashes, the most terrible being, of course, the one in 1812, when barely 6,000 buildings remained standing.

I was seized with a sudden urge to see this fire for myself.

"Can I come with you?" I begged the Chief of Police.

"If you promise not to delay me a single second."

I seized my hat as we ran together to the door. His troika, with its three mettlesome black horses, was waiting. We jumped in and shot off like lightning while the messenger, already in the saddle, spurred his own mount and led the way. I had no conception of how fast a troika can move behind three galloping horses, and for a moment I could not even draw breath. Dust from the macadamised country road billowed up in clouds above our heads; then, as we skimmed over the pointed cobbles of Moscow's streets, sparks struck by our flying hooves fell around us like rain and I clung desperately to the iron strut while the Chief of Police yelled: "Faster! Faster!"

As soon as we left Petrovsky Park we could see smoke hanging like an umbrella—fortunately there was no wind. In the town there were dense crowds, but the messenger, riding a horse's length ahead, cleared a path for us, using his knout on any bystanders who did not move fast enough to please him, and we passed between ranks of people like lightning between clouds. Every moment I feared that *someone would be run over, but by some miracle no one was even touched and five minutes later we were facing the fire, our horses trembling, their legs folding beneath then. A whole island of houses was burning fiercely. By good fortune the road in front of it was fifteen or twenty yards wide, but on every other side only narrow alleys separated it from neighbouring dwellings. Into one of these alleys rushed M. Schetchinsky, I at his heels. He urged me back–in vain. "Then hold fast to my sword-belt," he cried, "and don't let go!" For several seconds I was in the midst of flames and thought I should suffocate. My very lungs seemed on fire as I gasped for breath. Luckily another alley led off to our right. The Chief of Police ran into it, I followed and we both sank exhausted on a baulk of timber. "You've lost your hat," he laughed. "D'you feel inclined to go back for it?"*

"God! No! Let it lie! All I want is a drink."

At a gesture from my companion a woman standing by went back into her house and brought out a pitcher of water. Never did the finest wine taste so good! As I drank, we heard a rumble like thunder. The fire-engines had arrived!

Moscow's Fire Service is very well organised, and each of the 21 districts has its own engines. A man is stationed on the highest tower in the area, on the watch day and night, and at the first sign of fire he sets in motion a system of globes to indicate exactly where smoke is rising. So the engines arrive without losing a second, as they did on this occasion, but the fire was quicker still. It had started in the courtyard of an inn, where a carter had carelessly lit his cigar near a heap of straw. I looked into that courtyard. It was an inferno!

To my amazement, M. Schetchinsky directed the hoses not on the fire itself but on the roofs of the nearby houses. He explained that there could be no hope of saving the houses that were actually burning, but if the sheets of iron on neighbouring rooftops could be prevented from getting red hot there might be a chance of saving the homes they covered.

The only source of water in the district was 300 yards away, and soon the engines were racing to it to refill their tanks. "Why don't the people make a chain?" I asked.

"What is that?"

"In France, everyone in the street would volunteer to pass along buckets of water so that the engines could go on pumping."

"That's a very good idea! I can see how useful that would be. But we have no law to make people do that."

"Nor have we, but everyone rushes to lend a hand. When the Théâtre Italien *caught fire I saw princes working in the chain.*"

"My dear M. Dumas," said the Chief of Police, "that's your French fraternity in action. The people of Russia haven't reached that stage yet."

"What about the firemen?"

"They are under orders. Go and see how they are working and tell me what you think of them."

They were indeed working desperately hard. They had climbed into the attics of the nearby houses and with hatchets and levers, their left hands protected by gloves, they were trying to dislodge the metal roofing sheets, but they were too late. Smoke was already pouring from the top storey of the corner house and its roof glowed red. Still the men persisted like soldiers attacking an enemy position. They were really wonderful, quite unlike our French firemen who attack the destructive element on their own initiative, each finding his own way to conquer the flames. No! Theirs was a passive obedience, complete and unquestioning. If their chief had said "Jump in the fire!" they would have done so with the same devotion to duty, though they well knew that it meant certain death to no purpose. Brave? Yes, indeed, and bravery in action is always inspiring to see. But I was the only one to appreciate it. Three or four thousand people stood there watching, but they showed not the slightest concern at this great devastation, no sign of admiration for the courage of the firemen. In France there would have been cries of horror, encouragement, applause, pity, despair, but here—nothing! Complete silence, not of consternation but of utter indifference, and I realised the profound truth of M. Schetchinsky's comment that as yet the Russians have no conception of fraternity as we know it, no idea of brotherhood between a man and his fellows. God! How many revolutions must a people endure before they can reach our level of understanding?

Alexandre Dumas, Adventures in Czarist Russia

Giliarovsky, who wrote *Moscow and Moscovites*, lived at no. 9 for over half a century. The lane leads to Petrovka Street, a popular shopping area.

The side street to the left, Nezhdanovoi, leads to the **Church of the Resurrection**, founded by Czar Mikhail Romanov. It contains many beautiful 17th-century icons and is open daily for worship.

Sovietskaya Square is marked by the equestrian Statue of Yuri Dolgoruky, founder of Moscow. It was erected in 1954 to mark the 800th anniversary of the city. The building behind the square, in the small garden, holds the Party Archives of the Marxism-Leninism Institute, built in 1927. The archives contain more than 6,000 documents of Marx and Engels and over 30,000 of Lenin. In front is a granite statue of Lenin by Sergei Merkurov.

Directly across the street stands the large red-brick and white-columned **Moscow Soviet of People's Deputies**, the Mos-Soviet or City Council. The architect, Matvei Kazakov, designed the building as the residence for the first governor-general, appointed by Catherine the Great in 1782. Two of Moscow's governors were Prince Dmitri Golitsyn (1820-44), who paved the streets and installed water pipes, and Vladimir Dolgorukov, a descendent of Yuri Dolgoruky. In 1946, the building was moved back 42 feet (14 meters) and two more stories were added.

Farther up Tverskaya is the Tsentralnaya Hotel at no. 10. In the same building is the most famous bakery in Moscow, formerly known as Filippov's. Next door is the old **Gastronom No. 1**, another popular food store. Beautiful white sculptures and garlands line the shop's face, and the gilded interior is filled with stained glass and colorful displays. It is still known as Yeliseyev's, after the original owner, who also had a popular gourmet store by the same name in St. Petersburg on Nevsky Prospekt (which is also still there). The merchant bought the mansion from a princess in 1898 and opened the store in 1901. Even though delicacies are lacking, it is worth a visit to see the interior.

At no. 14 Tverskaya is the **Memorial Museum of Nikolai Ostrovsky** (1904-36) who wrote *How the Steel Was Tempered*. His house is now a museum with documents and photographs of the Soviet author. It is open 12 to 8 p.m. on Wed. and Fri., and on other days 10 a.m. to 6 p.m.; closed Mondays and the last day of the month. Next to the museum is the Central Actors Club and the All-Russia Theatrical Society.

Down the side street, at no. 6 Stanislavsky, is the **Stanislavsky Memorial House-Museum**. It is open on Wednesday and Fridays from

2 a.m. to 9 p.m. and others days 11 a.m. to 6 p.m. Closed on Mondays and Tuesdays.

At Tverskaya and no. 12 Shchukin St. is the **Sergei Konenkov Studio Museum** (1874-1971), displaying marble and wooden statues by this famous sculptor. Open on weekends 10 a.m. to 5 p.m. and other days 12 to 7 p.m. Closed on Mondays and Tuesdays. Nearby is the store Armenia, specializing in food from this republic.

As Tverskaya crosses the Boulevard Ring, it opens onto Pushkin Square. In the 16th century, the stone walls of the Beli-gorod, (Whitetown) stretched around what is now the Boulevard Ring. They were torn down in the 18th century. The Strastnoi Convent used to stand on what is now Pushkin Square—the square was named Strastnaya, after the Convent of the Passion of Our Lord. The convent was demolished in the 1930s. In the center of the square stands the **Statue of Alexander Pushkin**, by sculptor Alexander Opekulin. It was erected in 1880 with funds donated by the public. Pushkin lived over a third of his life in Moscow, where he predicted, "word of me shall spread across the Russian land." Dostoevsky laid a wreath on the statue at its unveiling; today it is still always covered with flowers and a popular spot for open-air readings.

Behind the square is the 3,000-seat Rossiya Cinema, built in 1961 for the 2nd International Moscow Film Festival. This area is also Moscow's major publishing center. Here are the newspaper offices of *Izvestia, Trud, Novosti* (*APN*) and *Moscow News*. A quick walk down Chekhov Street (behind *Izvestia*) leads to the tent-shaped **Church of the Nativity**, built in 1649-52. Legend had that a noblewoman gave birth in her carriage as she passed this spot and later commissioned a church to honor the Nativity. When it burned down, Czar Alexei Romanov donated money to have it rebuilt, along with a chapel dedicated to the icon that prevented fires, Our Lady of the Burning Bush, which is in the chapel.

The **Central Museum of the Revolution** is at no. 21 Tverskaya Street. This mansion was built for Count Razumovsky in 1780 by the architect Manelas. In 1832, when it was rebuilt after a fire by Adam Menelaws, the mansion was bought by the Angliisky (English) Club, formed in 1772 by a group of foreigners residing in Moscow. The club's members (all men) were made up of Russian aristocratic intellectuals and included the best minds in politics, science, art and literature. Tolstoy once lost 1,000 rubles in a card game in the "infernal" room.

Pushkin wrote of the club in his long poem *Evgeny Onegin*. When Tatiana arrived in Moscow, Evgeny described "the two frivolous looking lions" at the gates. The last *bolshoi* gala at the club was a banquet thrown for Nicholas II to celebrate the 300th anniversary of the Romanov Dynasty in 1913. The Museum, opened in 1924, exhibits over a million items from the Revolution. The gun outside was used to shell the White Guards in 1917. It is open from 11 a.m. to 7 p.m. on Wed. and Fri. Other days 10 a.m. to 6 p.m., and closed on Mondays.

Next to the museum, at no. 23, is the Stanislavky Drama Theater. Behind it, is the Young Spectator's Theater for children. The Baku Restaurant, at no. 24, serves delicious Azerbaijani food.

Passing the Minsk Hotel, whose restaurant specializes in Byelorussian cuisine, and a few other shops brings you to the corner of Tverskaya and Sadovoye Koltso (Garden Ring). On the corner stands a large building with ten columns, the Tchaikovsky Concert Hall, where orchestras and dance ensembles perform. The Mayakovsky Metro station is in front. Directly behind the Hall, at no. 18, is the circular-domed building of the Satire Theater. The Aquarium gardens are next with the Mossoviet Theater, at no. 16 Bolshaya Sadovaya Street. Also nearby is the

Sovremennik Theater, staging contemporary plays. Across the street is the Peking Hotel, with a Chinese restaurant.

A statue of the poet Vladimir Mayakovsky (1893-1930) stands in Mayakovsky Square. On the other side of the square is the Sofia Restaurant, with Bulgarian food. To the right is the Moskva Cinema. At no. 43 Tverskaya is the House of Children's Books, and at no. 46 is the Exhibition Hall of Artist Unions.

Gorky Street ends at Byelorusskaya Square. At the center of the square is a Monument to Maxim Tverskaya (1868-1935), erected in 1951. The Byelorusskaya Railway Station, over 100 years old, has trains to points west, including Warsaw, Berlin, Paris and London. The Metro station Byelorusskaya is in front. Here Gorky Street turns into Leningradsky Prospekt, which runs all the way to the international airport, Sheremetyevo.

On the next side street are the offices of the newspaper *Pravda*, with a daily distribution of 10 million. The Race Course is on Begovaya Street. A little farther up, at no. 25 Leningradsky, is the Hotel Sovetskaya with the Romany Gypsy Theater.

From here, head back into the center of town on the metro or continue by bus along Leningradsky Prospekt.

Kalinin Prospekt

Another main Moscow street, **Prospekt Kalinina**, begins across from the Kremlin Trinity and Kutufya Towers (by the Alexandrov Gardens) and runs westward toward the Moskva River. Here it turns into Kutuzovsky Prospekt and later the Minsk Highway.

The old route was known as Novodvizhenskaya, and stretched from the Kremlin to the outer walls of the city. A new thoroughfare was built along the old passage; in 1963, it was renamed Kalinin, after a leader of the Communist Party, Mikhail Kalinin. The old section *prospekt* runs from the Kremlin to the Boulevard Ring, where the more modern part begins.

The road starts by a large gray building off Prospekt Marxa, the **Lenin State Library**. The Library opened in the 1800s, when the book collector, Nikolai Rumyantsev, moved his collection from St. Petersburg into a Moscow mansion across from the Kremlin. A new building was constructed on the site in 1940, and now houses the largest collection of books in the USSR, over 36 million.

The first part of the street still contains a few 18th-century buildings. At no. 7 is the former **Monastery of the Holy Cross**. The house at no. 9 belonged to Tolstoy's grandfather.

At the corner of Granovsky is an early 18th-century mansion that belonged to the wealthy Count Sheremetev. Across the street, at no. 5, is another old mansion, built by Kazakov. It now houses the **Alexei Shchusev Museum of Architecture**, which features the history of Russian and Soviet architecture. It is open from 11 a.m. to 7 p.m. and closed on Mondays and Fridays. The nearest metro stop is Kalininskaya.

At no. 16 is the white, medieval former mansion of the merchant Morozov, who hired the designer Marizin in the 19th century to model his residence after a Spanish castle. In 1959, it was turned over to the House of Friendship, where delegations of foreign friendship societies meet.

Near the Metro stop Arbatskaya, on the side street Suvorov, is the Journalist Club. Across from the club is a monument to Gogol, standing in front of the house where the writer lived. On this corner is the large **Dom Svyazi** (House of Communications) with a post office, telephone center and video-phone links to a few other Russian cities.

The Arbat

The Prague Restaurant, on the other corner, marks the entrance to one of the city's oldest sections, the **Arbat**. Long ago, the Arbat Gates led into Moscow. *Arbad* is an old eastern Russian word meaning "beyond the town walls." The area was first mentioned in 15th-century chronicles. It lay along the Smolensk Road, making it a busy trade center. Many court artisans lived here in the 16th century; in the 19th century, many wealthy and educated residents chose to live in the Arbat. Today Arbat St. is a cobbled pedestrian passage and one of the most popular meeting and shopping spots in Moscow. Along with shops, cafes, art galleries, concert and theater halls and a museum tracing the history of the area are groups of painters that sketch portraits, performance artists and even demonstrators. It is also a frequent site for festivals and carnivals.

All the colorful buildings along the pedestrian mall and side streets have a rich and romantic history. Many poems, songs and novels, such as Anatoly Rybakov's *Children of the Arbat*, have been written about this area. The czar's stablemen once lived along Starokonivshenny, (Old-Stable Lane). An old church stood on the corner of Spasopekovsky Lane. Other small streets have the names Serebryany (Silversmith),

Plotnikov (Carpenter) and Kalachny (Pastrycook). Pushkin rented a house at no. 53 Arbat in 1831, and lived here with his new bride, Natalia Goncharova. The house is now the **Pushkin Museum**. It is open 12 to 6 p.m. and Saturdays and Sundays 11 a.m. to 5 p.m.; closed on Mondays and Tuesdays. The poet Lermontov, the writer Herzen, the composer Scriabin and the sculptress Golubkina lived in the Arbat neighborhood. Their residences are also museums (see museum listings for locations).

After a leisurely stroll down to Smolensky Square, you will better understand the lyrics to a popular song: "Oy, Arbat, a whole lifetime is not enough to travel through your length!"

New Arbat

The area along Kalinin Prospekt from Arbat Square on the Boulevard Ring to the Kalinin Bridge is better known as the New Arbat. This area consists of shops and flats built during Khrushchev's regime in the 1960s. Across the street from the Prague Restaurant (one of the oldest in Moscow) is the **Church of Simon Stylites**, now an exhibition hall. Down the side street, behind the church, at no. 2 Malaya Molchanovka, is the **House-Museum of Lermontov**. It is open 11 a.m. to 6 p.m. and on Wednesdays and Fridays 2 to 9 p.m.; closed on Mondays and Tuesdays.

Next to the church, on Kalinin, is **Dom Knigi** (House of Books), the city's largest bookstore. The Malachite Casket Jewelry Shop is also in this building. On the same side is the Melodia Record Shop and the 3,000-seat Oktyabr Cinema.

A series of shops and cafes line the left side of Kalinin. The block begins with the Valdai Cafe and the New Arbat Supermarket. Other shops include the Moskvichka (Miss Moscow) Fashion Shop, Sintetika Department Store, Metelitsa (Snowball) Ice Cream Cafe, Charodeika (Sorceress) Beauty Shop, Jazz Cafe Pechora and the Podarki (Gift) Shop. The block ends at the 2,000-seat Arbat Restaurant with a large globe on its roof.

The prospekt crosses the Garden Ring at Tchaikovsky Street and ends at the river. Before Kalinin Bridge, on the right, stands the 30-story **CMEA/COMECON** building, headquarters for the East European economic trade community. The Hotel Mir is behind it. Farther down, on the same side of the river, is the Sovincenter and Mezhdunarodny (International) Hotel, built with the help of Armand Hammer and used by foreign firms. Nearby is also the building of the Soviet Federal Republic's Council of Ministers.

Red Shirts and Black Bread

We plunged into plebeian Moscow, the world of red-shirted workmen and cheap frocked women; low vodka shops and bare, roomy traktirs, where the red-shirted workmen assemble each evening to gossip and swallow astonishing quantities of tea, inferior in quality and very, very weak.

Here was Moscow's social and material contrast to the big houses, with the sleeping dvorniks, and of the silent street of painted house fronts, curtained balconies and all the rest. Though day had not yet dawned for other sections of Moscow, it had long since dawned for the inhabitants of this. Employers of labor in Moscow know nothing of the vexed questions as to eight-hour laws, ten-hour laws, or even laws of twelve. Thousands of red shirts, issuing from the crowded hovels of this quarter, like rats from their hiding places, had scattered over the city long before our arrival on the scene; other thousands were still issuing forth, and streaming along the badly cobbled streets. Under their arms, or in tin pails, were loaves of black rye bread, their food for the day, which would be supplemented at meal times by a salted cucumber, or a slice of melon, from the nearest grocery.

Though Moscow can boast of its electric light as well as of gas, it is yet a city of petroleum. Coal is dear, and, in the matter of electric lights and similar innovations from the wide-awake Western world, Moscow is, as ever, doggedly conservative. So repugnant, indeed, to this stronghold of ancient and honorable Muscovite sluggishness, is the necessity of keeping abreast with the spirit of modern improvement, that the houses are not yet even numbered. There are no numbers to the houses in Moscow; only the streets are officially known by name. To find anybody's address, you must repair to the street, and inquire of the policeman or drosky driver, who are the most likely persons to know, for the house belonging to Mr. So-and-so, or in which that gentleman lives. It seems odd that in a country where the authorities deem it necessary to know where to put their hand on any person at a moment's notice, the second city of the empire should be, in 1890, without numbers to its houses.

T Stevens, Travelling Through Russia on a Mustang

The Boulevard Ring

Ulitsa Gerzena (Herzen Street), named after revolutionary writer Alexander Herzen, runs out from the Kremlin's Manezhnaya Square (in between Gorky and Kalinin streets) to the Boulevard Ring. In the 15th century, this was the passage to the town of Novgorod. At no. 13 is the Moscow Conservatory Grand Hall, built in 1901. The conservatory was founded in 1866 by Rubenstein. A statue of Tchaikovsky stands in front. Count Menschikov once lived in the palace at no. 12. Pushkin was married in the nearby Church of the Ascension. At no. 19 is the Mayakovsky Theater, and at no. 6 the **Zoological Museum**. It is open 10 a.m. to 5 p.m. and on Wednesdays and Fridays 12 to 8 p.m.; closed on Mondays.

During the 16th and 17th centuries, the stone walls of the Beli-gorod, (White-town), stretched around the area now known as the Boulevard Ring. During the Time of Troubles at the end of the 17th century, Boris Godunov fortified the walls and built 28 towers and gates. By 1800 the walls were taken down and the area was planted with trees and gardens, made up of a number of small connected boulevards. Ten *bulvari* make up the Bulvarnoye Koltso, or Boulevard Ring, a horseshoe shape that begins in the southwest off Kropotkinskaya Street and circles around to the back of the Rossiya Hotel on the other side of the Kremlin. Frequent buses run around the ring, stopping off at each intersecting boulevard.

The first bears the name of the writer Nikolai Gogol. Gogolevsky Bulvar stretches from the Moskva open-air swimming pool to Arbat Square. It was once known as the Immaculate Virgin Boulevard. At no. 14 is the Central Chess Club.

Suvorovsky Boulevard extends from Kalinin Street to Herzen Street. It was named after the famous Russian army commander Alexander Suvorov, who lived at the end of it. Gogol lived at no. 7; increasingly despondent in his later years, he burned the second volume of his novel *Dead Souls* in this house, and died here in 1852. A monument to Nikolai Gogol on which characters from his books are depicted stands in front. Built in Russian Empire style by Gilliardi in 1823, the Lunin House is at no. 12. It is now the **Museum of Oriental Art,** open 11 a.m. to 8 p.m., closed on Mondays. The Nikitskiye Gates used to stand at the junction of the boulevard and Herzen Street, which is named Nikitskaya Square after a monastery that was in the area.

Tverskoi Boulevard begins with the Monument to Kliment Timiryazev, a prominent Russian botanist. Built in 1796, it is the oldest

boulevard on the ring, and was once a very fashionable promenade. Pushkin, Turgenev and Tolstoy all mentioned the Tverskoi in their writings. The house (no. 11) where the great Russian actress Yermolova lived is now the **Maria Yermolova Museum.** It is open 1 to 8 p.m., Saturday and Sunday 12 to 7 p.m.; closed on Mondays and Tuesdays. At no. 23 is the Pushkin Drama Theater, and at no. 25 the Gorky Literature Institute. Across the street is the Theater of Friendship of the Peoples of the USSR.

The Strastnoi (Passion) Monastery used to be in the area of the Strastnoi Boulevard, which begins at Pushkin Square with a Statue of Pushkin. On Pushkin's birthday, June 6, many people crowd the square to honor the poet. Pushkin and Chekhov streets branch out from the center. The hospital at no. 15 was the Palace of the Gagarin Princes, also the English Club from 1802 to 1812.

The Petrovskiye Gates used to stand at what is now the beginning of Petrovsky Boulevard, which runs from Petrovsky Street to Trubnaya Square. A few buildings still remain from the 14th-century Vysoko-Petrovsky Monastery that once stood on the banks of the Neglinnaya River (now underground). Many of the old mansions on this boulevard were converted into hospitals and schools after the Revolution. At no. 13 Tsvetnoi Bulvar is the **Old Circus.**

Rozhdestvensky (Nativity) Boulevard ends at Sretenka Street, a popular shopping area. On the right are 14th-century walls from the Convent of the Nativity of God. An exhibit of the Soviet fleet is now in the 15th-century Church of the Assumption.

The Statue to Nadezhda Krupskaya (1869-1939), Lenin's wife, marks the beginning of Sretensky Boulevard. It ends on Turgenevskaya Square with a metro stop. In 1885, Moscow named its first public library, located here, after the writer Turgenev. The Central Post Office is on Kirov Street. To the right, one can make out the tower of the Church of the Archangel Gabriel. Prince Alexander Menschikov ordered it built on his estate in 1707; he wanted it to be taller than the Kremlin's Ivan the Great Bell tower. In 1723, the archangel at the top was struck by lightning; so, for a time, the tower was the second largest structure in Moscow. Today it is known as the **Menschikov Tower.**

A Statue of the writer Griboyedov (1795-1829), marks the beginning of Christoprudny Boulevard. The name "Clear Pond" comes from the artificial pond at its center, which offers boating and ice skating in winter. The Sovremennik Theater is at no. 19.

Pokrovsky (Intercession) Boulevard begins at Chernyshevsky Street. The czars often took this route to their estate in Izmailovo, now a popular 3,000-acre park with a theater, amusement park and summer tent-circus. It can be reached from Metro stop Izmailovo Park. The buildings on the left used to serve the Pokrovsky barracks. A highly decorative rococo-style house built here in 1766 was known as the "Chest of Drawers".

The Soviet Circus

"Oi, how I love the Circus," bellows Alexander Frish, a charismatic and eccentric clown, who has been clowning around in the Soviet Circus for almost 20 years. Frish believes that "the circus is the universal language of joy and laughter that lets us all become children again."

The Soviet Circus is a world of vibrant artistry, precision and grace. In the USSR, the circus is a highly respected art form taken as seriously as classical ballet. It's also the most popular entertainment: more than 100 million Soviets attend performances each year. The Soviet Circus employs more than 25,000 people, including 6,000 performing artists and 7,000 animals. Seventy permanent circus buildings, including ice and aquatic circuses, are scattered from Moscow to Siberia — more than in the rest of the world combined. Over 100 circus troupes (most are government regulated, others private collectives) give up to nine performances a week in over 30 countries a year.

The early traditions of the circus go back over three centuries. The first formalized circus was created in England in 1770 by an ex-cavalry officer and showman named Philip Astley. It consisted mostly of trick riding, rope dancers, tumblers and jugglers, staged within a circular ring. In 1793, one of Astley's horsemen and later competitors, Charles Hughes, introduced this novel form of entertainment to Russia, with a private circus for Catherine the Great in the Royal Palace in St. Petersburg. Russia's first permanent circus building was built in St. Petersburg in 1877 by Gaetano Ciniselli, an equestrian entrepreneur from Milan. The Ciniselli Circus was the center of performance activity up to the Revolution, and this classic building still houses today's Leningrad Circus. The second oldest circus was the Old Circus in Moscow (a new Old Circus has recently been built on the site where the original once stood). Moscow also boasts the New Circus and the summer Tent Circuses.

The last section of the Boulevard Ring is intersected by Yauzsky Boulevard. This ends by the Yauza River, where it joins the Moskva River. A few 18th-century mansions remain in this area. Continuing along the banks of the Moskva, past another one of Stalin's gothic skyscrapers, brings you round the back of the Kremlin. One of the best views of the Kremlin is from the **Bolshoi Kammeni Moct** (Large Stone Bridge).

Nowhere in Europe were circus performers as politically active as in turn-of-the-century Russia. The circus became a sort of political sanctuary where sketches depicting the tumultuous state of Russia were tolerated. The clowns, especially, took every opportunity to satirize the czars, landowners and merchants. During these years of intellectual and political intensity, some of Russia's finest writers and directors, such as Gorky, Chekhov, and Stanislavsky, turned their attention to the circus. In one of his short stories, Maxim Gorky wrote: "Everything I see in the arena blends into something triumphant, where skill and strength celebrate their victory over mortal danger." Later, even Lenin took time off from the Revolution to nationalize the circus; on September 22, 1919, the world's first government circus began its operations.

In order to provide a consistently high standard of training in the circus arts, the government founded the first professional circus school in 1927. Today, at hundreds of circus schools throughout the country, students train for up to four years, studying all facets of circus life. During his final year, the student creates his own act and utilizes the services of circus producers, directors and choreographers. Once the act is approved by a circus board, the performer's professional career begins—the State supplies everything needed, from costumes and equipment to animals and special effects. Employment for the State circus artist is guaranteed for 20 years with a full pension upon retirement.

The emblem of the Soviet Circus depicts a circus performer reaching for the stars. The language of the circus is without words, as beauty, courage and skill bridge the gap between generations and nationalities. The circus is the universal language of the heart.

The thrills of the Soviet Circus

SOVIET CIRCUS
СОВЕТСКИЙ ЦИРК

Oleg POPOV
Олег ПОПОВ

The Garden Ring

After much of Moscow burned in the great fire of 1812 (over 7,000 buildings were destroyed), it was decided to tear down all the old earthen ramparts and in their place build a circular road around the city. Anyone who had a house along the ring was required to plant a *sad* (garden); thus the passage was named Sadovaya Koltso (Garden Ring). The ring, Moscow's widest avenue, stretches for ten miles (16 km) around the city, with the Kremlin's bell tower at midpoint. It is less than a mile (two km) from the Boulevard Ring. The 16 squares and streets that make up this ring each have a garden in their name, such as Big Garden and Sloping Garden. Buses, trolleys and the Koltso Metro circle the route. Along the way, modern buildings are sprinkled with 18th- and 19th-century mansions and old manor homes.

Beginning by the river, near Metro stop Park Kultury, is Krymskaya (Crimean) Square, surrounded by old classically designed provisional warehouses, built by Stasov in 1832-35. Nearby is the Olympic Press Center, Novosti Press Agency and Progress Publishers, publishing books in foreign languages.

At Zubovsky Square, Bolshaya Pirogovskaya (named after Nikolai Pirogov, a renowned surgeon) leads to Novodevichy Monastery. Many of Moscow's clinics and research institutes are located here. The street begins at Devichye Park (Maiden's Field), where many carnivals were held; maidens would dance to Russian folk tunes. To the right, Kropotkinskaya Street leads down to the Kremlin. The area between the Boulevard and Garden rings was once an aristocratic residential district; many old mansions are still in the area. At no. 18 is the former estate of the wealthy merchant Morozov.

At Smolenskaya (formerly called Sennaya, the Haymarket) is the tall Ministry of Foreign Affairs. Nearby is Belgrade Hotel. Tchaikovsky Street leads off the square. In 1940, Novinsky Street was renamed after the composer who lived here. The poets Alexander Griboyedovs grew up at no. 17. The great singers Fyodor Chaliapins (1873-1938) lived at no. 25 for over a decade. The American Embassy is at no. 19-32 Tchaikovsky.

The next square, Vosstaniya (Uprising), was named after the heavy fighting that took place here during the Revolutions of 1905 and 1917. It was once called Kudrinskaya, after the local village of Kudrino. The side street off the square is still known as Kudrinskaya. The square is surrounded by large apartment complexes, except for the 18th-century

Widow's House, the residence of widows and orphans of czarist officers killed in battle. Once the home of writer Alexander Kuprin, it is now a medical institute.

Before the square, off to the right, is Vorovsky Street, once one of the most fashionable areas of the city. Centuries ago, when the czar's servants and cooks lived in this area, the street was known as Povarskaya (Cook). Other side streets were Khlebny (Bread), Nozhevoy (Knife), and Chashechny (Cup). The two lanes Skaterny (Tablecloth) and Stolovoy (Table) still branch off the street. In *War and Peace*, Tolstoy described the Rostov's estate at no. 52 Povarskaya St., where there is now a statue of Tolstoy. Next door is the Writer's Club, named after the Soviet writer, Alexander Fadeyev. The **Maxim Gorky Museum** at no. 25, recognizable by the statue of Gorky at the front, tells about the life of the Russian writer. It is open from 10 a.m. to 6 p.m. and on Wednesdays and Fridays 12 to 8 p.m.; closed on Mondays and Tuesdays. Gorky also spent his last years in a house on the neighboring street of Kachalov no. 6, which is also a museum, open the same times as the museum on Vorovsky.

On the other side of Vosstanaya Square is Barrikadnaya St., with a Metro stop by the same name. The Planetarium and Zoo are in the area. This street leads into Krasnaya Presnaya, once a working-class district and the scene of many revolutionary battles. On the nearby side street of Bolshevistskaya, at no. 4, the **Krasnaya Presnya Historical Revolutionary Museum** traces the history of the area. It is open 11 a.m. to 6 p.m., closed Monday. 1905 Street leads to the International Trade Center, along the Krasnopresnenskaya Embankment. It was built with the cooperation of the American firms, Occidental Petroleum and Welton-Becket, to promote cultural relations and international exhibits. Anton Chekhov lived in the small red house at no. 6 Sadovaya Kudrinskaya, now the **Chekhov House-Museum.** It is open on Tues. and Thurs. 12.30 to 8 p.m., other days 10 a.m. to 6 p.m., and closed on Fridays.

Bolshaya Sadovaya (Great Garden) Street once had a triumphal arch through which troops returned to Moscow. Past Mayakovsky Square (with a Metro stop of the same name) is the **All Russia Museum of Decorative, Applied and Folk Art** at no. 31 Delegatskaya Street. It is open 11 a.m. to 6 p.m., closed on Mondays. Along the next street at no. 3 Sadovaya Samotechnaya is the **Central Puppet Theater,** better known as the Obraztsov, its founder. The puppet clock on the front of the building has 12 little houses with a tiny rooster on top; every hour, one house opens. At noon, all the boxes open, each with an animal puppet dancing to an old Russian folk song. Tsvetnoi (Flower) Boulevard, branching off the square, has the Old Circus and popular Tsentralny Rinok (Central Market). Nearby is the Soviet Army Museum and Theater.

The next square, Kolkhoznaya (Collective Farm), used to be called Sukharevskaya, after Sukhorov, a popular commander of the czar's *streltsy* guards, quartered here. Peter the Great opened Russia's first navigational school in the center of the square where the Sukharov Tower had stood. Prospekt Mira leads to the **Exhibition Park of Economic Achievements.** At no. 28 are the oldest botanical gardens in the city, known in Peter the Great's time as the **Apothecary;** the Metro stop is Botanichesky Sad. At no. 94, near the Rizhskaya (Riga) Railway Station (with a Metro stop of the same name) is the popular Rizhsky marketplace. The **Museum of Cosmonautics** is on the Alley of Cosmonauts. It's open 12 to 8 p.m., on Friday, Saturdays and Sundays 11 a.m. to 5:30 p.m.; closed on Mondays. Prospekt Mira led to the old towns of Rostov and Suzdal; it now turns into the Yaroslavl Highway, which runs to Yaroslavl in the Golden Ring.

The next square, Lermontovskaya, is named after the Russian poet Lermontov, who was born in a house near the square on October 3, 1814; a plaque on a building marks where the house stood. The plaque is inscribed with Lermontov's words: "Moscow, Moscow, I love you deeply as a son, passionately and tenderly." The square was known as Krasniye Vorota (Red Gate), as red gates once marked the entrance to the square. The Metro station was given this name. The czar's kitchen gardens were in this area. Nearby is the **Academy of Agriculture,** housed in a 17th-century mansion once owned by Count Yusupov, a descendent of a Mongol Khan.

Chakalov is the longest street on the ring, named after the pilot, Valeri Chakalov, who made the first non-stop flight over the North Pole from the USSR to America in 1936. At no. 14-16 lived the poet Marshak, the composer Prokofiev and the violinist Oistrach. Tchaikovsky once lived at no. 47. Behind the Kursky Railway Station is an 18th-century stone mansion, the Naidyonov Estate. Gilliardi and Grigorev built the estate, whose gardens stretch down to the Yauza River; it is now a sanatorium. After crossing the Yauza River, the ring becomes Taganskaya Square (with a Metro stop of the same name), where the popular avant-garde theater **Taganka** is located.

The Conqueror

A t ten in the morning of the second of September, Napoleon was standing among his troops on the Poklónny Hill looking at the panorama spread out before him. From the twenty-sixth of August to the second of September, that is from the battle of Borodinó to the entry of the French into Moscow, during the whole of that agitating, memorable week, there had been the extraordinary autumn weather that always comes as a surprise, when the sun hangs low and gives more heat than in spring, when everything shines so brightly in the rare clear atmosphere that the eyes smart, when the lungs are strengthened and refreshed by inhaling the aromatic autumn air, when even the nights are warm, and when in those dark warm nights, golden stars startle and delight us continually by falling from the sky.

The view of the strange city with its peculiar architecture, such as he had never seen before, filled Napoleon with the rather envious and uneasy curiosity men feel when they see an alien form of life that has no knowledge of them. This city was evidently living with the full force of its own life. By the indefinite signs which, even at a distance, distinguish a living body from a dead one, Napoleon from the Poklónny Hill perceived the throb of life in the town and felt, as it were, the breathing of that great and beautiful body.

Every Russian looking at Moscow feels her to be a mother; every foreigner who sees her, even if ignorant of her significance as the mother city, must feel her feminine character, and Napoleon felt it.

"A town captured by the enemy is like a maid who has lost her honor," thought he, and from that point of view he gazed at the Oriental beauty he had not seen before. It seemed strange to him that his long-felt wish, which had seemed unattainable, had at last been realized. In the clear morning light he gazed now at the city and now at the plan, considering its details, and the assurance of possessing it agitated and awed him.

Leo Tolstoy, War and Peace

The Bolshaya Krasnokholmsky Bridge crosses the Moskva River off of Zetsepsky Street. Near the Pavletskaya Metro stop is Bakhrushina Street. At no. 31 is the **Bakhrushkin Theatrical Museum** (closed on Tuesdays) with collections on the history of Russian theater. It was named after the merchant Alexei Bakhruskin, who opened the museum in 1894.

Dobryninskaya Square was named after the revolutionary Dobrynin, killed in the 1917 revolution. The next square, Oktyabrskaya, leads to the entrance of **Gorky Park,** with two large ferris wheels. The Hotel Warsaw is also nearby. Across from the park is the **State Art Gallery** (a branch of the Tretyakov, closed on Mondays) and the **Park of Arts.** Krimsky Val (Crimean Rampart) is the last section of the ring. It crosses the Moskva River by way of the Krymsky suspension bridge that brings us back to Park Kultury.

The Lenin Hills

The Lenin Hills, in the southwest, are the highest point in Moscow and provide one of the best views of the city. Group tours usually include a stop on the hills, or they can easily be reached by taking the Metro to the stop Leninskiye Gory (Lenin Hills). The Metro here rides above ground and crosses the Moskva River, and pedestrian walkways are on each side of the bridge.

A short walk from the Metro is a glass-enclosed escalator to the top of the hill. The avenue to the right leads to an observation platform, about a 15-minute walk. The platform provides a spectacular view of the city; in good weather the golden domes of the Kremlin can be recognized. If you turn, with the Moskva River behind, back, you can see a massive 36-story building. This is Lomonosov University, more widely known as **Moscow University,** founded in 1755 by Russian scientist Mikhail Lomonosov. This new university building was put up in 1949-53 by Stalin, who had six other similar gothic-style structures built throughout the city. The top of the university's main tower is crowned by a golden star in the shape of ears of corn. It is the largest university in the Soviet Union, with students from over 100 countries. The campus consists of 40 buildings, including sports centers, an observatory, botanical gardens and a park. The Gorky Library has over six million volumes. Gorbachev graduated from Moscow University with a degree in law; his wife Raisa with a degree in Leninist philosophy. Lomonosov Prospekt stretches behind the university, and Universitetsky Prospekt lies in front.

A few blocks to the left, in between the two prospekts, is the circular building of the **Novi Tsirk** (New Circus) situated on Vernadsky Prospekt. The circus is one of the most popular forms of entertainment in the Soviet Union and the Moscow Circus is famous throughout the world. This circus building, opened in 1971, seats 3,400. Its ring has four interchangeable floors that can be switched in less than five minutes. One is the regular ring, another a special ring for magicians, and the others are a pool for the aquatic circus and a rink for the ice ballet. The Universitet Metro station is right behind the Circus.

The other main circus of Moscow is the **Stari Tsirk** (Old Circus) at no. 13 Tsvetnoi Boulevard. The Old Circus was the first circus built in Moscow. When it closed down, the New Circus took its place. But recently a circus was built on the site of the Old Circus to match the original building. The new Old Circus was reopened in 1989 and directed by the famous (now retired) clown, Yuri Nikulin. In summer, Tent Circuses operate in Gorky and Izmailovo Parks. Tickets can be booked for the circus through the Intourist Service Desk at your hotel.

In front of the New Circus is the Moscow Palace of Young Pioneers, referred to as **Pioneerland.** This is a large club and recreational center for the children who belong to the Communist Youth Organization known as the Young Pioneers. Older members belong to the Young Komsomol League. Over 25 million members in the Soviet Union belong to the Young Pioneers, and over 39 million to the Komsomol. The Young Pioneers are similar in structure to western scout organizations. The 400 rooms in the palace include clubs, laboratories and workshops. It also has its own concert hall, sports stadium, gardens, and even an artificial lake for learning how to row and sail. There are over 35 other branch Pioneer Houses in Moscow. The entrance to the palace is marked by the Statue of Malchish-Kibalchish, a character from a popular children's book. On the corner is the Children's Musical Theater.

The Lenin Hill Ski Jump is on your left. The hills are a favorite picnic spot in summer, and in winter there is skiing and tobogganing. Across the river are the white buildings of the **Lenin Central Stadium** in the wide meadow area known as Luzhniki. *Lug* in Russian means "meadow". The complex consists of the **Lenin Stadium** (seating 100,000), the Palace of Sport, Swimming and Tennis Stadiums, Friendship Hall and Museum of Physical Culture. Many events of the Moscow 1980 Olympics were held here. The Olympic Village was built behind the University on Lomonosov Prospekt. Glancing to the left of the stadium, you can make out the golden domes of the Novodevichy Convent. To the right of the stadium, on Komsomolky Prospekt, is the Church of St. Nicholas at Khamovniki, built in 1682. In the past weavers lived in this area. The old Russian word for weavers is *khamovniki*. A side street off the prospekt near the Garden Ring is **Leo Tolstoy Street,** where the Russian writer lived for 19 years. Some of the works that he wrote while living in the house at no. 21 were *Power of Darkness* and *Resurrection*. The museum is open 10 a.m. to 5 p.m., closed on Mondays.

Novodevichy Convent

Ride the Metro one stop from Lenin Hills back across the river to *Sportivnaya*, and get off in front of the Lenin Stadium. Walking a few blocks down Fruzensky Street you come to one of the oldest religious complexes in the city, the **Novodevichy Convent,** a baroque-style complex of 15 buildings and 16 gilded domes from the 16th and 17th centuries. Grand-Prince Vasily III founded the convent in 1514 to commemorate the capture of Smolensk from Lithuania, which had controlled the area for over a century. The convent was also one in the group of fortified monasteries that surrounded Moscow. Novodevichy served mainly as a religious retreat for Russian noblewomen. Peter the Great banished his half-sister, Sophia, and first wife, Evdokia, to the convent and forced them to wear the veil. Napoleon tried to blow up the convent before he fled the city, but a nun pulled out the fuses. The convent was converted into a museum in 1922.

The five-domed Smolensky Cathedral was the first stone building and lies at the center of the convent. It was dedicated to the Virgin of Smolensk, a much revered icon, and modeled after the Kremlin's Uspensky Cathedral. Many 16th-century interior frescos portray the life of Vasily III (the father of Ivan the Terrible). A copy of the *Icon of Our Lady of Smolenskaya* hangs over the altar. The beautiful five-tiered iconostasis (1683-86) was presented by Sophia. Ivan the Terrible's daughter, Anna, is one of the noblewomen in the burial vault. There are two Gate Churches: the Transfiguration Gate Church at the northern entrance and the Church of Pokrov at the southern. Other structures include the Refectory Church (1685-87), Bell Tower (1690) and four nun's residences. The Miloslavsky Chambers are named after Sophia's sister, Maria Miloslavskaya, who lived here until her death. Sofia's

Chamber Prison is where Peter the Great imprisoned his half-sister when he deposed her as Regent and took the throne. Irina Godunova had her chamber here. She was the sister of Boris Godunov and was married to Czar Fedor. When Fedor died, Irina refused the throne and her brother, Boris, was elected Czar. Peter the Great's first wife, Evdokia Lopukhina, lived in the Lopukhina Chamber. The Convent (with a large Beriozka next door) is open daily 10 a.m. to 5:30 p.m., closed on Tuesdays.

Many notable Russian personalities are buried in the Novodevichy Cemetery. These include Chekhov, Gogol, Scriabin, Stalin's first wife and Nikita Khrushchev. This part of the Convent is currently under restoration and closed to the public.

Gorky Park

Gorky Park lies a few minutes' walk over the Moskva River from the Metro station, Park Kultury, in the Frunze District. It can also be reached from the other side of the river at Metro stop Oktyabrskaya on the Square of the October Revolution, which has a bronze statue of Lenin. A large archway marks the entrance to the park. This large park has amusement rides, boat rentals and the Zelyoni (Green) open-air theater. In summer, the park is packed with strollers, along with performance artists and circus performers of the Tent Circus. In winter, the popular Gorky Park ice skating rink is operating. The park is open daily 9 a.m. to midnight.

Also part of the park are the Neskuchny Sadi (Not-Boring Gardens), originally part of the Alexandrov Estate and now used by the Academy of Sciences. The estate is part of the Main Botanical Gardens (with a collection of over 16,000 varieties of roses) that stretch all the way to the river.

Donskoi Monastery

Not far from Gorky Park near the Metro stop Shabolovskaya is the **Donskoi Monastery.** This monastery and seven churches were founded by Czar Fedor and Boris Godunov in 1591 on the spot of the Russian Army's defense line against the invading Mongols. Legend claims the protection of the city came from the Donskaya Virgin Icon, the icon that Prince Donskoi took for protection into battle against the Tatars in 1380.

In the 16th century, six fortified monasteries formed a defensive ring to protect the city from the Mongols. The monasteries were connected by an earthen rampart, today's Garden Ring. The Donskoi Monastery houses a branch of the **Shchusev Museum of Architecture,** opened in 1934; it has exhibits of pre-revolutionary Russian architecture. The Old Cathedral of the Donskaya Virgin was the first building of the monastery. The cube roof and onion domes are topped with golden half-moon crosses that symbolize the Christian victory over Islam. A copy of the Donskaya Virgin Icon is on the eight-tiered iconostasis. (The original is in the Tretyakov Gallery.) Patriarch Tikhon, who was appointed the head of the Orthodox Church on the eve of the October 1917 Revolution, is buried in a marble tomb at the southern wall.

The Naryshkin-Baroque style New Cathedral of the Donskaya Virgin was commissioned a century later by the Regent Sophia, Peter the Great's half-sister. The interior frescos were painted by the Italian artist, Antonio Claudio, between 1782 and 1785. At the southwest corner of the monastery is the classical Church of the Archangel Michael, built in 1806-09. The Church served as a memorial chapel for the Golitsyn family. Mikhail Golitsyn (1681-1764) was Peter the Great's star general who began his career as a service drummer. Fourteen Golitsyns are buried here, including Dmitri and his wife Natalia, who is the subject of

Pushkin's novel *Queen of Spades*. The Church is now the Museum of Monumental Sculpture. Some pieces include the *Sitting Christ* by Antokolsky and two lions from the old English Club. Some of the people buried in the cemetery are Turgenev, the architect Bovet and a few of Tolstoy's relatives. Other buildings include the Tikhvin Gate Church, the Abbot's residence, a bell tower and the 20th-century Church of St. Seraphim, now a crematorium. Outside the gates is the Church of Rizpolozhenie, whose priests also conduct mass in the Old Cathedral on Sundays and holidays.

At no. 56 Donskaya Street is the Moscow Baroque Church of the Deposition of the Lord's Robe, built in 1701. The Church is filled with interesting cherubs and contains a copy of the *Icon of the Deposition of the Lord's Robe* under a gilded canopy. In 1625, an envoy of a Persian shah presented Czar Mikhail Romanov and the Patriarch Filaret with a fragment of Jesus' robe. Filaret had an icon painted and declared a new church holiday. The icon shows Romanov and Filaret placing the gold box, containing the piece of cloth, on the altar of the Kremlin's Uspensky Cathedral. The original icon is now in the Tretyakov Gallery.

Danilovksy Monastery

This old monastery lies south of the Donskoi (Metro stop Danilovskaya) and was founded in 1276 by Prince Daniil (later cannonized), who is buried in a golden coffin in the Cathedral of the Holy Fathers of the Seven Ecumenical Councils. This church was built by Ivan the Terrible in 1565 on the original site of St. Daniil's Church. The fresco of St. Daniil is the oldest in the church. In 1983, the Soviet government returned the monastery to the Orthodox Church. It is now the residency of the Moscow Patriarchy and in the process of being restored.

Leninsky Prospekt runs in front of the Donskoi Monastery along the river and leads into Moscow's modern southwest district, which consists mostly of residential housing. It winds past the Soviet Academy of Sciences, formerly Neskuchny (Not-Boring) Castle, and Gagarin Square with its monument, cast from titanium, of Yuri Gagarin, the first Soviet man in space. At the base of the monument is a replica of the space capsule Vostok (East), in which Gagarin traveled on April 12, 1961. (Gagarin died in a plane crash in 1968.) This square used to mark the city limits in the 1950s. The prospekt continues past many department stores to the Lumumba People's Friendship University, with 6,000 students from around the world. It eventually turns into the Kievsky Highway and ends at the Vnukovo local airport.

Spaso-Andronikov Monastery

This monastery is situated along the River Yauza, a tributary of the Moskva, in the southeast part of the city, near the Metro station Ploshchad Ilicha. It was founded in 1359 by the Metropolitan Alexei during the reign of Prince Donskoi and has quite an interesting history. After Alexei was confirmed by the Byzantine Patriarch in Constantinople, a heavy storm occurred at sea during his return journey. Alexei promised God, if he should live, to build a monastery dedicated to the saint, whose feast day was celebrated on the day of his safe arrival in Moscow. Alexei returned on August 16, the "Saviour Day" or "Vernicle." When the Mongol Khan suddenly summoned Alexei to help his ailing wife in the south, the Metropolitan appointed Andronik, a monk at Zagorsk's Trinity-Sergius Monastery, to oversee the operation in his absence. His monastery was called the Spaso-Andronikov, after the Saviour and the first abbot of the monastery; it later became the stronghold for the Old Believers. The white Cathedral of the Saviour was built in 1420-27; the iconist Andrei Rublev, who also trained as a monk at the Trinity-St. Sergius Monastery in Zagorsk, painted the interior frescos. The baroque Church of the Archangel Michael was commissioned by Ustinia Lopukhina in 1694 to celebrate the birth of her grandson Alexei, son of Peter the Great and her daughter Evdokia. Peter later banished Evdokia to Novodevichy Monastery (a form of divorce in those days) and the Lopukhinas to Siberia. The church is now an icon restoration studio.

The **Andrei Rublev Museum of Religious Art** is housed in three separate buildings. The former Seminary Building contains many 15th- and early 16th-century icons by Rublev and his students. Some of the icons include St. Sergius, St. George, John the Baptist and the Saviour. Many of the icons found in the Monks' Quarters (behind the Saviour Cathedral) were painted in Novgorod in the 17th century. Nearby is a new Exhibition Hall of mainly 17th- and 18th-century icons that include Our Lady of Tikhvin. The museum is open daily 11 a.m. to 6 p.m. and closed on Wednesdays.

Exhibition of Economic Achievements

Known in Russian as *Vy'stavka Dostizhen'ii Narod'novo Khozyai'stva* (VDNKh), the exhibition (opened in l959) should be visited if you have the time; most group tours make a stop. The park is situated right across the street from the **Kosmos Hotel** at the end of Prospekt Mira, near the Metro station VDNKh. Nearly 100,000 objects are exhibited in 300 buildings and 80 pavilions which cover 545 acres, representing the latest achievements in science, industry, transport, building and culture. The first monuments that come into view are the 315-foot- (96-meter-) high **Sputnik Rocket** (1964) that appears to shoot into space, and the **Monument to the Worker and Collective Farm Girl,** a piece of l937 Soviet-realist architecture. Pavilions include the **Atomic Energy, Agriculture** and **Culture Pavilions**. The most interesting, located at the end of the park, is the **Kosmos Pavilion.** In front stands a replica of the Vostok rocket that carried Yuri Gagarin into space in l961. Inside are displays of rockets and space capsules, including the first Sputnik, Lunnik, Soyuz rockets and Salyut space stations. Pictures of Yuri Gargarin, Valentin Tereshkova (the first woman into space), Alexi Leonov (who took the first space walk), and the first dogs in space (Laika, Belka and Strelka) line the walls. One exhibit tells of the first joint US-USSR space mission, Soyuz-Apollo, undertaken in July 1975. Other buildings include an open-air theater, small zoo, amusement park, shopping center, the Circorama (standing-only) circular movie theater and restaurants. You can hire boats and go fishing in the ponds; fishing gear can be rented from booths along the bank. In the winter, especially during the Winter Festival, there is plenty of entertainment, including ice-skating and troika rides.

The park is open daily 10 a.m. to 10 p.m. and 10 a.m. to 11 p.m. on weekends; the pavilions are open 10 a.m. to 7 p.m. A half-hour tour of the park can be taken on electric trams.

Ostankino

Not far from Metro stop VDNKh near the Exhibition Park is the **Ostankino Palace.** At the close of the l8th century, Nikolai Sheremetev built a palace on the grounds of his family's Ostankino estate. The Palace (1792-97) was built of wood, but painted to resemble bricks and stone. Interesting rooms are the Blue Room, Egyptian Ballroom, Italian Reception Room and the Picture Gallery and Theater, which had over 200 serf actors, dancers and musicians. The palace also houses the **Museum of Serf Art.** The beautiful serf-actress Prashkovya Kovalyova-Zhemchugova later became the count's wife. One of the streets in Ostankino bears her name. The Trinity Church adjoins the palace. The Museum is open daily 10 a.m. to 5 p.m. (winter 10 a.m. to 3 p.m.) and closed on Tuesdays and Wednesdays. A short walk away is the **Ostankino TV Tower,** 160 feet (540 meters) high. The tower has an observation deck and the rotating restaurant, Sedmoye Nebo (Seventh Heaven).

Down The Moskva River

The Moskva River winds through the city for about 30 miles (48 km). If your tour does not include a trip on the river, the best **boat cruises** leave from Kievsky Railway Station and run eastward to Novospassky Bridge (May to October). To get there, take the Metro to Kievskaya, not far from Hotel Ukrainia. The boat pier is located on the Berezhkovskaya Embankment, at one end of Borodinsky Bridge. Some sites along the way are the Novodevichy Monastery, Lenin Hills and Stadium, Gorky Park, Srelka Rowing Club, Moscow Open-Air Pool, Kremlin, Hotel Rossiya, and many estates, palaces, and churches. The tour lasts about 80 minutes and ends at the Novospassky Monastery, founded in the 15th century.

A second boat also leaves from the same pier and runs westward to Kuntsevo-Krylatskoye in Fili-Kuntsevo Park, which has a river beach. This trip lasts about an hour.

Vicinity of Moscow

The privileged classes of Russia used to build their summer residences in the countryside around Moscow. Many of these palaces and parks have been preserved and turned into museums easily reached by Metro, bus or car. Excursions can also be booked through the Intourist Service Bureau at your hotel, which include transportation and a tour of the sights.

Abramtsevo

The **Abramtsevo Estate Museum** is located along the Yaroslavsky Highway near the town of Zagorsk, 37 miles (60 km) north of Moscow. In 1843, Russian writer Sergei Aksakov bought the country estate (built in the 1770s); over the next 15 years, it was frequented by many prominent writers, such as Gogol, Tyutchev and Turgenev. Here Gogol gave a reading of the first chapter from his second volume of *Dead Souls* which he later burned at his home in Moscow. In 1870, art patron, Savva Mamontov bought the estate and turned it into a popular meeting spot and artist colony. There were art, theater, writing and pottery workshops; Serov, Vrubel, Repin, Chaliapin and Stanislavsky all lived and worked here. The 12th century-style Orthodox church in the park was designed by Victor Vasnetsov and painted by Polenov and Repin. Vasnetsov also built the park's "Hut on Chick Legs," based on a popular fairy tale. Abramtsevo, now a museum, displays rooms as they were used by Aksakov and Mamontov. Paintings and art work, done on the estate, including many of Vrubel's, are on display in the art studio. The museum is open 11 a.m. to 5 p.m., closed on Mondays, Tuesdays, and the last day of each month.

Arkhangelskoye Estate Museum

This museum lies in the village of Arkhangelskoye, ten miles (16 km) west of Moscow. Take the Volokolamskoye Highway and then the left road toward Petrovo-Dalniye. The closest Metro station is Tushinskaya; then proceed with bus no. 549. The estate, situated along the banks of the Moskva River, took 40 years to complete. Prince Golitsyn originally founded the estate at the end of the 18th century. The mansion and park were designed in French style by the architect, Chevalier de Huerne, and built by serf craftsmen. In 1810, the estate passed into the hands of the wealthy landowner, Prince Yusupov (a descendent of one of the Khans), who was the director of the Hermitage Museum and Imperial Theater. He turned the classical palace into his own personal art museum. Today the palace (made into a state museum in 1919) contains work by such artists as Boucher, Hubert Robert, Roslin and Van Dyck. The rooms and halls are beautifully decorated with antique furniture, marble sculptures, tapestries, porcelain and chandeliers; much of the china and glassware were produced on the estate. The palace is surrounded on three sides by a park, lined with sculptures, pavilions and arbors. The Temple to the Memory of Catherine the Great depicts her as Themis, Goddess of Justice. There is also a monument to Pushkin, who enjoyed visiting the grounds. The triumphal arch over the entrance was built in 1817.

A short distance from the palace is the wooden **Serf Theater,** exhibiting theatrical and original set designs by Pietro Gottardo Gonzaga.

Built in 1819 by the serf-architect Ivanov, the theater had one of the largest companies of serf actors. Nearby is the Russkaya Izba (Russian Cottage) Restaurant, fashioned after Russian peasant rooms. The cooking is also Old Russian; the menu offers bear meat and venison along with *kvas*, mead, and tea served from a bubbling samovar. Arkhangelskoye is open 11 a.m. to 6 p.m., closed on Mondays, Tuesdays and the last Friday of each month.

Borodino

Borodino, site of the most famous battle in the War of 1812, lies on the Moscow-Minsk Road, 75 miles (120 km) from Moscow. On August 26, 1812, Napoleon's troops fought the Russian Army, commanded by Mikhail Kutuzov, on a large field near the village. Napoleon's army numbered 135,000 soldiers and 600 guns. After 15 hours of fighting, Napoleon was forced to retreat. The Battle of Borodino was the turning point of the war. In 1912, to mark the 100-year anniversary, 34 monuments were erected throughout the battlefield. The polished granite obelisk (1966) crowned by a bronze eagle is dedicated to Field-Marshall Kutuzov. Leo Tolstoy visited the battlefield in 1876 while writing *War and Peace*. Other memorials commemorate WW II battles that took place here in 1941. The **Borodino Military History Museum,** with exhibits of the Battle of Borodino, is open 10 a.m. to 6 p.m., closed on Mondays and the last Friday of each month.

Istra River Museum Of Wooden Architecture

The museum is located 35 miles (56 km) west of Moscow near the Novoyerusalimsky (New Jerusalem) Monastery. The main building in the monastery is the Resurrection Cathedral (1656-85), built as an exact replica of the Christian church in Jerusalem. A collection of Russian paintings and porcelain is on display in the Refectory. The **Museum of Wooden Architecture** is on display in the park along the River Istra. It contains a wooden 17th-century church and farmstead, cottages, granaries and windmills brought in from nearby areas. The museums are open from 10 a.m. to 6 p.m., closed on Mondays and the last Friday of each month.

Klin

The old Russian town of Klin, founded on the banks of the Sestra River (a tributary of the Volga) in 1318, is located 50 miles (80 km) northwest of Moscow along the Leningrad Highway. Only two Naryshkin Baroque style churches remain from the town's monastery. Klin is widely known as the home of the great Russian composer, Pyotr Tchaikovsky (1840-93). His house, surrounded by a lovely garden, is now a museum that contains his personal belongings and grand piano. Here Tchaikovsky composed *The Nutcracker*, *Sleeping Beauty*, and the Fifth and Sixth Symphonies. Twice a year, on the anniversary of Tchaikovsky's birth and death, composers and musicians come to Klin to play his music. On his birthday, May 7, the winners of the Moscow Tchaikovsky International Competition play works on his grand piano. Concerts are also given year round in a hall near the museum. In Tchaikovsky's own words, "I just can't imagine myself living anywhere else. I find no words to express how much I feel the charm of the Russian countryside, the Russian landscape and the quiet that I need more than anything else." The museum is open 10 a.m. to 6 p.m., closed on Wednesdays, Thursdays and the last Mondays of each month.

Kolomenskoye Museum Preserve

This preserve is on the southern side of Moscow on the banks of the Moskva River and can be reached from the Metro station Proletarsky Prospekt. Kolomenskoye was once the estate of numerous Russian princes and czars, including Ivan the Terrible and Peter the Great. It is now an open-air museum of 16th- and 17th-century architecture. The tent-shaped Church of the Ascension, decorated with *kokoshnik* gables, was the highest structure in Moscow, 189 feet (60 meters) when it was built in 1532. Other structures of interest are the Dyakovskaya and Kazanskaya churches (open for services), the water and clock towers, a Siberian watch tower (1631), and a cottage used by Peter the Great (built in 1702), which was brought from Archangel. These buildings now exhibit 16th- to 19th-century Russian applied and decorative art that includes collections of paintings, ceramics, woodcarvings and clocks. The museum is open September through April from 11 a.m. to 5 p.m., May through August 1-8 p.m. on Wed. and Thurs. and other days 11 a.m. to 5 p.m., closed on Mondays and Tuesdays.

Kuskovo Palace Museum

This museum is located within the city limits and can be reached easily from Metro station Zhdanovskaya. The Kuskovo Estate was in the Sheremetev family since the 16th century. In the early 18th century,

Cows of Moscow

*T*he proceedings of these cows in the early morning in the heart of the city, wandering alone, was a mystery. On inquiring I was told that throughout Moscow various families possess, among their worldy goods, a cow. Vast numbers of the larger houses have considerable spaces enclosed in the rear of their dwellings— gardens, courts, grassy places. Likewise the innumerable cottages in the by-streets have within their gates green plots and outhouses. In very many of these there is a cow. During the summer time, when there is a pasture, the first duty to be observed in all these dwellings is to open the gates and let out the cow. If there is a delay in this performance a loud warning from the outhouse or court awakes the servant to it. The cow let out, he may go to bed again. She knows her way by certain streets towards a certain barrier of the city. As she goes other cows join her from other cottages or houses, and by the time they all arrive near the barrier they are a considerable body. Here they find a man blowing a horn, whose business it is to conduct them to some pasture outside the town, to take care of them during the day, to collect them by his horn in the afternoon, and to bring them back to the barrier at a given time. When he has done this his business is over. Each cow knows her way home, and finds it unmolested up to the very heart of the city, the Kremlin. What a simple and convenient method for insuring good and pure and fresh milk to the family! Each mater-familias *can water it according to her wants or tastes, and she can omit the chalk—a blessed privilege!*

G T Lowth, Across the Kremlin, *1868*

Count Pyotr Sheremetev, who had over 200,000 serfs, transformed Kuskovo into his summer residence. His wooden mansion (1769-75), designed by Karl Blank and the serf-architect Alexei Mironov, is faced with white stone and decorated with parquet floors, antique furniture and crystal chandeliers; it also houses an excellent collection of 18th-century Russian art. Other buildings of special interest in the gardens are Hermitage (1767), Dutch Cottage (1750), Italian Cottage (1755), Grotto Pavilion (1771) and the Greenhouse. The **Ceramics Museum** exhibits a fine collection of Russian and European porcelain, faience and glass. The museum is open 11 a.m. to 7 p.m. or 10 a.m. to 4 p.m. depending on time of year, and closed on Mondays and Tuesdays and the last Wednesday of each month.

Nahabino
Located about 18 miles (28 km) northwest of Moscow, Nahabino is the Soviet Union's first golf course. It was designed by Robert Trent Jones II who, along with Dr. Armand Hammer, spent nearly 15 years negotiating authorization permits. Nahabino is an 18-hole, 7,000-plus-yard, (6,735-meter) par-72 championship course, with an adjoining sport and hotel complex. It is scheduled to open in 1991.

Peredelkino
A few stops from Moscow's Kievsky Railway Station is Peredelkino. Here you can visit the estate and grave of the great Russian writer, Boris Pasternak, who received the Nobel Prize for Literature for his novel *Dr. Zhivago*.

Yasnaya Polyana
This town lies south of Moscow along the Simferopolskoye Highway. The great Russian writer, Leo Tolstoy, was born in Yasnaya Polyana and lived and worked here for over 60 years. Everything on the estate has been preserved as he left it — his study, library and parlor, where his wife Sofia Andreyevna meticulously copied his manuscripts. Here he wrote *Anna Karenina*, *War and Peace* and chapters of *The Resurrection*. Peasants would gather under the "Tree of the Poor" to ask his advice. Nearby, Tolstoy opened a school for peasant children. He is buried on the estate grounds. The museum is open 10 a.m. to 5:30 p.m. and closed on Mondays and Tuesdays.

The Golden Ring

The ancient towns of the Golden Ring, built between the 11th and 17th centuries, were the cradle of Russian culture. During Russia's early history, the two most important cities were Kiev in the south and Novgorod in the north. Both, situated in what is now western Russia, lay along important commerce routes to the Black and Baltic seas. The settlements that sprang up along the trade routes between these two cities prospered and grew into large towns of major political and religious importance. From the 11th to 15th centuries, the towns of Rostov, Yaroslavl, Vladimir, and Suzdal became capitals of the northern principalities, and Zagorsk served as the center of Russian Orthodoxy. In the 12th century, Moscow was established as a small protective outpost of the Rostov-Suzdal principality. By the 16th century, Moscow had grown so big and affluent that it was named the capital of the Russian empire. At the turn of the 18th century, St. Petersburg became the center of Russian power. The prominent towns that lay in a circular formation between Moscow and Leningrad became known as the Golden Ring.

The Russian Town

Up to the end of the 18th century, a typical Russian town consisted of a *kremlin*, a protective fortress surrounding the area. Watchtowers were built in strategic points along the *kremlin* wall and contained vaulted carriageways, which served as the gates to the city. The "timber town" within the kremlin contained the governmental and administrative offices. The *boyars* (noble class) had homes here too that were used only in time of war — otherwise they lived outside the town on their own country estates, where the peasants or serfs worked the land. The *posad* (earth town) was the settlement of traders and craftsmen. The *posad* also contained the *rinoks* — the markets and bazaars, as well as the storage-houses for the town. The merchants and boyars used their wealth to help build the churches and commissioned artists to paint elaborate frescos and icons. The number of churches and monasteries mirrored the prosperity of the town. The rest of the townspeople lived in settlements around the *kremlin* known as the *slobody*. The historical nucleus and heart of the town was known as the *strelka*. The regions were separated into principalities with their own governing princes. The ruler of the united principalites was known as the Grand-Prince and later

Czar. The head of the Orthodox Church was called the Metropolitan or Patriarch.

The Golden Ring area provides an excellent opportunity to view typical old Russian towns, which are still surrounded by ancient *kremlins*, churches and monasteries. The towns of Rostov, Vladimir, Suzdal and Pereslavl-Zalessky retain much of their original layouts. Outside Zagorsk and Kostroma are open-air architectural museums — entire wooden villages built to typify old Russian life. All the towns of the Golden Ring have been well-restored, and many of the buildings are now museums that trace the history of the area that was the center of the Golden Age of Rus for more than four centuries.

Religion and the Church

Before Prince Vladimir introduced Byzantine Christianity to the Kievan principality in AD988, Russia was a pagan state; the people of Rus worshipped numerous gods. Festivals were held according to the seasons, planting and harvest cycles, and life passages. Special offerings of eggs, wheat and honey were presented to the gods of water, soil and sun. Carved figures of mermaids and suns adorned the roofs of houses. When Prince Vladimir married the sister of the Byzantine Emperor and introduced Christianity, Russia finally united under one God, and Kiev became the center of the Orthodox Church. But it took almost a century to convert the many pagan areas, especially in the north. Early church architecture (llth century) was based on the Byzantine cube-shaped building with one low rounded cupola on the roof bearing an Orthodox cross facing east. The domes gradually evolved into helmet drums on tent-shaped or square sloping roofs. These drums eventually took on the distinctive onion shape suitable to the heavy snowfalls. By the end of the 16th century, three or five domes, with one dominant central dome, were commonly installed atop Orthodox places of worship. The next two centuries witnessed Classical and Baroque influences, and the onion domes become elaborately shaped and decorated. During your tour of the Golden Ring, try dating the churches by the shape of their domes.

The outer walls were divided into three sections by protruding vertical strips, which indicated the position of the piers inside the church. A few centuries later, the churches expanded considerably, and were built from white stone or brick instead of wood. (Unfortunately, many of the wooden buildings did not survive and stone churches were built on their original sites.) The main body of the church was tiered into different levels and adjoined by chapels, galleries and porches. A large tent-shaped bell tower usually dominated one side.

During the two and a half centuries of Mongol occupation (beginning in the mid-13th century), Russia was cut off from any outside influence. Monasteries united the Russian people and acted as shelters and fortresses against attacks. They became the educational centers and housed the historical manuscripts, which monks wrote on birch-bark parchment. During this period, Russian church architecture developed a unique style. Some distinctive features were the decorative *zakomara*, semi-circular arches that lined the tops of the outer walls where they joined the roof. The *trapeza* porch was built outside the western entrance of the church and other carved designs were copied from the decorations on peasant houses. Elaborate carved gables around doors, windows and archways were called *kokoshnik*, named after the large headdresses worn by young married women. Even though, through the years, the architecture took on elements of European Classical, Gothic and Baroque elements, the designs always retained a distinctive Russian flare. Each entrance of the *kremlin* had its own Gate Church. The most elaborate stood by the Holy Gates, the main entrance to the town. Many cathedrals took years to build and twin churches were also a common sight — one was used in winter and the other, more elaborate, for summer services and festivals.

The interior of the church was highly decorated with frescos. Images of Christ were painted inside the central dome, surrounded by angels. Beneath the dome came the pictures of saints, apostles and prophets. Images of the patron saint of the church might appear on the pillars. Special religious scenes and the earthly life of Christ or the Virgin Mary were depicted on the walls and vaults. The Transfiguration was usually painted on the east wall by the altar and scenes from the Last Judgment and Old Testament were illustrated on the west wall, where the people would exit the church. The iconostasis was an elaborate tiered structure, filled with icons, that stretched behind the altar from the floor toward the ceiling. The top tiers held Christ, the middle the saints and prophets, and the lower tiers were reserved for scenes from church history. Fresco painting was a highly respected skill and many master craftsmen, such as Andrei Rublev and Daniil Chorny, produced beautiful works of art. The plaster was applied to the wall of the church, and then the artists would sketch the main outline of the fresco right on to the damp plaster. The master supervised the work and filled in the more intricate and

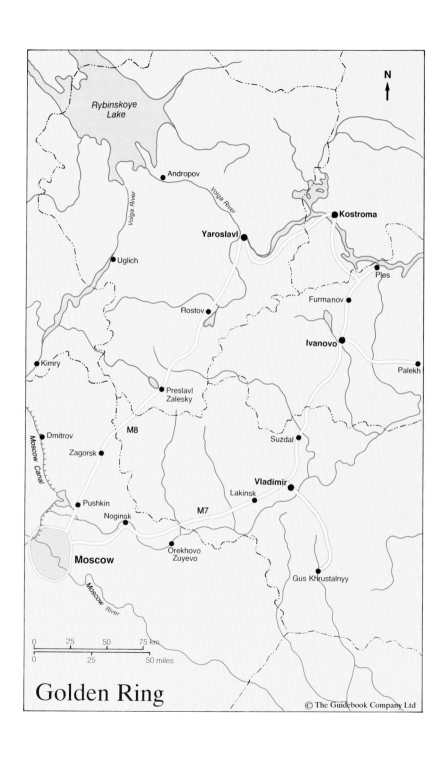

N

Rybinskoye
Lake

Androppov

Volga River

Volga River

Kostroma

Yaroslavl

Uglich

Ples

Rostov

Furmanov

Ivanovo

Kimry

Palekh

Preslavl
Zalesky

M8

Dmitrov

Moscow Canal

Zagorsk

Suzdal

Vladimir

Pushkin

Lakinsk

Noginsk

M7

Orekhovo
Zuyevo

Moscow

Gus Khrustalnyy

Moscow River

| 0 | 25 | 50 | 75 km |

| 0 | 25 | | 50 miles |

Golden Ring

important parts of the composition, while the apprentices added the background detail.

The building of elaborate churches and painting of exquisite icons and frescos reached its zenith in the prosperous towns of the Golden Ring. Even cathedrals in the Moscow Kremlin were copied from church designs that originated in Rostov, Vladimir and Suzdal. Today these churches and works of art stand as monuments to an extraordinary era of Russian history.

Religion after the Revolution

For nearly 1,000 years, the Russian Orthodox Church dominated the life of Russia and, as Tolstoy observed, for most of the Russian people, "faith was the force of life." But after the 1917 Revolution, when Marx proclaimed that "religion is the opium of the people," all churches were closed to religious use and their property confiscated and redistributed by the government. Article 124 of the Soviet Constitution states that "church is separate from state" and provides "freedom of worship for all citizens." Before the Revolution, Russia had almost 100,000 churches and monasteries; today the country has less than 10,000 (with an increase of 3,000 in the last few years) that are open for religious activities. There are about 50 million Orthodox believers, 15 percent of whom are regular church attenders. Leningrad, a city of five million people, has only 18 churches.

In 1988, the Millenium of Russian Christianity was officially celebrated throughout the Soviet Union and government decrees provided a new legal status for the Orthodox Church and other religions. The Russian Orthodox Church is still headed by the Patriarch, assisted by the Holy Synod, whose seats are in Zagorsk and Moscow. But the government continues to control and dictate the moves of the Church. The topic of religion is scheduled to be discussed in future meetings of the Supreme Soviet. Positive signs of increased religious tolerance and freedom are emerging; a small number of churches, for example, have been officially given back for religious use. More people, especially the younger generation, are attending church services and being baptized. Theological seminaries are training monks and priests and church charity organizations are now permitted to help the poor, unemployed and homeless, the new paradox of Soviet society.

One well-respected Leningrad rector of the Orthodox Church and city seminary (who was recently allowed to visit Rome for an audience with the Pope) remarked that "in principle, even with perestroika, nothing has changed. We've been waiting for 70 years for a law allowing the church to govern itself. But I'm an optimist. People aren't only interested in bettering themselves economically, but also morally and spiritually. The powers of the State cannot extend to the soul. And in these uncertain times, we would like to help the new generation find their way."

Many other religious groups are also enjoying a new period of openness. There are 1.5 million officially registered Jews (given as their nationality), 4 million Roman Catholics, 5 million Uniates (Catholics of Eastern Rite), over 1 million Baptists, 2 million Lutherans, 250,000 Pentecostalists, 50,000 Mennonites, 50,000 Seventh-Day Adventists and 50,000 Jehovah's Witnesses, 500,000 Buddhists, 5.5 million Moslems and about 1 million Old Believers, a sect resulting from the 1666 schism of the Orthodox Church.

Getting There

Many travel organizations offer packaged tours specifically to the Golden Ring area that include stops in Moscow and Leningrad; most tour the Golden Ring by bus — also an excellent way to see the Russian countryside. Intourist can help book excursions to cities along the Golden Ring route from Moscow or Leningrad once you're in the USSR — they also add the towns to your visa. Some places, such as Zagorsk, can be visited in a day from Moscow. In others you may stay overnight, as long as you have prebooked the hotel through Intourist. You can travel quite comfortably to the areas via bus, train or car. There are restaurants along the way, but bring some food and drink for the bus rides.

The towns of the Golden Ring are a majestic mirror of Russia's past grandeur. The churches and monasteries are beautifully preserved and their frescos and icons have been painstakingly restored. Many of the churches still hold religious services, which you are welcome to attend, as long as you are not wearing shorts or sleeveless shirts. Other religious buildings have been converted into museums that house the art and history of the regions. A splendid skyline of golden-domed churches, tent-shaped towers, ornamental belfries, picturesque old wooden buildings and rolling countryside sprinkled with birch trees greets you — as it did the visitor more than seven centuries ago.

A variety of church architecture in the Golden Ring

Zagorsk

A 45-mile (70-km) ride north of Moscow on the Yaroslavskoye Highway leads to Zagorsk, the most popular town on the Golden Ring route.
As soon as the road leaves Moscow, it winds back in time through dense
forests of spruce and birch, past old wooden *dacha* (country homes) and
collective farms, and eventually opens onto a magical view, upon which
fairy tales are based. Once upon a time on a hilltop in a large white
fortress surrounded by the rivers Koshura and Glimitza and filled with
star-studded golden onion domes, sparkling in the sunlight and dusted
lightly with glistening snow, an obscure monk, who was destined to
become a saint, founded the small settlement of Sergiev Posad and a
monastery that was to be the center of Russian Orthodoxy for centuries
to come. Zagorsk, the jewel of old Russian towns, gives the visitor a
marvelous glimpse into the Russian life of six centuries ago.

History

In order to unify the Russian territories during the Mongol invasions
(beginning in the 13th century), Sergius and his pupils founded 23
monasteries across Russia that also acted as regional strongholds.
Moscow princes, czars and rich *boyars* contributed heavily to the
Troitse Lavra until the monastery became not only the wealthiest in all
Russia, but also the most revered pilgrimage shrine in Moscovy. For
centuries, it was the center of the Church and today still seats the Patriarch of the Orthodox Faith.

Grand Prince Dmitri Donskoi defeated the Khan Mamai's hordes in
1380. At the monastery, one of St. Sergius' pupils, the famous iconist
Andrei Rublev, painted the *Old Testament Trinity* (now in Moscow's
Tretyakov Gallery) to commemorate this famous battle at Kulikovo on
the Don. The town's original name of Sergiyev Posad (Settlement of
Sergius) was changed to Zagorsk, after the revolutionary Vladimir
Zagorsk, in 1930. It has a population of over 100,000.

The art of carving wooden toys has long been a tradition in Zagorsk;
the first toys were made and distributed by St. Sergius to the children of
the town. Many painters, sculptors and folk artists trace their heritage
back to the 17th century, when the first toy and craft workshops were set
up in the town. The Beriozka, to the left as you pass through the main
gates, sells many locally made wooden toys.

The thick *kremlin* walls were built around the monastery in 1540
during the reign of Ivan the Terrible to protect it from attack. A half-

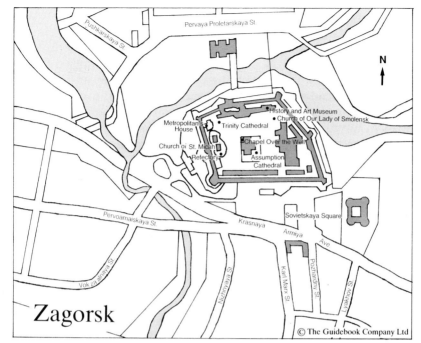

Zagorsk

© The Guidebook Company Ltd

century later, the *Lavra* (as large monasteries were called in Russia) withstood a 16-month seige by Polish forces. The monastery complex was such an important center for the Russian people that its fall would have meant the end of Rus. The monastery remained an important fortress that defended Moscow well into the 17th century. Eleven octagonal towers were built into the walls as key defense points. The most famous, the northeast tower, is known as the Utichya (Duck) Tower; the duck atop its spire symbolizes Peter the Great's hunting expeditions in Zagorsk.

Sights

The parking square, near the main gates of the monastery complex, looks out over many ancient settlements that dot the landscape, and the large *kremlin* citadel that houses priceless relics of old Russian architecture. Enter the main gates at the eastern entrance through the Pilgrim Tower; paintings of the Holy Pilgrims depict the life of Sergius Radonezhsky (from the town of Radonezh), the 14th-century monk who established the Troitse-Sergiyev Lavra — the Trinity Monastery of St. Sergius, lying beyond the gates. The small **Church of St. John the Baptist**, built in 1693 by the Stroganov family (a wealthy princely family), stands over the main or Holy Gates.

The first large structure that catches the eye is the monastery's main **Assumption Cathedral**. This blue and gold-starred, five-domed church, with elegant sloping *zakomara* archways was consecrated in 1585 to commemorate Ivan the Terrible's defeat of the Mongols in the Asian territory of Astrakhan. Yaroslavl artists, whose names are inscribed on the west wall, painted the interior frescos in 1684. The burial chambers of the Godunov family (Boris Godunov was czar from 1598 to 1605) are located in the northwest corner.

Many of these churches are open for worship and conduct services throughout the day. Respectfully-dressed visitors are welcome. Picture taking without flash is usually permitted.

The brightly painted **Chapel-over-the-Well**, located outside by the cathedral's west wall, is built in the Naryshkin cube-shaped octagonal style. Near the riverbank stands the **Sergius Well Chapel**. It was customary for small chapels to be built over sacred wells; today pilgrims still bring bottles to fill with holy water.

Directly beyond the cathedral is the five-tiered turquoise and white baroque bell tower (1740-70) designed by Prince Ukhtomsky and Rastrelli. Topped with a dome in the form of a crown, it once held 40 bells.

Head directly left of the cathedral to the southern end of the complex. A stroll in this direction to the **Refectory** may lead past long-bearded monks dressed in the traditional black robes and *klobuki* tall hats. The Refectory, rebuilt in 1686, is painted in colorful checkerboard patterns of red, blue, green and yellow. It has a large open gallery with 19th-century paintings and wide staircases, and is decorated with carved columns and gables. The small chapel at the end of the hall has a carved iconostasis by the altar and a beautiful red jasper inlaid floor.

Another quaint church, standing next to the Refectory, is the **Church of St. Micah** (1734).

Behind the Refectory, in the southwest corner, is the one-domed **Trinity Cathedral**, which the Abbot Nikon erected over the site of the original Church of St. Sergius in 1422 (the year Sergius was cannonized). Pilgrims still visit the remains of St. Sergius, which lie in a silver sarcophagus donated by Ivan the Terrible. An embroidered portrait of St. Sergius that covered his coffin is now preserved in the History and Art Museum, a short walk away. In 1425, Andrei Rublev and Daniil Chorny painted the icons on the cathedral's iconostasis, which include a copy of Rublev's *Holy Testament Trinity*. The cathedral contains 42

The Old Aristocracy

**W**ealth was measured in those times by the number of 'souls' which a landed proprietor owned. So many 'souls' meant so many male serfs: women did not count. My father, who owned nearly twelve hundred souls, in three different provinces, and who had, in addition to his peasants' holdings, large tracts of land which were cultivated by these peasants, was accounted a rich man. He lived up to his reputation, which meant that his house was open to any number of visitors, and that he kept a very large household.

We were a family of eight, occasionally of ten or twelve; but fifty servants at Moscow, and half as many more in the country, were considered not one too many. Four coachmen to attend a dozen horses, three cooks for the masters and two more for the servants, a dozen men to wait upon us at dinner-time (one man, plate in hand, standing behind each person seated at the table), and girls innumerable in the maid-servants' room, —how could anyone do with less than this?

Besides, the ambition of every landed proprietor was that everything required for his household should be made at home by his own men.

'How nicely your piano is always tuned! I suppose Herr Schimmel must be your tuner?' perhaps a visitor would remark.

To be able to answer, 'I have my own piano-tuner,' was in those times the correct thing.

'What a beautiful pastry!' the guests would exclaim, when a work of art, composed of ices and pastry, appeared toward the end of the dinner. 'Confess, prince, that it comes from Tremblé ' (the fashionable pastry-cook).

'It is made by my own confectioner, a pupil of Tremblé, whom I have allowed to show what he can do,' was a reply which elicited general admiration.

As soon as the children of the servants attained the age of ten, they were sent as apprentices to the fashionable shops, where they were obliged to spend five or seven years chiefly in sweeping, in receiving an incredible number of thrashings, and in running about town on errands of all sorts. I must own that few of them became masters of their respective arts. The tailors and the shoemakers were found only skilful enough to make clothes or shoes for the servants, and when a really good pastry was required for a dinner-party it was ordered at Tremblé's, while our own confectioner was beating the drum in the music band.

That band was another of my father's ambitions, and almost every one of his male servants, in addition to other accomplishments, was a bass-viol or a clarinet in the band. Makar, the piano-tuner, alias under-butler, was also a flutist; Andrei, the tailor, played the French horn; the confectioner was first put to beat the drum, but he misused his instrument to such a deafening degree that a tremendous trumpet was bought for him, in the hope that his lungs would not have the power to make the same noise as his hands; when, however, this last hope had to be abandoned, he was sent to be a soldier. As to 'spotted Tikhon', in addition to his numerous functions in the household as lamp-cleaner, floor-polisher, and footman, he made himself useful in the band—today as a trombone, tomorrow as a bassoon, and occasionally as second violin. . . .

Dancing-parties were not infrequent, to say nothing of a couple of obligatory balls every winter. Father's way, in such cases, was to have everything done in a good style, whatever the expense. But at the same time such niggardliness was practised in our house in daily life that if I were to recount it, I should be accused of exaggeration. However, in the Old Equerries' Quarter such a mode of life only raised my father in public esteem. 'The old prince,' it was said, 'seems to be sharp over money at home; but he knows how a nobleman ought to live'.

Prince Peter Kropotkin, Memoirs of a Revolutionist, *1899* works by Rublev and is joined by the smaller **Church of St. Nikon** (1548).

Across from the cathedral is the slender **Church of the Holy Spirit** with the long bell tower under its dome. It was built in 1476 by stone masons from Pskov.

Past the belfry along the northwestern wall is the softly rounded **Church of Our Lady of Smolensk** (1745), built to house the icon of the same name. It was designed by the Russian architect, Prince Okhtomsky, and decorated in the Elizabethan baroque fashion.

Behind this church stands the **Trinity Monastery of St. Sergius**, one of the most important monuments of medieval

Russia. The **Metro- politan's House**, vestry and adjoining monastery buildings now house the **Zagorsk History and Art Museum**. The museum, which displays gifts in the order presented to the monastery, contains one of the Soviet Union's richest collections of early religious art. The exhibits include icons from the 14th to 19th centuries, and portraits, chalices, china, crowns, furniture, jewelry and handicrafts from the 14th to 20th centuries. The museum is open daily from 10 a.m. to 5 p.m. and closed on Mondays.

The monastery also served as the town's hospital and school. Next to the museum is the red brick, yellow-and-white sandstone hospital building with the adjoining all-white tent-roofed **Church of Saints Zosimus and Savvaty** (1635).

In the opposite northeast corner, behind the Duck Tower, is the colorfully painted and tiled **Chertogi Palace**, built at the end of the 17th century for Czar Alexei, who often came to Zagorsk with an entourage of over 500 people. One of the ceilings in the palace is covered with paintings that honor his son's (Peter the Great) victories in battle. It now houses the Theological College.

Exiting through the main gate make a right, and walk toward the **Kelarskiye Ponds**, situated beyond the southeast Pyatnitskaya Tower. There you may find artists sketching and people strolling among the old garden walls. Two churches built in 1547 stand outside the walls — the **Church of St. Parasceva Pyatnitsa** and the **Church of the Presentation of the Mother of God**, nearest the pond. The Zolotoye Koltso (Golden Ring Restaurant), is only a few minutes' walk away.

The craft of wood carving is still carried out in Zagorsk. The famous *matryoshka*, the nest of carved dolls, has its origins here. The history of toys and folk art can be viewed at the **Zagorsk Toy Museum** at no. 136 Krasnoi Armii Prospekt. The Zagorsk Art Workshop Collective continues to produce wooden folk art. A special souvenir section contains carved wooden dolls, boxes and jewelry.

Vicinity of Zagorsk

Not far outside Zagorsk is the small town of **Alexandrov**, whose history is connected with Ivan the Terrible. The Alexandrova Sloboda was a residence of Ivan the Terrible for 17 years and one of the headquarters for his select army of *oprichniki*. The oldest buildings in the village are the (non-functioning) convent and **Trinity Cathedral** that women helped build in the 15th century.

After Ivan's *oprichniki* sacked Novgorod, he brought the golden oak doors from the Hagia Sophia Cathedral to adorn the Trinity's entrance. The daughters of Czar Alexei are buried in the Church of the Purification. The Church of the Intercession was Ivan the Terrible's court chapel. Next to this chapel is a bell tower and residential quarters, where Marfa, the step-sister of Peter the Great, who forced her to take the veil, was exiled from 1698 to 1707. The future Empress Elizabeth was also banished to the Alexandrova Sloboda for nine years.

Pereslavl-Zalessky

The tranquil town of Pereslavl-Zalessky is situated on a hilltop by the southeastern shores of Lake Pleshcheyevo about 35 miles (56 km) northeast of Zagorsk. Approaching Pereslavl from the road, pleasantly scented by the surrounding groves of pine and birch, you have an enchanting view of the shimmering azure waters of the lake, three old monasteries on the side of the road, and golden crosses atop painted onion domes that loom up from sprawling green fields dusted with blue and yellow wildflowers. Young boys wave at passersby as they fish in the lake with long reed poles. The River Trubezh meanders through the old earthen kremlin that winds around the center of town. These ramparts date back over eight centuries. One of Russia's most ancient towns, Pereslavl Zalessky is a charming place, sprinkled with well-preserved churches and monasteries that at one time numbered over 50. After checking into your hotel and having a meal at the *Skazka* (Fairy Tale) Restaurant, take a pleasant walk along the dirt roads and imagine that Peter the Great may have traversed the same footpaths before you.

History

Pereslavl-Zalessky's long and fascinating history is traced back to the year 1152, when Prince Yuri Dolgoruky (who founded Moscow five years earlier) fortified the small village of Kleschchin on the banks of the Trubezh, and renamed it Pereslavl after an old Kievan town. Situated in an area on the *zalasye* (beyond the dense woods of Moscow), it became known as Pereslavl-Zalessky. The area was an important outpost of Moscow; Prince Alexander Nevsky set out from Pereslavl to win his decisive battle with the Swedes in 1240. Since the town also lay on important White Sea trade routes, it quickly prospered; by 1302, Pereslavl had grown large enough to be annexed to the principality of Moscovy.

Sights

Ivan the Terrible later consolidated Pereslavl, along with the nearby village of Alexandrov, into a strategic military outpost to headquarter his *oprichniki* bodyguards. In 1688, the young Czar Peter I came here from Moscow to build his first *poteshny* (amusement) boats on Lake Pleshcheyevo. It was in a small shed near the lake that Peter discovered a wrecked English boat that he learned to sail against the wind. In 1692, Peter paraded these boats (forerunners of the Russian fleet) for members of the Moscow court. One of them, the *Fortuna*, can be found in the **Botik Museum**, which lies about two miles (three km) from Pereslavl (by the south bank of the lake) near the village of Veskovo. Other relics from the Russian flotilla are also displayed here. Two large anchors mark the entrance and a monument to Peter the Great by Campioni stands nearby. It is open 10 to 4 and closed on Tuesdays.

Make your way to the central Krasnaya Square. The small grassy hills circling around you are the remains of the towns's 12th-century earthen protective walls. In front of the **Statue of Alexander Nevsky** is the white stone **Cathedral of the Transfiguration**, the oldest architectural monument in northeastern Russia. Yuri Dolgoruky himself laid the foundation of this church, which was completed by his son, Andrei Bogoliubsky; (God-Loving) in ll57. This refined structure with its one massive fringed dome became the burial place for the local princes. Each side of the Cathedral is decorated with simple friezes. The *zakomara*, the semi-circular rounded shape of the upper walls, distinguish the Russian-style from the original simpler cube-shaped Byzantine design. Frescos and icons from inside the cathedral, like the 14th-century *Transfiguration* by Theophanes the Greek and Yuri Dolgoruky's silver chalice, are now in Moscow's Tretyakov Gallery and Kremlin Armory. The other frescos were done during the cathedral's restoration in 1894. Across from the cathedral is the **Church of St. Peter the Metropolitan**. Built in 1585 (with a l9th-century bell tower), the octagonal frame is topped with a long white tent-shaped roof. This design in stone and brick was copied from the traditional Russian log-cabin churches of the north.

Off in the distance, across the river, is the **Church of St. Semion** (1771). In between this church and the Lenin Monument on Svoboda Street are the early 19th-century shopping arcades, Gostiny Dvor. Religious services are held at the **Church of the Intercession** on Pleshcheyevskaya Street.

Take a leisurely stroll towards the river and follow it down to the lake. Scattered along the paths are brightly painted wooden *dachas* with carved windows covered by lace curtains. Children can be found playing outside with their kittens or a *babushka* (accent on first syllable) hauling water from the well. Many times the *dedushka* is picking apples and wild strawberries or carving a small toy for his grandchildren out of wood. Stop for a chat; it is amazing how far a few common words can go — before you know it, an invitation for *chai* may follow! At the

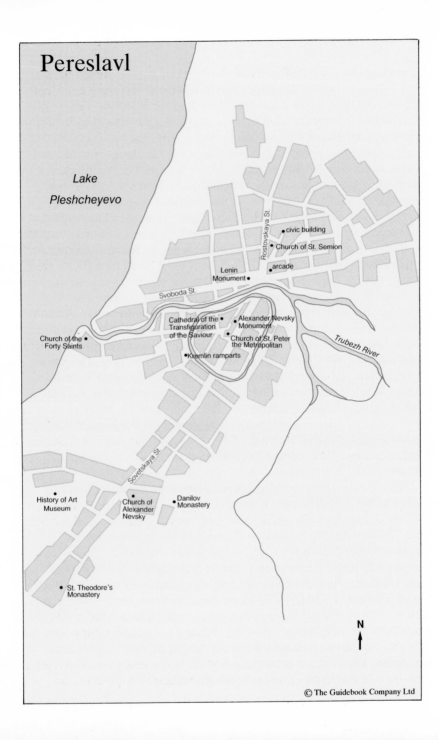

point where the Trubezh flows into the lake stands the **Church of the Forty Saints** (1781) on Riibnaya Sloboda, the old fish quarter. With a little bargaining or a smile, get a rowboat to take out on the lake — or go out with the fishermen. On a warm day, it is a perfect place for a picnic; try taking a dip in the water!

On a little sidetrip out of the town are a number of monasteries and chapels that you may have glimpsed if you arrived from Zagorsk. The four monasteries lining the road into and out of Pereslavl also acted as protective strongholds, guarding the town from invasions. The one farthest away is the **Convent of St. Theodore**, about 4 miles (6.5 km) south of town on Sovetskaya Street. Ivan the Terrible built this convent and the **Chapel of St. Theodore** to honor his wife Anastasia, who gave birth to their first son, Fedor (Theodore), in 1557. Ivan often stopped at the shrine to pray when he visited his bodyguard army, which resided in the town.

About a mile closer to the town is the memorial **Church of Alexander Nevsky** (1778). A few minutes' walk from this church, set in a woody rustic setting, is the **Danilov Monastery**. A few buildings remain from this l6th-century structure. The **Trinity Cathedral** was commissioned by Grand-Prince Vasily III in 1532. The single-domed cathedral, with 17th-century frescos by renowned Kostroma artists Nikitin and Savin, was built by Rostov architect Grigory Borisov in honor of Vasily's son, Ivan the Terrible. The Abbot Daniel, who founded the monastery in l508, was in charge of the cathedral's construction and present at Ivan's christening. The smaller **Church of All Saints** was built in l687 by Prince Bariatinsky, who later became a monk (Ephriam) at the monastery and was buried near the south wall. Other surviving structures are the two-storey Refectory (l695) and the large tent-roofed bell tower (l689), whose bell is now in the Moscow Kremlin's Ivan the Great Bell Tower.

On the other side of the road, behind the **Monument to Yuri Dolgoruky**, is the **Goritsky Monastery**, surrounded by a large red-brick *kremlin*. On the hilltop, a mass of sparkling onion domes rise up from inside the fortified walls.The monastery is now the **Museum of History and Art** (open 10 a.m. to 4 p.m., closed on Tuesdays). The monastery, founded during the reign of Ivan I in the l4th century (rebuilt in the 18th), is a fine example of medieval architecture with its octagonal towers, large cube-shaped walls and ornamental stone entrance gates The tiny white gate-church next to the gatekeeper's lodge was once known as the "casket studded with precious stones", for it was richly decorated with gilded carvings and colorful tiles. The large seven-domed **Cathedral of the Assumption** was built in 1757. The exquisite golden-framed and figured iconostasis, designed by Karl Blank, was carved and painted by the same team of artists who decorated the churches in the Moscow Kremlin.

The monastery, with 47 rooms filled with local treasures, is now one of the largest regional museums in the USSR. The rooms include a unique collection of ancient Russian art, sculptures and rare books. The museum also exhibits the plaster face mask of Peter the Great by Rastrelli (1719) and Falconnet's original model of the Bronze Horseman. The elaborately carved wooden gates from the Church of the Presentation won the Gold Medal at the 1867 Paris World Exhibition. May 2nd is a town holiday, Museum Day, at the Goritsky Monastery.

Heading north toward Rostov and Yaroslavl, you will find the last monument structure of Pereslavl-Zalessky, the 12th-century **Monastery of St. Nicetas**, encased in a long white-bricked *kremlin*. In 1561, Ivan the Terrible added stone buildings and the five-domed Cathedral. He intended to convert the Monastery into the headquarters for his Oprichniki, but later transferred their residence to the village of Alexandrov.

Rostov Veliky

Approaching Rostov on the road from Moscow (34 miles/54 km north of Pereslavl-Zalessky), the visitor is greeted with a breathtaking view of silvery aspen domes, white stone churches and high *kremlin* towers. Rostov is one of Russia's ancient towns and has stood along the picturesque banks of Lake Nero for more than 11 centuries. Named after Prince Rosta, a powerful governing lord, the town was mentioned in chronicles as far back as AD862. Rostov's size and splendor grew to equal the two great towns of Novgorod and Kiev. By the 12th century, Rostov was named *Veliky* "The Great" and became the capital of the Russian north. Rostov later came under the jurisdiction of Moscow and lost its importance as a trade and religious center by the end of the 18th century.

Today Rostov is the district center of the Yaroslavl region, and considered a historical preserve, heralding the glory of old Russian art and architecture. The town, with a population of about 50,000, has been restored to much of its original grandeur after a tornado destroyed many of the buildings in 1953. The oldest section of town, set by the lake, is

The End of the Line

As usual, Marya Sidorovna Tyutina got up at eight, had oatmeal for breakfast, and cleaned up the dishes after herself and her husband. Then she went off to the corner grocery, a half-flight down from the street, where yesterday they had definitely promised that they would have cod filet in the morning.

Marya Sidorovna didn't bother to get a receipt beforehand. She just took a place in line at the fish and meat department so they could weigh it out first. After standing there half the day— half an hour, anyway—she finally wound up at the counter, and then the sales girl told her they won't serve you without a receipt. Marya Sidorovna begged her to weigh out half a kilo anyway, for an invalid, because she'd been in line there since they opened, and it was too crowded at the cashier; but the salesgirl didn't even bother discussing it, took a receipt from some man, and turned her back. Someone in line yelled at Marya Sidorovna to stop holding things up—they all had to get to work; so she went straight over to the cashier without even waiting in line, said she just had to pay a bit extra on her bill and took out several kopeks. But despite the receipt, they wouldn't let her up to the counter because she'd missed her turn, and the filet was almost gone.

When Marya Sidorovna said that she'd been standing there, one woman declared that personally she hadn't seen anyone. What people! Marya Sidorovna didn't want to get mixed up in anything, so she went to the end of the line and waited another twenty minutes; but three people ahead of her they ran out of cod.

Nina Katerli, The Barsukov Triangle

still surrounded by low earthen walls, built around 1630. From the hotel and restaurant on Karl Marx Street, it is just a few minutes' walk to the ancient cathedrals inside the Kremlin.

History

Rostov Veliky was one of the wealthiest towns in all of Russia and the most important trade center between Kiev and the White Sea. Rostov became not only the capital of its own principality, but also the northern ecclesiastical center of early Christianity and the seat of the Metropolitan, head of the Orthodox Church. In the 17th century, the Metropolitans Jonah and Ion Sisoyevich built a large number of magnificent cathedrals and church residences, decorated with the Byzantine influence of icons and frescos. The many religious shrines of a Russian town symbolized its wealth and status.

Unlike other Russian towns, the Rostov kremlin was not originally built as a protective fortress, but served as a decorative feature that surrounded the palace of the Metropolitan. Also the main cathedral stood outside the kremlin walls and not in the town's center.

Sights

The *kremlin* itself, built in 1670, has 11 rounded towers and encompasses an area of about 5 acres. At the west gate is the **Church of St. John Divine** (1683). The five-domed **Church of the Resurrection** (1670) at the northern gates is designed with intricate white-stone patterns and the classic Russian *zakomara*, forming the 24 slopes of the roof. The towers on either side of both churches are made from aspen and sparkle with a silken sheen. Stone iconostasis (instead of traditional wooden ones) inside both churches are decorated with beautiful frescos painted by artists Nikitin and Savin from the Golden Ring town of Kostroma. The Church of the Resurrection stands over the Holy Gates, so named because the Metropolitan passed through them on the way from his residence inside the *kremlin* to the main cathedral.

The first stone of the massive **Cathedral of the Assumption** was laid by Prince Andrei Bogoliubsky (son of Yuri Dolgoruky who founded Moscow) in 1162. Bogoliubsky ruled the Russian north from Rostov. The 11th-century Vladimir Virgin hangs to the left of the Holy Doors. A few of the 12th-century frescos have survived, along with the original lion mask handles that guard the western doors. Rostov frescos were known for their soft color combinations of turquoise, blue, yellow and

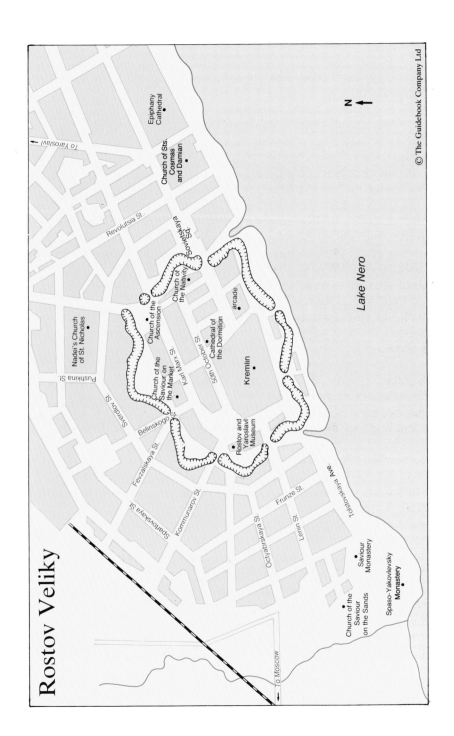

Rostov Veliky

To Yaroslavl →

Epiphany Cathedral

Church of Sts. Cosmas and Damian

Revolutsia St.

Nadel's Church of St. Nicholas

Pushkina St.

Sverdlov St.

Sovietskaya Sq.

Church of the Nativity

Church of the Ascension

Church of the Saviour on the Market

Karl Marx St.

50th October St.

arcade

Cathedral of the Dormition

Kremlin

Belinskogo St.

Fevzalskaya St.

Spartovskaya St.

Kommunarov St.

Rostov and Yaroslavl Museum

Frunze St.

Lake Nero

Octyabrskaya St.

Lenin St.

Tolstovskaya Ave.

To Moscow →

Church of the Saviour on the Sands

Saviour Monastery

Spaso-Yakovlevsky Monastery

N ←

© The Guidebook Company Ltd

white. Five large aspen-hewn onion domes and beautiful white-stone friezes decorate the outside of the structure. The four-tiered bell tower (1687), standing atop the Assumption Cathedral, was the most famous in all of Russia. Bells played an important role in the life of Russian towns. The 13 bells (the heaviest weighing 32 tons) can be heard 15 miles away.

Other churches inside the *kremlin* include the one-domed **Church of the Savior-on-the-Marketplace** (1690) that stands across 25th October Street; it is now the town library. In the northeast, at the end of Karl Marx Street, is the five-domed **Church of St. Isodore the Blessed** (1566), built during the reign of Ivan the Terrible. Right behind this church, on the other side of the earthern walls, stands the **Church of St. Nicholas-in-the-Field** (1830) on Gogol Street. This is one of the few places in town open for religious services. At the southeastern end by the water is the **Church of the Nativity**. *Gostiny Dvor* (Traders' Row) marks the town's center. This long yellow arcade, marked by many carved white archways, is still the shopping and market district of Rostov.

The large main complex at the western end by the Cathedral of the Assumption is the **Metropolitan's Palace** (1680), with its highly decorated Otdatochnaya Hall; here people gathered to pay their respects to the prince and Metropolitan. The **White Chambers** were built for the prince and later visiting czars. The **Red Chambers** accommodated other church and civil dignitaries. This complex of buildings now houses the **Rostov Museum Preserve of Art and Architecture**. The chambers are filled with collections of icons, woodcarvings and enamels from the 14th to 20th centuries. Rostov enamels were famous throughout Russia. Craftsmen painted miniature icons and other decorative enamels for church books and clergy robes. Today Rostov craftsmen still produce elegant enamel jewelry, ornaments and small paintings that are sold in Beriozka stores.

Heading west out of the *kremlin* along Lenin Street brings you to the small three-domed **Church of the Savior-on-the-Sands**. This is all that has survived of a monastery built by Princess Maria, whose husband was killed by invading Mongols in the 14th century. Princess Maria and other noblewomen of Rostov chronicled many of the events of medieval Russia. During the 17th century, the library of Countess Irina Musina-Pushkina was one of the largest in Russia.

Down on the banks of Lake Nero are the 17th-century remains of **St. Jacob's Monastery of Our Savior**; the original walls are still standing.

The Immaculate Conception Cathedral (1686) and Church of St. Demetrius (1800) are designed in the Russian Classical style. Along the water is a park, where boats can be rented. Fishing is also a pleasant pastime. Along the shores of the lake at the eastern end of town (at the end of Proletarskaya Street) is the **Church of Saints Cosma and Damian** (1775). Next to this small church stands the larger **Epiphany Cathedral** (1553), part of the **Monastery of St. Barlaam** (Abraham); this is one of the oldest surviving monasteries in Russia, dating back to the 11th century.

Outside of Rostov, in the northwestern suburbs of the village of Bogoslov, is the lovely red **Church of St. John upon Ishnya**, one of the last wooden churches left in the region. It stands on the River Ishnya and legend has that it miraculously appeared from the lake and was washed up on the shores of its present location. It is open daily for visits and closed on Wednesdays.

Vicinity of Rostov Veliky

About 15 miles (24 km) outside of Rostov Veliky on the way to Yaroslavl lies the **Borisoglebsky Monastery**. Built in the early 16th century, it was later surrounded by a fortified *kremlin* during the reign of Boris Godunov to protect it from Polish invasions. The famous Rostov architect, Grigory Borisov, built the **Cathedral of Saints Boris and Gleb** in 1524 and decorated it with colorful tiles. Boris and Gleb, sons of Prince Vladimir (who introduced Christianity to Russia in AD988), were the first saints of Russia. As political and religious turmoil swept Kiev, they passively accepted their death without fighting, believing in Christ's redemption. Borisov also built the five-domed Gate Church of St. Sergius (1545) and the Church of the Annunciation (1526).

Yaroslavl

The English writer and adventurer Robert Byron wrote of his first visit to Yaroslavl in the early 1930s, "While Veliki Novgorod retains something of the character of early Russia before the Tatar invasion, the monuments of Yaroslavl commemorate the expansion of commerce that marked the 17th century... The English built a shipyard here; Dutch, Germans, French and Spaniards followed them. Great prosperity came to the town, and found expression in a series of churches whose spacious proportions and richness of architectural decoration had no rival in the Russia of their time."

Today Yaroslavl, lying 175 miles (280 km) northeast of Moscow on the M8 Highway (and by train from Moscow's Yaroslavl Station), is still an important commercial center with a population of almost a million. It occupies the land on both sides of the Volga, where the River Kotorosl flows into it. Yaroslavl, the oldest city on the Volga, celebrated its 975th birthday in 1985, commemorated by a monument in the city center. The seven-ton Ice Age boulder was unearthed on the site of the Strelka and the inscription reads, "On this spot in 1010 Yaroslavl the Wise founded Yaroslavl". The oldest part of town, located at the confluence of the two rivers, contains many grandiose churches and residencies, erected by the many prosperous merchants. Not far from the city is the Estate-Museum of the poet Nekrasov and the Cosmos Museum, dedicated to the first Soviet woman cosmonaut, Valentina Tereshkova.

History

The city has the symbol of a bear, worshipped by pagan inhabitants as their sacred animal, on its crest. In the ninth century, a small outpost arose on the right bank of the Volga River and became known as Bear Corner, forming the northern border of the Rostov region. When Kievan Grand-Prince Yaroslavl the Wise visited the settlement in 1010, its named was changed to honor the Grand Prince. It grew as large as Rostov; an early chronicle entry stated that in one great fire 17 churches burned to the ground. By the 13th century, Yaroslavl had become the capital of its own principality along the Volga and remained politically independent for another 250 years.

The hordes of the Mongol Khan Batu invaded in 1238 and destroyed a great part of the city. Later, in 1463, when Prince Alexander handed over his ancestral lands to the Grand-Prince of Moscow, Ivan III, Yaroslavl was finally annexed to the Moscovy principality. For a short time, Yaroslavl regained its political importance when it was made the temporary capital during the Time of Troubles from 1598 to 1613.

The city reached the height of its prosperity in the 17th century when it became known for its handicrafts. Located along important trade routes, merchants journeyed from as far away as England and the Netherlands to purchase leather goods, silverware, woodcarvings and fabrics. At one point, one-sixth of Russia's most prosperous merchant families lived in Yaroslavl. These families, in turn, put their wealth back into the city; by the middle of the 17th century, more than 30 new churches had been built. Yaroslavl was also Moscow's Volga port until the Moscow-Volga canal was built in 1937.

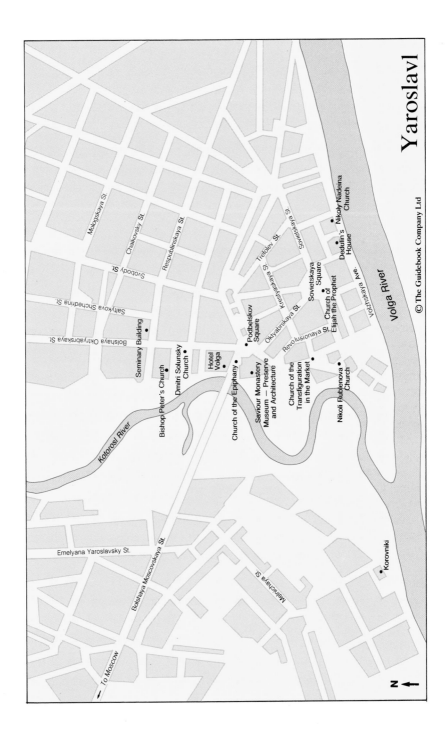

Yaroslavl

Molodgskaya St.

Chaikovsky St.

Svobody St.

Respublinskaya St.

Saltykova Shchedrina St.

Bolshaya Oktyabrskaya St.

Seminary Building

Bishop Peter's Church

Dmitri Solunsky Church

Hotel Volga

Church of the Epiphany

Kotorosl River

Saviour Monastery Museum — Preserve and Architecture

Church of the Transfiguration in the Market

Nikoli Rublenova Church

Podbelskov Square

Trefoley St.

Kresyaskaya St.

Oktyabrskaya St.

Revolusionaya St.

Sovietskaya Square

Church of Elijah the Prophet

Sovietskaya St.

Nikoly Nadeina Church

Dedulin's House

Volzhskaya Ave.

Volga River

© The Guidebook Company Ltd

Emelyana Yaroslavsky St.

Bolshaya Moscovskaya St.

To Moscow

Melnchaya St.

Korovniki

N

The *burlaki* (barge haulers) were a common sight, as portrayed in Repin's famous portrait, *Barge Haulers on the Volga*. In 1795, Count Musin-Pushkin discovered, in the Saviour Monastery, the famous 12th-century chronicle, *The Lay of Igor's Host*, based on the fighting campaigns of Prince Igor of Novgorod who, in the words of the chronicle, "did not let loose ten falcons on a flock of swans, but laid down his own wizard fingers on living strings, which themselves throbbed out praises..." Later Borodin composed the opera, *Prince Igor*, based on this chronicle.

Sights

A tour of Yaroslavl begins at the oldest part of town, the Strelka (arrow or spit of land), lying along the right bank of the Volga, where the Kotorosl empties into it; the Bear Ravine (now Peace Blvd) once separated the Timber Town from the Earth Town or *posad*.

By the Kotorosl, on Podbelskov Square, is the oldest surviving structure in Yaroslavl, the **Transfiguration of Our Saviour Monastery**, founded at the end of the 12th century. It grew into a large feudal power; by the end of the 16th century, the monastery was one of the strongest fortresses in the northern states with a permanent garrison of its own *streltsy* (musketeer marksmen) to protect it. The *kremlin* walls were fortified to nine feet thick (three meters) in 1621. During an attack, the defenders would pour boiling water or hot tar on their enemies.

The Holy Gates of the monastery were built at the southern entrance in 1516. The archway frescos include details from the Apocalypse. The 16th-century bell tower stands in front of the gates; climb up to the observation platform along its upper tier for a breathtaking panorama of the city.

The monastery's gold-domed **Cathedral of the Transfiguration of the Saviour** (1506) was one of the wealthiest churches in all of Russia. Frescos cover the entire interior, the oldest wall paintings in Yaroslavl. The fresco of the *Last Judgment*, painted in 1564, is on the west wall; the east side contains scenes of the *Transfiguration and Adoration of the Virgin*. It served as the burial chamber for the Yaroslavl princes. The vestry exhibits icons and old vestments that were used during church rituals and services.

Behind the bell-clock tower are two buildings of the Refectory and the Chambers of the Father Superior and Monks, which now house branches of the **Yaroslavl Museums of Art, History and Architec-**

ture. The museums are open daily 10 a.m. to 5 p.m. and closed on Mondays and the first Wednesday of each month. The Refectory exhibits the history of the Yaroslavl region up to the present day. The monk cells contain collections of Old Russian art, which include icons, folk-art, manuscripts, costumes, armor and jewelry. Here is also the **Museum of The Lay of Igor's Host**. The story of this famous epic, along with ancient birch-bark documents and early printed books, are on display. Twelve years after Count Musin-Pushkin discovered the epic and other old rare manuscripts in the monastery library, the great fire of Moscow, during Napoleon's invasion, destroyed all these originals. The **Church of the Yaroslavl Miracle Workers** (1827), at the south end of the cathedral, is the museum's cinema and lecture hall.

The red-brick and blue five-domed **Church of the Ephiphany** (1684) stands on the square behind the monastery. The church is open from May 1 to October 1 (10 to 5, closed on Tuesdays). It is festively decorated with *kokoshniki* and glazed colored tiles, a tradition of Yaroslavl church architecture. The interior is a rich tapestry of frescos illustrating the life of Christ; they were painted by Yaroslavl artists in 1692. It also has an impressive gilded seven-tiered iconostasis.

Crossing the square and walking up Pervomaiskaya St.(away from the Volga) leads to the early l9th-century **Central Bazaar**. Today this area is still a busy shopping district. A short walk behind the walls of the arcade brings you to the Znamenskaya (Sign) Tower of the *kremlin*. Towers in Russia were usually named after the icon that was displayed over its entrance. This tower once held the Sign of the Mother of God Icon.

Directly behind the tower on Ushinskov Street is the Yaroslavl Hotel. Here you can stop at the café and have a quick cup of *chai* or a meal in the Medvyed (Bear) Restaurant. Across from the hotel on Volkov Square is the **Volkov Drama Theater**, founded by Fyodor Volkov, who opened Russia's first professional theater to the general public in 1729; he formed his own drama company in 1748.

At the end of the Ushinskov Street is a statue of Lenin on Krasnaya Ploshchad (Red Square). Circle back down toward the Volga on Sovietskaya Street until it intersects with Sovietskaya Square. Dominating the town's main square is the **Church of Elijah the Prophet**, now a Museum of Architecture. The church is open from May 1 to October 1 (from 10 to 6, closed on Wednesdays). Built in 1647, the white-stone church is decorated with ornamental tiles and surrounded by a gallery with chapels and a bell tower. The wooden iconostasis is carved in Baroque fashion; the frescos were painted in 1680 by Kostroma artists, Savin and Nikitin. These murals depict Christ's ascension, his life on earth, the lives of his Apostles, and the prophet Elijah. Prayer benches carved for Czar Alexei (father of Peter the Great) and Patriarch Nikon are also found inside.

Behind this church is a **Branch Museum of Russian Art** from the 18th to 20th centuries (23 Volzhsky Emb.), housed in the former governor's residence. It is open 10 a.m. to 5 p.m. and closed on Fridays. Across the street from the museum is **Nadei's Church of St. Nicholas** (1620), a gift to the city from a wealthy merchant named Nadei Sveteshnikov. This church is open from 1 May to 1 October (9 a.m. to 5 p.m., closed on Thursdays). Ten churches in Yaroslavl were dedicated to St. Nicholas, the patron saint of commerce.

The impressive **Vakhrameyev Mansion** is also right by the water, in the other direction, off Revolution Street. The house was built in the 1780s in the Baroque fashion. This wealthy noble family were avid patrons of the arts in Yaroslavl. Behind the mansion (at 17 Volzhsky Emb.) is a small Branch Museum of Local History. It is open from 10 a.m. to 5:30 p.m. and closed on Mondays.

Walking directly along the Volga, on the Volzhsky Embankment, leads to the two-storey building of the **Metropolitan's Chambers** (1690), located in the old Timber Town. It was originally built to accommodate the Metropolitan of Rostov Veliky when he visited. The chambers are now a **Museum of Old Russian Art**, displaying many icons, paintings and ceramic tiles. The museum is open from 10 a.m. to 5 p.m. and closed on Fridays. Of interest is the icon *The Lay of the Bloody Battle with Khan Mamai*, a portrait of Count Musin-Pushkin and a bronze sculpture of Yaroslavl the Wise.

Making your way back up toward the Savior Monastery, along the Kotorosl Embankment, leads past three distinctive churches. The first (at 8 Kotorosl) is the simple white cube-shaped **Church** of St. Nicholas in the Timber (1695), built by the local shipbuilders who lived in this part of the Timber Town. Next (no. 10) is the **Church of the Transfiguraton in the Marketplace** (1672). It was built from funds collected by the townspeople in the old marketplace of the original Earth Town, where the local merchants and artisans lived. In the summer of 1693, 22 Yaroslavl artists helped paint the interior frescos. The red-brick **Church of the Archangel Michael**, (1658) directly across from the monastery (at 14), is filled with brightly colored frescos painted by local Yaroslavl artists in 1730.

Outside the Strelka in the village of Tolchkovo (in the northern part of the city) is the picturesque 15-domed **Church of St. John the Baptist** (1671), located at 69 Kotorosl Embankment on the right bank of the river. The five central green domes with a tulip-shaped dome in the middle, gold crosses, and ornamental tiles, are prime examples of the

architecture of the Golden Age of Yaroslavl. The whole principality of Yaroslavl donated funds to build the church. Fifteen masters from around Russia painted the frescos and icons that adorn every part of the interior, in 1694. The Baroque-style iconostasis was carved in 1701. The complex also includes a seven-tiered bell tower. The church is open from 10 to 6 and closed on Tuesdays.

Also on the Kotorosl's right bank, but down the Volga (at 2 Port Embankment), is a delightful architectural ensemble in the **Village of Korovniki**. The most impressive structure is the five-domed **Church of St. John Chrysostom** (1649). Its tent-shaped bell tower is known as the "Candle of Yaroslavl." The **Church of Our Lady of Vladimir** (1669) was used as the winter church.

If you have time, take a boat ride along the Volga; cruises last about an hour. For an evening's entertainment, book tickets at your hotel for the Yaroslavl Circus (located at 69 Svobody Street across from Truda Square). The Puppet Theater is at 25 Svobody Street.

Each summer, beginning August 1, the Yaroslavl Sunsets Music Festival is held, which usually opens with the overture to Borodin's *Prince Igor*.

Vicinity of Yaroslavl

On the Uglich Highway 15 miles (29 km) southwest of Yaroslavl is the **Cosmos Museum**, dedicated to Valentina Tereshkova, the first female cosmonaut. Valentina's flight, in 1963, lasted 70 hours and orbited the earth 48 times. The museum, near the house where she was born in the village of Nikulskoye, displays her space capsule and the history of Soviet space travel. It is open from 10 a.m. to 5 p.m. and closed on Mondays. The Intourist Office in your hotel can arrange excursions to these places.

About 10 miles (16 km) from Yaroslavl, along the Moscow-Yaroslavl Highway, is the **Nekrasov Estate-Museum** in the village of Karabikha. The famous Russian writer, Nikolai Nekrasov, stayed on the estate in the summer months; it retains its former appearance. His poems and other works are on display. The museum is open from 10 a.m. to 5 p.m. and closed on Mondays. Each summer there is a Nekrasov Poetry Festival at Karabhikha.

Kostroma

Kostroma, 80 miles (128 km) northeast of Yaroslavl, is the only city in the Soviet Union which has retained the original layout of its city center. Constructed in the early 18th century, it is one of the country's finest examples of old Russian classic design. Once a bustling trade center known as the "Flax Capital of the North," Kostroma (pronounced with last syllable accented) supplied Russia and Europe with the finest sail cloth. The emblem of this picturesque town set along the Volga River depicts a small boat on silvery waters with sails billowing in the wind. The central mercantile square was situated right by the banks of the Volga. The Krasniye (Beautiful) and Bolshiye (Large) stalls were connected by covered galleries where fabrics and other goods were sold. Today, the modernized **Arcade** still houses the town's markets and stores. The **Borschchov Mansion** (home of a general who fought in the War of 1812), the largest of the older residential buildings, stands nearby.

The oldest building in Kostroma is the octagon-roofed **Cathedral of the Epiphany** (1592) in the village of Krasnoye-on-the-Volga. The most beautiful structure is the **Church of the Resurrection on-the-Debre**, situated on the outskirts of town. In 1652, the merchant Kiril Isakov built this elaborate red-brick and green-domed church from money found in a shipment of English dyes. When informed of the discovery of gold pieces, the London company told Isakov to keep the money for "charitable deeds". Some of the bas-reliefs on the outside of the church illustrate the British lion and unicorn. The towering five-domed church has a gallery running along the sides; at the northwestern end is the **Chapel of Three Bishops**, with a magnificently carved iconostasis. The gates of the church are surrounded by ornamental *kokoshniki*, and the interior is ornately decorated with frescos and icons from the 15th century.

The real gem of the town is the **Ipatyevsky Monastery**, founded in the 14th century by the Zernov Boyars, ancestors of the Godunovs. This large structure is enclosed by a white brick *kremlin* and topped by green tent-shaped domes. Later, the relatives of Boris Godunov built the monastery's golden-domed **Trinity Cathedral**. While Boris Godunov was czar (1598-1605), the Ipatyevsky Monastery became the wealthiest in the country, containing over 100 icons. The Godunov family had its own mansion (the rose-colored building with the small windows) within the monastery, and most members were buried in the cathedral. The monastery was continually ravaged by internal strife, blackened by Polish invasions, and captured by the second False Dmitri in 1605, who claimed the throne of the Russian Empire. Later, the Romanovs who,

like the Godunovs, were powerful feudal lords in Kostroma, got the young Mikhail elected czar after the Time of Troubles. In 1613, Mikhail Romonov left the monastery to be crowned in the Moscow Kremlin. Today, the famous *Ipatyevsky Chronicles* are displayed here; this valuable document, found in the monastery's archives, traces the fascinating history of the area.

The **Church of St. John the Divine** (1687), which functioned as the winter church, stands nearby. From the monastery's five-tiered bell tower, one has a lovely view of the countryside and of the **Museum of Wooden Architecture**, open daily to the public. Intricately carved old wooden buildings gathered from nearby villages include the **Church of the Virgin** (1552), a typical peasant dwelling, a windmill and a bathhouse.

Other churches on the right bank of the Volga are the **Church of the Transfiguration** (1685), **Church of St. Elijah-at-the-Gorodishche** (1683-85) and the lovely hilltop **Church of the Prophet Elijah**. The Kostroma Hotel, with restaurant, overlooks the Volga (request a room on the riverside with balcony). There are paths along the river and even swimming in summer.

Ivanovo

Ivanovo, an industrial and regional center 180 miles (288 km) northeast of Moscow, began as a small village on the right bank of the River Uvod. The River Talka also crosses the town; both rivers flow into the River Kliyazma, a tributary of the Moskva. The village of Voznesensk,on the left bank, was annexed by Ivanovo in 1871. In 1561, a chronicle mentioned that Ivan the Terrible presented the village of Ivanovo to a powerful princely family. When, two centuries later, an Ivanovo princess married a Sheremetev, the town then passed over to this powerful aristocratic family. In 1710, Peter the Great ordered weaving mills and printing factories built here. Soon the town grew into a major textile and commercial center, with little religious significance. Ivanovo calico was famous worldwide; by the mid-1800s, it was known as the Russian Manchester. Today, almost 20 percent of the country's cloth is produced in this city of more than half a million people. Ivanovo is nicknamed the "City of Brides" — since a high percentage of textile workers are women, many men come to the city looking for a catch!

Ivanovo participated actively in the revolutionary campaigns and was called the Third Proletarian Capital after Moscow and Leningrad. Major strikes were held in the city in 1883 and 1885; in 1897, 14,000 workers held a strike against the appalling conditions in the factories. The 1905 strike, with over 80,000 participants, was headed by the famous Bolshevik leader Mikhail Frunze, who established the town's first Workers' Soviet, which provided assistance to the strikers and their families during the three-month protest.

Compared to other Golden Ring towns, Ivanovo is relatively new and modern, with only a few places of particular interest. On Lenin Prospekt, the **Ivanovo Museums of Art and History** portray the city's historical events and display collections of textiles, old printing blocks and other traditional folk arts. Off Kuznetsov St. is the **Museum-Study of Mikhail Frunze**. On Smirnov Street is the 17th-century **Shudrovskaya Chapel**; on nearby Sadovaya Street stands the large red-bricked **House-Museum of the Ivanovo-Voznesensk City Soviet**. Other locations of interest in the city are the circus, puppet theater, a 17th-century wooden church and **Stepanov Park**, with an open-air theater, planetarium, and boat rentals. The Zarya Restaurant is on Lenin Prospekt and the Tsentralnaya Hotel on Engels Street.

Palekh

This village lies 30 miles (48 km) east of Ivanovo and is famous for colorfully painted lacquer boxes.

After the revolution, when icon production was halted, it became popular to paint small miniatures on lacquer papier-mâché boxes, which combined the art of ancient Russian painting with the local folkcrafts. Ivan Golivko (1886-1937), the Master of Palekh Folk Art, created many beautiful lacquer scenes drawn from traditional Russian fairy tales, folk epics and songs. The **Museum of Palekh Art** displays a magnificent collection of painted boxes and other lacquer art by the folk artists of Palekh. These include works by the masters Vatagin, Bakanov, Vakurov, Butorin, Zubkov and Golivko. The **Timber House of Golivko**, where he lived and worked, is also open to the public.

The 17th-century **Cathedral of the Exaltation of the Holy Cross**, now a museum, stands in the town's center. A plaque on the outside of the west wall shows the builder to be Master Yegor Dubov. Local craftsmen carved and painted the Baroque-style golden iconostasis inside the church, which is covered with almost 50 colorful icons. The highly respected Palekh artists were sent all over Russia to paint beautiful icons and frescoes in the Central Russian style. Today, the artists of Palekh carry on the traditions of lacquer design and 270 craftsmen are employed at the Palekh Art Studio.

Vladimir

Vladimir lies 120 miles (190 km) northeast of Moscow along the M7 Highway. Trains also leave from Moscow's Kursk Station and pass through the cultivated countryside, strewn with collective farms that raise corn and livestock. The same rural scenes of farmers, dressed in embroidered peasant shirts with wide leather belts and *valenki* (black felt boots), plowing the fertile land, were painted by Russian artists such as Kramskoi, Vrubel and Repin over a century ago. It is recommended to spend at least a few days in the Vladimir region. After visiting Vladimir (overnight in the Vladimir Hotel), spend the next day in the ancient town of Suzdal, only 16 miles (26 km) to the north. Between these two cities is the historic village of Bogoliubovo and the Church-of-the-Intercession on the River Nerl.

History

Even though Vladimir is now a bustling city of 325,000 and the administrative head of the region, it is still one of the best preserved centers of 12th- and 13th-century Old Russian architecture. Eight centuries ago, Vladimir was the most powerful town of ancient Rus. Located on the banks of the Klyazma River, a small tributary of the Volga, Vladimir was an important stop on the trade routes between Europe and Asia. Greeks from Constantinople, Vikings from the north, Bulgars from the Volga, and Central Asian merchants all journeyed through the Vladimir-Suzdal principality.

Vsevolod, the son of Kievan Grand-Prince Yaroslavl the Wise, first began to settle the area of Vladimir in northeastern Rus while Kiev was being attacked by numerous hostile tribes in the late 11th century. Many Russians, at this time, began to migrate northward; this exodus is described in one of Russia's earliest epic chronicles, *The Lay of Igor's Host*. With the death of his father, Vsevolod became the most powerful prince in all the land. Prince Vsevolod built a small fortress near the village of Suzdal on the road from Kiev. Later, a trading settlement was established around the fort by Vsevolod's son, who also built the first stone church. The town was named after Vladimir Monomakh in 1108. After Monomakh's death in 1125, the Kievan states in the south began to lose their political and economic importance; under Monomakh's son Yuri Dolgoruky, the northern territories began to flourish. Vladimir grew so large and prosperous that it became the capital of northern Rus by the middle of the 12th century.

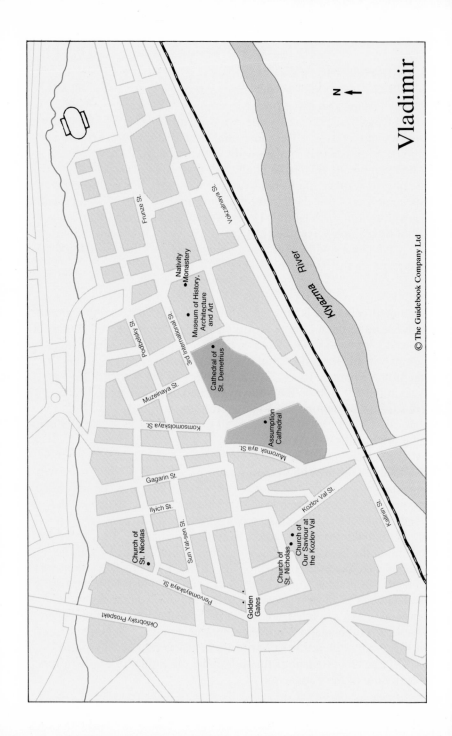

Vladimir

N

Kiyazma River

© The Guidebook Company Ltd

Vokzalnaya St.

Frunze St.

Nativity Monastery

Museum of History, Architecture and Art

Podbelsky St.

3rd International St.

Cathedral of St. Demetrius

Muzeinaya St.

Komsomolskaya St.

Assumption Cathedral

Muromskaya St.

Gagarin St.

Ilyich St.

Kozlov Val St.

Kalinin St.

Church of St. Nicetas

Sun Yat-sen St.

Church of St. Nicholas

Church of Our Saviour at the Kozlov Val

Pervomayskaya St.

Golden Gates

Oktiabrsky Prospekt

Dolgoruky's heir, Andrei Bogoliubsky, decided to rule Russia from a more centralized and peaceful area, and transferred the throne of the Grand-Prince from Kiev to Vladimir in 1157, after a vision of the Blessed Virgin directed him to do so. Bogoliubsky left Kiev under the protection of a holy icon, said to have been painted by St. Luke from Constantinople, known as Our Lady of Vladimir. This revered icon became the sacred palladium of the Vladimir region; the prince even took it on his military campaigns. As the protectorate of the city, it became the symbol of divine intervention and power of the grand-princes.

Andrei brought in master artists and craftsmen to recreate the splendors of Kiev in the new town of Vladimir. A crowned lion carrying a cross was the town's coat-of-arms. Under his brother, Vsevolod III (who ruled 1174-1212), the Vladimir-Suzdal principality, with Vladimir as its capital, reached the zenith of its political power.

When the Mongol Tatars invaded in 1238, Vladimir, like many other towns in Russia, suffered extensive damage. For a while, Vladimir retained the seat of the Church Metropolitan, and the Grand-Princes were still crowned in the town's Uspensky Cathedral. But eventually the princes of Moscovy began governing Russia through the Khans. When Vladimir was annexed to the principality of Moscovy and Moscow became the capital of the country in the 16th century, its importance slowly declined; by 1668, the population numbered only 990. After the revolution, the city grew with industrialization and today it is a large producer of electrical machinery. The Vladimiret tractor, sold around the world, recently won a Gold Medal at a Brussels Machinery Exhibition.

Sights

To enter the old part of town along the river, pass through the **Golden Gates** (the only surviving gates of the city), built in 1158 by Prince Bogoliubsky, who modeled them after the Golden Gates of Kiev. The oak doors of the now white gates were once covered with gilded copper; the golden-domed structure on top of the gates was the Church of the Deposition of the Robe. These gates were used as a defense fortification for the western part of town and also served as a triumphal arch — Alexander Nevsky, Dmitri Donskoi (in 1380) and troops on their way to fight Napoleon in the Battle of Borodino in 1812 all passed through the

The Brotherhood Grave

*L*ate in the night we went through the empty streets and under the Iberian Gate to the great Red Square in front of the Kremlin. The church of Vasili Blazhenny loomed fantastic, its bright coloured, convoluted, and blazoned cupolas vague in the darkness. There was no sign of any damage. . . Along one side of the square the dark towers and walls of the Kremlin stood up. On the high walls flickered redly the light of hidden flames; voices reached us across the immense place, and the sound of picks and shovels. We crossed over.

Mountains of dirt and rock were piled high near the base of the wall. Climbing these we looked down into two massive pits, ten or fifteen feet deep and fifty yards long, where hundreds of soldiers and workers were digging in the light of huge fires.

A young soldier spoke to us in German. 'The Brotherhood Grave,' he explained. 'Tomorrow we shall bury here five hundred proletarians who died for the Revolution.'

He tooks us down into the pit. In frantic haste swung the picks and shovels, and the earth-mountains grew. No one spoke. Overhead the night was thick with stars, and the ancient Imperial Kremlin wall towered up immeasurably.

'Here in this holy place,' said the student, 'holiest of all Russia, we shall bury our most holy. Here where are the tombs of the Tsars, our Tsar—the People—shall sleep. . . . ' His arm was in a sling from a bullet wound gained in the fighting. He looked at it. 'You foreigners look down on us Russians because so long we tolerated a medieval monarchy,' he said. 'But we saw that the Tsar was not the only tyrant in the world; capitalism was worse, and in all the countries of the world capitalism was Emperor. . . . Russian revolutionary tactics are best. . . .'

As we left, the workers in the pit, exhausted and running with sweat in spite of the cold, began to climb wearily out. Across the Red Square a dark knot of men came hurrying. They swarmed into the pits, picked up the tools and began digging, digging, without a word.

So, all the long night volunteers of the People relieved each other, never halting in their driving speed, and the cold light of the dawn laid bare the great square, white with snow, and the yawning brown pits of the Brotherhood Grave, quite finished.

We rose before sunrise, and hurried through the dark streets to Skobeliev Square. In all the great city not a human being could be seen; but there was a faint sound of stirring, far and near, like a deep wind coming. In the pale half-light a little group of men and women were gathered before the Soviet headquarters, with a sheaf of gold-lettered red banners—the Central Executive Committee of the Moscow Soviets. It grew light. From afar the vague stirring sound deepened and became louder, a steady and tremendous bass. The city was rising. We set out down the Tverskaya, the banners flapping overhead.

A bitter wind swept the square, lifting the banners. Now from the far quarters of the city the workers of the different factories were arriving, with their dead. They could be seen coming through the Gate, the blare of their banners, and the dull red—like blood—of the coffins they carried. These were rude boxes, made of unplaned wood and daubed with crimson, borne high on the shoulders of rough men who marched with tears streaming down their faces, and followed by women who sobbed and screamed, or walked stiffly, with white, dead faces. Some of the coffins were open, the lid carried behind them; others were covered with gilded or silvered cloth, or had a soldier's hat nailed on the top. There were many wreaths of hideous artificial flowers.

All the long day the funeral procession passed, coming in by the Iberian Gate and leaving the square by way of the Nikolskaya, a river of red banners, bearing words of hope and brotherhood and stupendous prophecies, against a background of fifty thousand people—under the eyes of the world's workers and their descendants for ever. . . .

John Reed, Ten Days that Shook the World

arch. The gates were damaged many times through the years, and were reconstructed in the 18th century. Today the Golden Gates house the local **Military Historical Museum**. Next to the Gates, in the red brick building (formerly a church) and the fire observation tower, are the **Museums of Contemporary Artists and Ancient Town Life**. The latter has many interesting old illustrations and black and white photographs, tracing the history of the region.

The oldest buildings of the city were constructed on the hills by the water, which served as a defensive wall. Walk right through the gates and a cluster of golden-domed white churches come into view. In 1158, Andrei Bogoliubsky brought in master craftsmen from all over Russia and Europe to build the triple-domed *Spensky Sobor,* the **Assumption Cathedral**. Built to rival Kiev's St. Sophia, the cathedral was decorated with gold, silver and precious stones. It was the tallest building in all of Rus. Filled with frescos and icons, the iconostasis was also the largest of its kind in Russia. A tenth of the Grand-Prince's revenue was contributed to the upkeep of the cathedral. After much of it was destroyed by fire in 1185 (along with 33 other churches), Prince Vsevolod III had it rebuilt with five domes. Since the original walls were encased within a larger structure, the cathedral doubled in size, with an area for a congregation of 4,000 people. The Italian architect Fioravanti used it as his model for the Moscow Kremlin's own Assumption Cathedral. After more fires blackened the walls, the famous iconists, Andrei Rublev and Daniil Chorny, were sent in 1408 to restore the interior. Frescoes from the 12th and 13th centuries are still evident on the western and northern walls. Rublev's and Chorny's frescos, including scenes from the *Last Judgment*, decorate two vaults beneath the choir gallery and the altar pillars. The famed icon of the *Virgin of Vladimir*, that once hung by the altar, was transferred in 1380 to Moscow's Assumption Cathedral; it is now in the Moscow Tretyakov Gallery.

This cathedral was one of the most revered churches in Russia; all the Vladimir and Moscow Grand-Princes were crowned inside it, from the son of Yuri Dolgoruky to Ivan III, in the early 15th century. It was the main center of the Church Metropolitan in the 14th century. The Assumption Cathedral was also the burial place of the Princes of Vladimir, including Andrei Bogoliubsky and Vsevolod III. The three-story belfry was built in 1810. The cathedral has been under continuous restoration during the last century. Mass is celebrated on Saturday evenings, Sundays and Orthodox feast days. Visitors are welcome in proper attire. Taking flash pictures is not permitted.

A short walk away to the right of the cathedral (with your back to the river) leads to one of the most splendid examples of old Russian architecture, the **Cathedral of St. Demetrius** (1193-97). It was built by Vsevolod III as his court church; his palace once stood nearby. The cathedral, with its one large helmut drum, was named after "Big Nest" Vsevolod's patron saint (St. Demetrius of Thessaloniki) and new-born son Dmitri. (Vsevolod was nicknamed "Big Nest" for his large family of 12 children.) It is built from blocks of white limestone and decorated with intricate *kokoshniki* along the doorways and arches. Over 1,300 bas-reliefs cover the outer walls: decorative beasts, birds, griffins, saints, prophets, the labors of Hercules, and many elaborate floral patterns all glorify the might of Vladimir. The friezes of King David and Alexander the Great symbolize Vsevolod's cunning military exploits. At the top of the left section of the northern façade is Prince Vsevolod seated on the throne with his young son; the other sons are bowing to their father. The interior frescos date back to the 12th century. In 1834, Nicholas I ordered the cathedral restored; it is now part of the local museum complex.

Across from this cathedral at 64 IIIrd International Street is the **Vladimir Museum of Art and Architecture**, with displays of old religious paintings, manuscripts and architectural designs. Directly across the street is the **Museum of History**. A rich collection of artifacts, archeological materials, old fabrics and weapons, princely possessions, and the white stone tomb of Alexander Nevsky are on display. Another branch of the museum with lacquered art, crystal and embroidery is located at the end of IIIrd International Street past the Golden Gates. The museums are open daily and closed on Thursdays.

Directly behind this last branch museum is the simple white **Church of the St. Nicholas** and the **Church of the Saviour at the Kozlov Val**, both built in the late 17th century. Across from them, nearer the water, is the **Church of St. Nicholas-at-Galeya**, with its tent-shaped bell tower. The church was built by a wealthy citizen of Vladimir in the early 18th century.

At the opposite end of IIIrd International Street toward Frunze Square is the **Nativity Monastery** (1191-1196), one of Russia's most important religious complexes up until the end of the 16th century; it was closed in 1744. Alexander Nevsky was buried here in 1263; his remains were transferred to St. Petersburg by Peter the Great in 1724. The Nikolskaya Church next door is now the Planetarium.

Next to the Vladimir Hotel (across from the Planetarium on Frunze St.) is the brick and five-domed **Assumption Church** (1644), built from donations given by rich local merchants. At the end of Frunze St. is the Eternal Flame, commemorating the soldiers who lost their lives during World War II.

Right in front of the Golden Gates on Gagarin Street is the city's main shopping district, the *Torgoviye Ryady*. Across the street is the **Monument to the 850th Anniversary of Vladimir**.

Stroll down Gagarin Street and look out over the old section of Vladimir. In the distance are many old squat wooden houses with long sloping roofs and stone floors. Many of the town's inhabitants have lived in these homes for generations. The people enjoy a simple town life. During the day you may see residents hanging out laundry, perhaps painting the lattice work around their windows a pastel blue-green, chopping wood, or gathering fruits and mushrooms. The children enjoy having their picture taken. Bring a few souvenirs from home to trade.

At the end of Gagarin St. is the **Knyaginin (Princess) Convent**, founded by the wife of Vsevolod III, Maria Shvarnovna, in 1200. The grand-princesses of the court were buried in the convent's Assumption Cathedral, rebuilt in the 16th century. The cathedral's three-tiered walls are lined with fancy *zakamora* and topped with a single helmet drum. In 1648, Moscow artists painted the colorful interior frescos. The north and south walls depict the life of the Virgin Mary, and the west wall shows scenes from the *Last Judgement*. Paintings of Vladimir princesses, portrayed as saints, are on the southwest side, and the pillars recount the lives of the grand-princes. The cathedral is the only remaining building of the convent complex and now houses a restoration organization. Next to the convent stands the **Church of St. Nicetas** (1762). This Baroque green and white, three-tiered church was built by the merchant, Semion Lazarev. The interior is divided into three separate churches on each floor. It was restored in 1970. In front of this church is a bust of the writer, Gogol. Pervomaiskaya (First of May) Street leads back to the Golden Gates.

At the end of the day, your group tour may stop at the rustic log-hewn Traktir Restaurant for an enjoyable meal of the local cuisine.

Vicinity of Vladimir

The quaint village of Bogoliubovo lies five miles (eight km) from Vladimir. Group tours sometime stop; if not, a car can be hired in the

town. One legend says that when Prince Andrei was traveling from Kiev to Vladimir, carrying the sacred icon of Our Lady of Vladimir, his horses stopped on a large hill and would move no farther. At this junction, by the confluence of the Klyazma and Nerl rivers, Andrei decided to build a fortress and royal residence. He named the town Bogoliubovo (Loved by God) and took the name of Bogoliubsky; he was canonized by the Church in 1702. Supposedly, after the Virgin appeared to him in a dream, he built the **Nativity of the Virgin Church**. This cathedral was still standing in the 18th century, but when one Father Superior decided to renovate it in 1722 by adding more windows, the cathedral collapsed; it was partially rebuilt in 1751. Only a few of the 12th-century palace walls remain, of which chronicles wrote, "it was hard to look at all the gold." On the staircase tower are pictures depicting the death of Andrei Bogoliubsky — assassinated by jealous nobles in this tower in 1174. The coffins of his assassins were said to have been buried in the surrounding marshes and their wailing cries heard at night. The buildings in Bogoliubovo are now museums, which are closed on Mondays. About one mile southeast of Bogoliubovo on the River Nerl is the graceful **Church of the Intercession-on-the-Nerl**, built during the Golden Age of Vladimir architecture. Standing alone in the green summer meadows or snowy winter landscape, it is reflected in the quiet waters of the river that is filled with delicate lilies. It has come down from legends that Andrei built this church in 1164 to celebrate his victory over the Volga Bulgars. The Virgin of the Intercession was thought to have protected the rulers of Vladimir. With the building of this church, Andrei proclaimed a new church holiday of the Feast of the Intercession.

Suzdal

Suzdal is a pleasant half-hour ride from Vladimir through open fields dotted with hay stacks and mounds of dark rich soil. Vladimir was the younger rival of Suzdal which, along with Rostov Veliky, was founded a full century earlier. The town was settled along the banks of the Kamenka River, which empties into the Nerl a few miles downstream. Over 100 examples of Old Russian architecture attract half a million visitors each year to this remarkable medieval museum. Just outside Suzdal is Kideksha, a small preserved village that dates back to the beginning of the 12th century. On the left bank of the river is the lovely **Suzdal Museum of Wooden Architecture**, portraying the typical Russian life-style of centuries ago.

The first view of Suzdal from the road encompasses towering silhouettes of gleaming domes and pinkish walls atop Poklonnaya Hill, rising up amidst green patches of woods and gardens. Time seems to have stopped around this fantastic creation — a perfection of spatial harmony. Today, Suzdal is a quiet town with no industrial enterprises. Crop and orchard farming is the main occupation of the residents who still live in the predominant *izba* wooden houses. The scenic town is a popular site for filmmaking. The American production of *Peter the Great* used Suzdal as one of its locations.

Traveling along the Golden Ring route, you may have noticed that the distances between towns are similar. When these towns were settled, one unit of length was measured by how much ground a team of horses could cover in 24 hours. Most towns were laid out about one post-unit apart. So the distance between Moscow and Pereslavl-Zalessky, Pereslavl and Rostov, or Rostov and Yaroslavl could easily be covered in one day's time. Distances in medieval Russia, from Kiev to the White Sea, were measured by these units; thus, the traveler knew how many days it took to arrive at his destination — from Moscow to Suzdal took about three days.

History

The area of Suzdalia was first mentioned in the chronicles in 1024, when Kievan Grand-Prince Yaroslavl the Wise came to suppress the rebellions. By 1096, a small *kremlin* had been built around the settlement, which one chronicle already described as a "town". As Suzdal grew, princes and rich nobles from Kiev settled here, bringing with them spiritual representatives from the church, who introduced Christianity to the region. The town slowly gained prominence; Grand-Prince Yuri Dolgoruky named it the capital of the northern provinces in 1125. From Suzdal, the seat of his royal residence, he went on to establish the small settlement of Moscow in 1147. His son, Andrei Bogoliubsky, transferred the capital to Vladimir in 1157.

After the Kievan States crumbled in the 12th century, Suzdal, along with Rostov Veliky, became the religious center of medieval Rus. The princes and boyars donated vast sums of money to build splendid churches and monasteries; by the 14th century, Suzdal had over 50 churches, 400 dwellings and a famous school of icon painting. No other place in all of Russia had such a high proportion of religious buildings. The crest of Suzdal was a white falcon contained in a prince's crown.

Since the town itself was not situated along important trade routes, the monks (and not the merchants) grew in wealth from large donations to the monasteries. The Church eventually took over the fertile lands and controlled the serf-peasants.

Suzdal was invaded many times, first by the Mongols in 1238, then by Lithuanians and Poles. After the Mongol occupation, no new stone buildings were erected until well into the 16th century. When it was annexed to Moscovy in the late 14th century, Suzdal lost its political importance, but remained a religious center.

During the 1700s, Peter the Great's reforms undermined ecclestiastical power and the Church in Suzdal lost much of its land and wealth. Churches and monasteries were mainly used to house religious fanatics and political prisoners. Many barren or unpopular wives were forced to take the veil and exiled to Suzdal's convents. By the end of the 19th century, only 6,000 residents remained, and one account described Suzdal as "a town of churches, bell towers, old folk legends and tombstones." But today, this enthralling poetic spot has been restored to the majesty of its former days. As one 13th-century chronicler observed, "Oi, most radiant and bountiful, how wondrous art thou with thy beauty vast."

Sights

Approaching Suzdal from Vladimir, as horse coaches once did, two churches are passed on the right before crossing the Kamenka River. These are the **Church of Our Lady of the Sign** (1749) and **Church of the Deposition of the Robe** (1777). The former houses the Suzdal Excursion Bureau.

The *kremlin* was well protected on three sides by the river; along the eastern wall ran a large moat. Remnants from the 11th-century earthen walls are still evident today. These ramparts are topped with wooden walls and towers.

A tour of Suzdal begins on the right bank of the river, where much of the old architecture is clustered. Take a moment to gaze out along the fertile plains and meandering waters of the river. The rich arable land in this area first attracted settlers seeking greater freedoms from Novogorod, where pagan priests were still leading uprisings against Kievan attempts to Christianize and feudalize the northern lands. In Old Russian, *suzdal* meant to "give judgement or justice." Today, several streets still carry the names of Slavic pagan gods, such as Kupala, Netyoka and Yarunova.

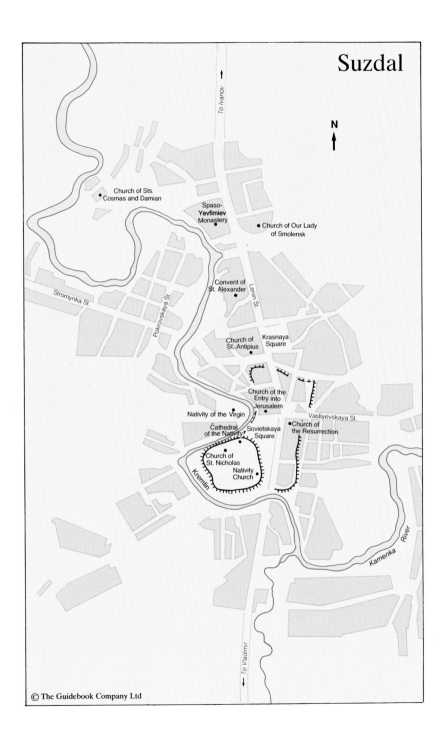

Suzdal

N

To Ivanov

Church of Sts.
Cosmas and Damian

Spaso-
Yevfimiev
Monastery

Church of Our Lady
of Smolensk

Stromynka St.

Pokrovskaya St.

Convent of
St. Alexander

Lenin St.

Church of
St. Antipius

Krasnaya
Square

Church of the
Entry into
Jerusalem

Vasliyevskaya St.

Nativity of the Virgin

Cathedral
of the Nativity

Sovietskaya
Square

Church of
the Resurrection

Church of
St. Nicholas

Nativity
Church

Kremlin

Kamenka River

To Vladimir

© The Guidebook Company Ltd

As you cross the river, a simple white church with red outlines, comes to view on the left side of Lenin Street. This was used as the summer church; the slender helmet-domed building behind it was used in winter.

The 13th-century **Korsunsky Gates** lead to the main cathedral and are covered with Byzantine patterns; religious scenes from the New Testament were engraved and etched with acid on copper sheets and then gilded.

Prince Vladimir Monomakh laid the first stone of the town's main **Cathedral of the Nativity** at the end of the 11th century. This structure was rebuilt many times; in 1528, Grand-Prince Vasily III of Moscow reconstructed it from brick and white stone and topped it with five helmet-shaped domes. In 1748, the domes were altered to the present blue onion and gold-star pattern.

The southern doors, surrounded by elaborate stone decorations, were the official entrance of the princes. Lions, carved along the portals, were the emblems of the princes of Vladimir. The carved female faces symbolize the Virgin Mary, whose nativity is celebrated. The southern and western doors (1230-33) are made of gilded copper and depict scenes from the life of St. George, the patron saint of both Prince Georgi and his grandfather, Yuri Dolgoruky.

Early 13th-century frescos of saints and other ornamental floral patterns are still visible in the vestry. Most of the other murals and frescos are from the 17th century. Tombs of early bishops and princes from as far back as 1023 are also found inside. The burial vaults of the early princesses are near the west wall. The octagonal bell tower was built in 1635 by order of Czar Mikhail Romanov and repaired in 1967. Old Slavonic letters correspond to numbers of the face of the clock.

The Archbishop's Palace, now the **Suzdal Museum**, was built next to the cathedral on the bank of the Kamenka between the 15th and 17th centuries. The main chamber of the palace, a large pillarless hall, held important meetings and banquets. In the 17th century, this *Krestovaya* (Cross-Vaulted) Chamber was considered one of the most elegant rooms in all Russia. The museum contains collections of ancient art and traces the evolution of architecture in the Suzdal region.

Enter the palace chamber through the western entrance. In the center stands a long wooden table, topped by a rich red cloth, once used by the archbishop and his clergy. An 18th-century tiled stove stands in one corner. The walls are decorated with many 15th-century icons. Suzdal developed its own school of icon painting in the early 13th century. Its use of lyrical flowing outlines, detailed facial qualities and soft designs in red and gold, were later adopted by the Moscow school, headed by Andrei Rublev. Both the Moscow Tretyakov Gallery and the Leningrad Russian Museum include Suzdal icons in their exhibits.

Pass through the gateway to the left of the palace to reach another art section of the museum. Here are more displays of icons, paintings, sculptures, ivory carvings, embroideries and other crafts.

In front of the palace by the river is the wooden **Church of St. Nicholas** (1766). It represents one of the oldest types of Old Russian wooden architecture and is built from logs into a square frame with a long sloping roof. The early architects used only an axe, chisel and plane to build these designs. No nails were needed; the logs were held together by wooden pegs and filled with moss. It was transferred from the village of Glotovo in 1960. Beside it, in lovely contrast, stands the red and white-trimmed **Church of the Assumption** (1732), with its green rounded roof and horseshoe *kokoshniki*.

Farther up the riverbank by Sovietskaya Square (formerly Trade Square) is the yellow-white brick summer **Church of the Entry into Jerusalem** (1707), topped with a half-dome drum and a gilded cross. The white-washed winter **Church of St. Paraskeva** (1772) stands next to it.

Many of the local citizens built their own churches. Across the river are four churches constructed between the 16th and 18th centuries with money raised by the local tanners who lived and worked by the river near the marketplace. The local blacksmiths, who lived at the northern end of town, built the **Churches of Saints Cosmas and Damian**, the patron saint of blacksmiths.

The long trading stalls of the *Torg* (marketplace), built in 1806, mark the center of town. During holidays, the grounds were opened to fairs and exhibitions, and were filled with jolly jesters, merry-go-rounds and craft booths. Horses were tied up along the arcade. Today, the colonnade has over 100 stores, where the townspeople congregate, especially around mid-day.

(For a lunch break, try dining at the Trapeznaya restaurant, located in the Refectory of the Archbishop's Palace (closed on Mondays; sometimes advance reservations are needed). Sample the splendors of ancient Suzdalian monastic cooking — the local fish-soup and home-brewed mead are especially tasty. On Lenin Street are the Sokol restaurant and a tearoom. The Suzdal Hotel and Restaurant are near the central square and the Pogrebok (Cellar) Cafe is on Kremlyovskaya Street.)

Behind the trading stalls on Lenin St. is the **Church of the Resur-rection on-the-Marketplace**, now a branch of the Suzdal Museum. Here are exhibits of architectural decorations, wooden carvings and colorful tiles used to adorn buildings in the 17th and 18th centuries. Continuing west along Lenin St. brings you by two other sets of church complexes. Not only did the number of churches in a town symbolize the wealth, but it was also customary in medieval Russia to build twin churches; this added even more to the cluster of religious structures. These twin churches stood usually in close proximity to each other — one cool, high-vaulted and richly decorated church was used only in summer; the other, simpler and smaller, held the congregation in winter. The first set is comprised of the **Church of the Emperor Constantine** (1707), topped by five slender drum domes, a unique feature of Suzdalian architecture. The glazed green-roofed and white-bricked **Church of Our Lady of Sorrows** (1787), with the large bell tower, was for the winter. The next set is made up of the **Church of St. Antipus** (1745), recognized by its unusual multicolored octagonal red-roofed belltower, and the **Church of St. Lazarus** (1667), topped with beautiful forged crosses on five domes.

Suzdal had the largest monasteries and convents in the region, which served as protective citadels for the citizens during times of war. These institutions, besides being religious, became the educational centers for the town. Husbands could also force their wives to take the veil, a quick way to divorce. Fathers would also place daughters in a convent until they were married. In front of the twin churches, back down by the water, is the **Convent of the Deposition of the Robe,** founded by Bishop John of Rostov Veliky in 1207. The convent was rebuilt of stone in the 17th century. The white Holy Gates are topped with two red and white octagonal towers covered with glazed tile. The convent's church was built by Ivan Shigonia-Podzhogin, a rich boyar who served Czar Vasily III. The citizens of Suzdal erected the 72-meter (312-foot) bell tower in 1813 to commemorate Napoleon's defeat.

The neighboring red-brick **Convent of St. Alexander** was built in 1240 in honor of Prince Alexander Nevsky, who defeated the Swedes on the Neva River that same year. After it was burned down by the Poles in the 17th century, the Mother Superior had Peter the Great rebuild it. In 1682, the Ascension Cathedral was constructed from funds donated by Peter's mother, Natalya Naryshkina. The convent closed in 1764, but the church remains open to the public.

Behind this convent is a 17th-century gabled-roof tailor's house, nestled in the former *posad*. It now contains a domestic museum with displays of furniture and utensils from the 17th to 19th centuries. The rooms represent a typical peasant hut. Across from the *pechka* (stove), over which the eldest member of the family slept, was the *krasnaya ugol* (beautiful corner), where the family icons were kept. Usually the *gornitsa* (living area) was comprised of one or two rooms. Here were found a few beds, chairs, tables and a clothes chest. The kitchen was situated in the corner nearest to the *kamin* (fireplace) or stove. A small storage-house was also built into the hut. This house stands next to the summer **Church of Our Lady of Smolensk** (1696) on Krasnaya Square.

The largest architectural complex on the right bank of the river is the **Spaso-Yevfimiev Monastery**, built in 1350 by a Suzdal Prince; the monks eventually owned vast amounts of land and their monastery became the wealthiest in the region. It is enclosed by a massive, mile-long, red *kremlin* that has 20 decorated towers. The Cathedral of the Transfiguration was built in 1594. Inside, 17th-century frescos depict the history of the monastery. Prince Dmitry Pozharsky, hero of the 1612 Polish war and Governor of Suzdal, is buried beside the altar; a monument to him, standing outside the cathedral, says "To Dmitri Mikhailovsky 1578-1642". Adjoining the cathedral is a small chapel that stands over the grave of the Abbot Yevfimy.

The Church of the Assumption, built in 1526, was decorated with *kokoshniki* and a large tent-shaped dome. The Kostroma artists Nikitin and Savin painted the frescoes on the outside southern and western walls. At one point, Catherine the Great had it converted into a prison to house those who committed crimes against the church and state. The Decembrist Shakhovskoi died in this prison. Leo Tolstoy, excommunicated by the Church, was almost sent here too. The monk cells contain an exhibit of Contemporary Folk Art that includes works by local painters, potters, sculptors and glass blowers.

The large complex across the river is the **Convent of the Intercession**, built by Prince Andrei in 1364. Prince Vasily III built the convent's churches in 1510. The white three-domed Cathedral of the Intercession served as the burial place for Suzdal noblewomen. Vasily used the convent to exile his wife, Solomonia Saburova. Vasily wanted to divorce his wife on the grounds that she was barren; Solomonia accused Vasily of sterility. The Metropolitan granted Vasily his divorce and sent Solomonia to the Pokrovsky (Intercession) Convent to live out her life as a nun. He remarried a Polish girl named Elena Glinskaya. Sometime later news reached Moscow that Solomonia had given birth to a son. Fearing for her son's life, Solomonia hid him with friends and then staged a fake burial. For centuries this tale was regarded only as legend; but in 1934 a small casket was unearthed beside Solomonia's tomb, (d. 1594). There was no skeleton, only a stuffed silk shirt embroidered with pearls. The small white tomb and pieces of clothing are on display in the Suzdal Museum. Ivan the Terrible also sent his wife , Anna, to this convent in l575. Later, Peter the Great even exiled his first wife, Yevdokia Lopukhina, here in l698.

At the southern end of town on the left bank of the Kamenka is the **Suzdal Museum of Wooden Architecture**. Old wooden villages were brought in from all around the Vladimir-Suzdal region and reassembled at this location on Dmitriyevskaya Hill, to give an idea of the way of life in a typical Russian village. This open-air museum consists of log-built churches covered with aspen-shingled roofs, residential houses, windmills, barns and bath-houses.

At the end of the day, return to your hotel, probably at the Main Tourist Complex behind the Convent of the Intercession. Before dinner, take a walk along the river as the sun sets over the town. Young boys can be seen swimming and fishing in the warmer months or skating in winter. Many small side streets are filled with the local wooden dachas, covered with elaborate wood carvings and latticework. Ask your driver to stop by the **House of Merchant Bibanov**, the most lavishly decorated house in town. If you are lucky, a pink full moon will rise above the magical display of gabled roofs and towers, to call an end to the delightful Suzdalian day! Try taking a *banya* or a dip in the hotel's indoor pool. The hotel also offers *troika* rides in winter.

Vicinity of Suzdal

A few miles to the north of Suzdal is the small **Village of Kideksha**. According to chronicles, in 1015 the brothers Boris and Gleb, sons of the Kievan Prince Vladimir who brought Christianity to Russia, had a meeting here, where the Kamenka River empties into the Nerl. They were later assassinated by their brother, but died defending the Christian faith; they became the first Russian saints. In 1152, Prince Yuri Dolgoruky chose to build his country estate on this spot. Dolgoruky also erected the simple white-stone **Church of Saints Boris and Gleb**, where his son Boris, and daughter-in-law Maria are buried. The winter Church of St. Stephan was erected in the l8th century.

Practical Information

Holidays and Festivals

The Soviet Union celebrates only a few of the traditional holidays common in the West. Most of the national holidays are connected with Lenin and the Revolution. Still, holidays are holidays, especially May Day (International Labor Day) and the Anniversary of the October Revolution.

Soviet Holidays

January 1: **New Year's Day**. The last week in December is quite festive, culminating with New Year's Eve. Presents are given on New Year's Day.

March 8: **International Women's Day**. Established after the Second International Conference of Socialist Women in Copenhagen in 1910, women receive gifts and usually do not have to work!

May 1-2: **International Workers Solidarity Day**. This holiday, better known as **May Day**, has massive parades and demonstrations, especially in Moscow's Red Square and Leningrad's Palace Square. All the leaders come out to watch the pageant and sport displays.

May 9: **Victory Day**. Parades are held at war memorials such as the Piskar-yovskoye Cemetery in Leningrad to celebrate VE Day at the end of World War II in Europe.

October 7: **Constitution Day**. Commemorates the adoption of the 1977 Constitution.

November 7-8: **Anniversary of the October 1917 Revolution**. So called because the Revolution on the old calendar took place on October 25, which differs from the Gregorian Calendar by 13 days. These celebrations are the most festive of the year, with colorful parades and marching bands. Firework displays go on at night, the streets are lit up and people are out late into the evening. In Leningrad, the Baltic fleet sails up the Neva and drops anchor by the Winter Palace; torches are lit atop the Rostral columns and Peter and Paul Fortress.

(Be aware that hotels must be booked far in advance during May and Revolution Days.)

Festivals

February 23: **Soviet Army Day**

April 22: **Lenin's Birthday**

May 5 to 13: **Festival of Moscow Stars**

June 6: **Pushkin's Birthday**. Poetry readings by Pushkin monuments. The Soviet fleet, including ships, submarines and sailors parade around the city.

June 21 to July 11: **Leningrad White Nights Festival**. While the sun does not set, many musical concerts, theatrical performances, street events and celebrations take place throughout the city. On June 21-29, there is the **Festival of the Arts**, which includes ballet and theater performances in front of the fountains of Petrodvorets, Peter the Great's summer palace. (In August, the **Festival of Fountains** is held here too.) On some evenings during the summer, the Neva River is turned into a giant theatrical stage— hundreds of boats fill the river, cannons fire, fireworks flare and fountains soar into the air. Every night people gather to watch the bridges of the city open at 2 a.m. Additional performances and celebrations are held on the Kirov Islands in the Gulf of Finland. Similar white night festivals are held in Vladimir, Suzdal and Novgorod.

Sept 8: **Seige of Leningrad Day**. This day marks the end of the 900-day seige of Leningrad, and includes special ceremonies at the Piskarovskoye Cemetery.

Sept 19: **Moscow Day**. A day for merry-making in the city.

Dec 25-Jan 5: **Russian Winter Festival**. Events are held to celebrate the coming new year especially in Moscow, Leningrad, Novgorod, Vladimir and Suzdal. In Leningrad's Kirov Central Park of Culture and Rest, *troika* rides, along with other traditional Russian folk customs, take place.

Many church holidays are celebrated by the Russian Orthodox Church, such as Easter, Orthodox New Year (usually in January) and church name days.

A few Saturdays each year, especially the Saturday before Lenin's birthday on April 22, Soviets practice the **Subbotnik**, voluntary and non-paid work on a day off. (*Subbota* means Saturday.) The first Subbotnik was held on May 1, 1920, when citizens of Moscow and Leningrad planted trees and worked together to clean up their city, neighborhoods, schools and work places.

Moscow and Leningrad have many other art, music and sports festivals during the year. Every other summer, Moscow hosts the **Moscow International Film Festival**. Every August, the **Moscow International Marathon** is run through the city.

Moscow Metro

Ⓜ

N ←

Planernaya
ПЛАНЕРНАЯ

Skhodnenskaya
СХОДНЕНСКАЯ

Tushinskaya
ТУШИНСКАЯ

Shchukinskaya
ЩУКИНСКАЯ

Oktyabrskoye Pole
ОКТЯБРЬСКОЕ ПОЛЕ

Polezhayevskaya
ПОЛЕЖАЕВСКАЯ

Begovaya
БЕГОВАЯ

Molodyozhnaya
МОЛОДЁЖНАЯ

Kuntsevskaya
КУНЦЕВСКАЯ

Pionerskaya
ПИОНЕРСКАЯ

Filevsky Park
ФИЛЕВСКИЙ ПАРК

Bagrationovskaya
БАГРАТИОНОВСКАЯ

Fili
ФИЛИ

Kutuzovskaya
КУТУЗОВСКАЯ

Studencheskaya
СТУДЕНЧЕСКАЯ

Kievskaya
КИЕВСКАЯ

Arbatskaya
АРБАТСКАЯ

Smolenskaya
СМОЛЕНСКАЯ

Ulitsa 1905 Goda
УЛИЦА 1905 ГОДА

Barrikadnaya
БАРРИКАДНАЯ

Krasnopresnenskaya
КРАСНОПРЕСНЕНСКАЯ

Belorusskaya
БЕЛОРУССКАЯ

Rechnoi Vokzal
РЕЧНОЙ ВОКЗАЛ

Vodny Stadion
ВОДНЫЙ СТАДИОН

Voikovskaya
ВОЙКОВСКАЯ

Sokol
СОКОЛ

Aeroport
АЭРОПОРТ

Dinamo
ДИНАМО

Medvedkovo
МЕДВЕДКОВО

Babushkinskaya
БАБУШКИНСКАЯ

Svitbovo
СВИБЛОВО

Botanichesky Sad
БОТАНИЧЕСКИЙ САД

VDNKh
ВДНХ

Shcherbakovskaya
ЩЕРБАКОВСКАЯ

Rizhskaya
РЫЖСКАЯ

Prospekt Mira
ПРОСПЕКТ МИРА

Novoslobodskaya
НОВОСЛОБОДСКАЯ

Mayakovskaya
МАЯКОВСКАЯ

Gorkovskaya
ГОРЬКОВСКАЯ

Pushkinskaya
ПУШКИНСКАЯ

Ploshchad Sverdlova
ПЛОЩАДЬ СВЕРДЛОВА

Kolkhoznaya
КОЛХОЗНАЯ

Turgenevskaya
ТУРГЕНЕВСКАЯ

Kuznetsky Most
КУЗНЕЦКИЙ МОСТ

Dzerzhinskaya
ДЗЕРЖИНСКАЯ

Prospekt Marksa
ПРОСПЕКТ МАРКСА

Ploshchad Revolutsii
ПЛОЩАДЬ РЕВОЛЮЦИИ

Biblioteka imeni Lenina
БИБЛИОТЕКА ИМЕНИ ЛЕНИНА

Preobrazhenskaya Ploshchad
ПРЕОБРАЖЕНСКАЯ ПЛОЩАДЬ

Sokolniki
СОКОЛЬНИКИ

Krasnoselskaya
КРАСНОСЕЛЬСКАЯ

Komsomolskaya
КОМСОМОЛЬСКАЯ

Krasnye Vorota
КРАСНЫЕ ВОРОТА

Kirovskaya
КИРОВСКАЯ

Ploshchad Nogina
ПЛОЩАДЬ НОГИНА

Shchelkovskaya
ЩЁЛКОВСКАЯ

Pervomaiskaya
ПЕРВОМАЙСКАЯ

Izmailovskaya
ИЗМАЙЛОВСКАЯ

Izmailovsky Park
ИЗМАЙЛОВСКИЙ ПАРК

Semyonovskaya
СЕМЁНОВСКАЯ

Electrozavodskaya
ЕЛЕКТРОЗАВОДСКАЯ

Baumanskaya
БАУМАНСКАЯ

Kurskaya
КУРСКАЯ

Taganskaya
ТАГАНСКАЯ

Novogireyevo
НОВОГИРЕЕВО

Perovo
ПЕРОВО

Shosse Entuziastov
ШОССЕ ЭНТУЗИАСТОВ

Aviamotornaya
АВИАМОТОРНАЯ

Ploshchad Ilicha
ПЛОЩАДЬ ИЛИЧА

Marksistskaya
МАРКСИТСКАЯ

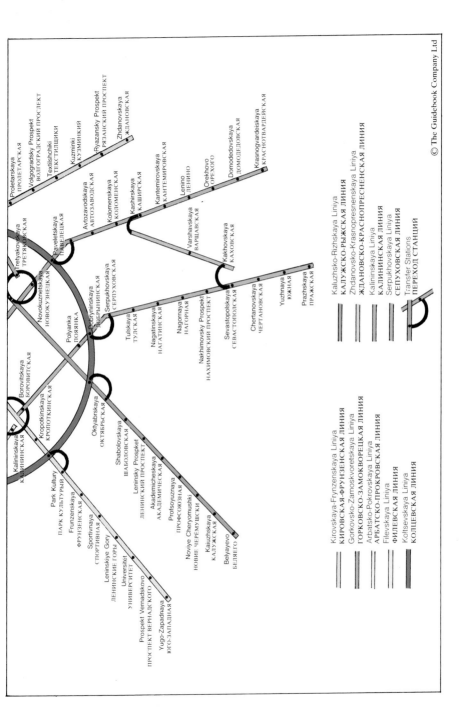

© The Guidebook Company Ltd

Proletarskaya ПРОЛЕТАРСКАЯ
Volgogradsky Prospekt ВОЛГОГРАДСКИЙ ПРОСПЕКТ
Textilshchiki ТЕКСТИЛЬЩИКИ
Kuzminki КУЗЬМИНКИ
Ryazansky Prospekt РЯЗАНСКИЙ ПРОСПЕКТ
Zhdanovskaya ЖДАНОВСКАЯ

Avtozavodskaya АВТОЗАВОДСКАЯ
Kolomenskaya КОЛОМЕНСКАЯ
Kashirskaya КАШИРСКАЯ
Kantemirovskaya КАНТЕМИРОВСКАЯ
Lenino ЛЕНИНО
Orekhovo ОРЕХОВО
Domodedovskaya ДОМОДЕДОВСКАЯ
Krasnogvardeiskaya КРАСНОГВАРДЕЙСКАЯ

Tretyakovskaya ТРЕТЬЯКОВСКАЯ
Paveletskaya ПАВЕЛЕЦКАЯ
Novokuznetskaya НОВОКУЗНЕЦКАЯ
Varshavskaya ВАРШАВСКАЯ
Kakhovskaya КАХОВСКАЯ

Polyanka ПОЛЯНКА
Dobryninskaya ДОБРЫНИНСКАЯ
Serpukhovskaya СЕРПУХОВСКАЯ
Tulskaya ТУЛЬСКАЯ
Nagatinskaya НАГАТИНСКАЯ
Nagornaya НАГОРНАЯ
Nakhimovsky Prospekt НАХИМОВСКИЙ ПРОСПЕКТ
Sevastopolskaya СЕВАСТОПОЛЬСКАЯ
Yuzhnaya ЮЖНАЯ
Chertanovskaya ЧЕРТАНОВСКАЯ
Prazhskaya ПРАЖСКАЯ

Borovitskaya БОРОВИЦКАЯ
Kalininskaya КАЛИНИНСКАЯ
Kropotkinskaya КРОПОТКИНСКАЯ
Oktyabrskaya ОКТЯБРЬСКАЯ
Shabolovskaya ШАБОЛОВСКАЯ

Park Kultury ПАРК КУЛЬТУРЫ
Frunzenskaya ФРУНЗЕНСКАЯ
Sportivnaya СПОРТИВНАЯ
Leninskiye Gory ЛЕНИНСКИЕ ГОРЫ
Universitet УНИВЕРСИТЕТ
Prospekt Vernadskovo ПРОСПЕКТ ВЕРНАДСКОГО
Yugo-Zapadnaya ЮГО-ЗАПАДНАЯ

Akademicheskaya АКАДЕМИЧЕСКАЯ
Leninsky Prospekt ЛЕНИНСКИЙ ПРОСПЕКТ
Profsoyuznaya ПРОФСОЮЗНАЯ
Noviye Cheryomushki НОВЫЕ ЧЕРЕМУШКИ
Kaluzhskaya КАЛУЖСКАЯ
Belyayevo БЕЛЯЕВО

Kirovskaya-Frunzenskaya Liniya
КИРОВСКАЯ-ФРУНЗЕНСКАЯ ЛИНИЯ
Gorkovsko-Zamoskvoretskaya Liniya
ГОРКОВСКО-ЗАМОСКВОРЕЦКАЯ ЛИНИЯ
Arbatsko-Pokrovskaya Liniya
АРБАТСКО-ПРОКРОВСКАЯ ЛИНИЯ
Filevskaya Liniya
ФИЛЕВСКАЯ ЛИНИЯ
Koltsevskaya Liniya
КОЛЬЦЕВСКАЯ ЛИНИЯ

Kaluzhsko-Rizhskaya Liniya
КАЛУЖСКО-РЫЖСКАЯ ЛИНИЯ
Zhdanovsko-Krasnopresnenskaya Liniya
ЖДАНОВСКО-КРАСНОПРЕСНЕНСКАЯ ЛИНИЯ
Kalininskaya Liniya
КАЛИНИНСКАЯ ЛИНИЯ
Serpukhovskaya Liniya
СЕПУХОВСКАЯ ЛИНИЯ
Transfer Stations
ПЕРЕХОД СТАНЦИИ

Hotels

Most foreigners are required to stay in Intourist hotels (prebooked before you enter the USSR). These have restaurants, cafés, Beriozkas, post offices, and usually nightly entertainment.

Belgrade, 5 Smolensky St., tel. 248-6692, nearest Metro station Smolenskaya. First-class hotel near the Arbat and Kalinin Prospect.

Kosmos, 150 Prospect Mira (across from Park of Economic Achievements), tel. 217-0785, nearest Metro station VDNKh). Deluxe hotel, with bowling alley, sauna and pool; built by French. Far from center, but close to Metro.

Intourist: 3 Gorky St., tel. 203-4008, nearest Metro Prospekt Marxa. First-class hotel; centrally located right on Gorky Street and a few minutes' walk to Red Square.

Metropole: 1 Prospekt Marxa (near Bolshoi Ballet), tel. 225-6673, nearest Metro Prospekt Marxa. First-class prerevolutionary hotel; recently renovated. Short walk to Red Square.

Leningradskaya: 21 Kalanchovsky St., tel. 975-3008. One of Stalin's wedding-cake buildings, traditional rooms, restaurants. About 15 minutes from downtown.

Mozhaiskaya: 165 Mozhaisky St., tel. 447-3434. Standard hotel, less expensive, away from downtown; also has camping facilities available in summer (must pre-book before arrival in country).

Mezhdunarodnaya: Kracnopresnensky Emb., tel. 253-7708/2378. The "International Hotel" or *Mezh*, as it is nicknamed, is part of the Sovincenter, known as the Armand Hammer Center. Used mainly for businessmen and delegations. Has every modern convenience, an expensive Japanese restaurant and Baskin-Robbins ice cream. It is a bit outside of town near the Moscow River.

National: 14 Prospekt Marxa, tel. 203-6539, nearest Metro Prospekt Marxa. Old charming deluxe hotel right across the street from Red Square; Lenin lived here after the Revolution.

Rossiya: 6 Razin St., tel. 298-5530/5437, nearest Metro Ploshchad Revolutsii. The world's largest hotel, accommodates 6,000 people. First-class; overlooks St. Basil's and Kremlin.

Savoy: 3 Zhdanov St., tel. 928-9169/230-2625, nearest Metro Smolenskaya. Deluxe hotel, remodeled by the Finns (used to be Hotel Berlin). Even has 24-hour CNN cable channel. Bookings can be made through Finnair.

Sevastopol: 1-A Bolshaya Yushunskaya St., tel. 110-4659/318-2827. First-class/standard hotel; less expensive, since not centrally located, but near Metro.

Ukraine: 2 Kutuzovsky Prospekt, tel. 243-3030. Modern first-class hotel on the Moscow River. A close hop to the center by Metro (nearest stop Kievskaya).

Useful Addresses

In the U S

Airlines: **Finnair** tel. (800) 950-5000;
Pan Am tel. (800) 221-1111; **British
Air** tel. (800) 247-9297; **Aeroflot**, 630
Fifth Ave. Suite 241, New York, NY
10111 tel. (212) 397-1660.

Soviet Embassy: 1115-1125 16th St.
NW, Washington, D.C. 20036, tel.
(202) 628-7551/7554; Visa/Consular
Office, 1825 Phelps Place NW,
Washington, D.C. 20009, tel. (202)
332-1513.

Soviet Consulate General in New
York: 9 E. 91st St., New York, NY
10020, tel. (212)348-6772. Soviet
Consulate General in San Francisco:
2790 Green St., San Francisco, CA
94123, tel. (415) 922-6642.

**Travel Organizations: Pan Am
Tours to USSR.** Call 1-800-843-8687
and press 2.
  Intourist. 630 Fifth Ave. Suite
868, New York, NY 10111 tel. (212)
757-3884/5.
  **American Express Travel
Services.** World Financial Center, 200
Vesey St., New York, NY 10285-
0320, tel. (212) 640-2000.
  **Council on International Ex-
change (CIEE).** 205 E 42nd St., New
York, NY 10017, tel. (212) 661-1414.
  Tour Designs Inc. 510 H St. SW,
Washington, D.C. 20024, tel. (800)
432-8687/(202) 554-5820.
  **Vega International Travel
Service Inc.** 201 N Wells St. Suite

430, Chicago, Illinois 60606, tel.
(312) 332-7211.
  **Beverly International Travel
Inc.** 9465 Wilshire Blvd. Suite 432,
Beverly Hills, CA 90212, tel. (213)
271-4116/272-3011.
  Center for US-USSR Initiatives.
3268 Sacramento St., San Francisco,
CA 94115, tel. (415) 346-1875 (Exec.
Dir. Sharon Tennison). For more
information on the work of citizen
diplomacy and trips to the USSR, you
may write the above address.

In the U K

Airlines in London: **British Air** tel.
(71) 897-4000; **Finnair** tel. (71) 408-
1222; **Pan Am** tel. (71) 409-0688;
Aeroflot 69-72 Piccadilly W1, tel.
(71) 493-7436/492-1756.

Soviet Embassy: 18 Kensington Place
Gardens, London W8 4QP tel (71)
229-6412/727-6888.

Soviet Visa Consulate: 5 Kensington
Place Gardens, tel. (71) 229-3215/16.

Travel Organizations:**Intourist.** 292
Regent St., London W1R, tel.(71)
580-1221/631-1252.
  Barry Martin Travel, Ltd. 342/
346 Linen Hall, 162/168 Regent St.,
London W1X 1RA, tel. (71) 439-
1271.
  Progressive Tours, Ltd. 12
Porchester Pl., Connaught Square,
London W2 2BS, tel. (71) 262-1676.

In the USSR

Airlines in Moscow: **Finnair** 5
Proyezd Khudozhestvennovo Teatra,

tel. 292-8788. Open Mon.-Fri. 9 to 5;
Pan Am, Hotel Mezhdunarodnaya II,
Krasnopresnenskaya 12, Rm. 1102, tel.
253-2658/59. Open Mon.-Fri. 9 to 6;
British Air Hotel Mezhdunarodnaya
II, Krasnopresnenskaya 12 Rm. 1905,
tel. 253-2482; **Aeroflot** Head Office
Frunzenskaya Emb. 4 tel. 241-9947.

Airlines in Leningrad: **Finnair** 19
Gogol St., tel. 315-9736/312-8987;
Pan Am 36 Herzen St. (in Aeroflot
office), tel. 311-5819.

Embassies: U S, in Moscow, 19/23
Tchaikovsky St., tel. 252-245159.
U S, in Leningrad, Consulate, 15
Petra Lavrova St., tel. 274-8235.
U K, in Moscow, 14 Morisa Toreza
Emb., tel. 231-8511/12.

Travel Agencies:
Intourist, Moscow Main Office, 16
Prospekt Marxa, tel. 203-6962, telex
411211. At Airport Sheremetievo II
156-9435 (Each Intourist Hotel has an
Intourist Service Desk.)
American Express Co., Moscow,
21-A Sadovo-Kudrinskaya St., tel.
254-0671. Open Mon.-Fri. 9 to 5:30.
Barry Martin Travel, Moscow,
Hotel Mezhdunarodnaya II,
Krasnopresnenskaya Emb. 12 Rm.
940, tel. 253-2940.

Moscow
Airports: **Sheremetyevo,** Leningradskoe Shosse (Sheremetyevo II is
the international airport about 20
miles/32 km outside the city);
Vnukovo and **Domodedovo** (both
local airports). Domodedovo is the
largest airport in the Soviet Union.

Train Stations: **Byelorussky,** Byelo-
russky Square, tel. 253-4908 (trains to
and from Berlin, Warsaw, London,
Paris, Vilnius, Minsk, Smolensk and
Brest); **Kazansky,** Komsomolsky
Square, tel. 266-2542 (trains to and
from Siberia and Central Asian
Republics); **Kievsky,** Kievsky Square,
tel. 240-7622, (trains to and from the
Ukraine and Eastern Europe);
Kursky, 29 Chkalov St., tel. 266-
5652 (trains to and from Armenia,
Azerbaijan, the Crimea and the
Caucasus); **Leningradsky,** 1 Komso-
molsky Square, tel. 262-4281 (trains
to and from Leningrad, Finland,
Novgorod, Pskov and Tallinn,
Estonia); **Paveletsky,** Leninsky
Square, tel. 235-4673 (trains to and
from the Volgograd region); **Rizhsky,**
Rizhsky Square, tel. 266-1176 (trains
to and from the Baltic); **Savyolovsky,**
Butyrskoi Zastavy Square, tel. 285-
9000 (trains to Uglich); **Yaroslavsky,**
Komsomolsky Square, tel. 266-0595
(trains to and from the Far East. The
Trans-Siberian departs daily at 10
a.m.)

Leningrad
Airports: **Pulkovo** (Pulkovo II is
international)

Train Stations: **Baltiisky,** 120
Obvodnov Kanal (trains to and from
Petrodvorets and Lomonosov);
Finlandsky, 6 Lenin Square (trains to
and from Repino and Finland);
Moskovsky, 2 Vosstaniya (Uprising)
Square (trains to and from Moscow

and points south); **Varshavsky,** Izmailovsky Prospekt (trains to and from Warsaw, Eastern Europe and Berlin); **Vitebsk,** 52 Zagorodny Prospekt (trains to and from Pushkin and Pavlovsk).

Useful Numbers: Fire dial (01); Police (02); Medical Ambulance (03) (In case of medical emergency contact your hotel or embassy for staff doctor); Local long-distance asst. (07); Local long-distance line dial 8—wait for tone and then dial city code and number; information inquiries (business 09) (private 00); correct time (Moscow 100) (Leningrad 08) (Leningrad weather 001); taxi (Moscow 2250000) (Leningrad 3120022; ordering an international call (Moscow 8-194) (Leningrad 3144747)—or order through your Intourist Hotel Service Desk.

City Area Codes: Moscow 095; Leningrad 812; Yaroslavl 0852; Kostroma 09422; Ivanovo 09322; Vladimir 09222; Novgorod 816; Pskov 81122.

Restaurants

A boom in co-operative restaurants over the last several years has increased the total of eating establishments in Moscow to well over 9,000. Every Intourist hotel has several restaurants (that usually offer nightly entertainment), cafés and bars. It is advisable to reserve a place in the restaurant in advance through the hotel service desk. The restaurants are usually open for lunch and dinner from 11 a.m. to midnight, with a few hours' break in the late afternoon. Two types of bars, ruble and *valutni* (hard-currency only), are usually open till midnight or 2 a.m. More and more hotels are now offering the *Svetsky Stol*, Swedish Table. This smorgasbord-style cafeteria is open for breakfast, lunch and dinner and an excellent way to get a quick, filling meal, in contrast to the slow service found in many restaurants. Remember that Russians expect to spend a full evening when dining out in a good establishment (an expensive luxury). Often the service is slow (to stretch out the night), the music can be loud, and other people may be seated at your table. Anticipate a dinner with entertainment to last all evening.

Try a few of the restaurants and cafés outside the hotel. Even though the menu is in Russian and the waiters speak only Russian, be ready for an adventure and some fun. Bring your phrasebook and a good time will be had by all! Many of the co-operatives have delicious regional food, fast service, and some offer floor shows, folk music or dance bands. For the more popular ones, advance reservations are recommended.

Abkhazia, 28 Novocheremushkinsky St., tel. 128-8040. Northern Georgian food, such as chicken *abkhaz* and *hachapuri* , a bread and cottage cheese dish. Nightly music and dancing. Moderate.

Alma-Alta, 13 Shvernika St., tel. 127-3283. Kazakh Asian food. Music and dancing in evening. Moderate.

Aragvi, 6 Gorky St., tel. 229-3762. The most popular Georgian restaurant in town. (Winston Churchill once ate here.) Among the specialities are *lavash* (bread) with hot *sulguni* (cheese), *kharcho* spicy meat soup, *satsivi* chicken in walnut and coriander sauce, *shashlik* and tasty Georgian wines. Music, dancing in evenings. Expensive. Reservations essential.

Arbat, 29 Kalinin Prospekt, tel. 291-1403. One of Moscow's largest restaurants. Lively music, dancing. Expensive. Reservations necessary.

Baku, 24 Gorky St., tel. 299-8506. Azerbaijani food, wine and music. Try *piti* (lamb and potato soup in a clay pot), *narkurma* (roast lamb with pomegranates), chicken, lamb or beef *pilau*. Expensive. Make a reservation.

Bega, 22 Begovava (in Hippodrome "Race" Track), tel. 259-9947. One of the oldest restaurants in Moscow, specializing in Tatar food, such as *tebe* lamb and *kalzha* spicy meat. Music nightly, except Wednesday. Moderate.

Belgrade, 8 Smolensky Square (in Belgrade Hotel), tel. 248-2696. Yugoslavian dishes and nightly entertainment. Expensive.

Bombay, 61 Rublyobsky Hwy., tel. 141-5502. Indian food and decor. Music and dancing. Moderate.

Bucharest, 1 Balchug St., tel. 223-7854. Romanian and Transylvanian cooking. Moderate.

Budapest, 2/18 Petrovsky Linii, tel. 221-4044. Hungarian cuisine and nightly entertainment; dance orchestra. Moderate.

Bukhara, 2/34 Sadovo-Sukharevsky, tel. 221-5259. Delicious Uzbek food. No music. Moderate.

Delhi, 23b Krasnaya Presnya St., tel. 252-1766. Indian food.

Dubrava, 150 Prospekt Mira (Hotel Cosmos), tel. 217-0495. A lively night spot with dancing. Speciality is chicken Kiev. Expensive.

Havana, 88 Leninsky Prospekt, tel. 138-0091. Cuban food and decor. Rock 'n' roll music and dancing. Moderate.

Hanoy, 60 Prospekt Let Oktyabr 20, tel. 124-4884. Vietnamese food. Music and dancing (except Wed.). Moderate.

Izba Rybaka, 48 Baumansky St., tel. 261-5685. The "Fisherman's Hut" serves seafood only. Inexpensive.

Jaltarang, 12 Chistoprudny Blvd. Indian food. Reasonable.

Labirint, 29 Kalinin Prospekt, tel. 291-1172. Nightly dancing and dining under Arbat nightclub. Moderate.

Kropotkinskaya 36, 36 Kropotkinsky St., tel. 201-7500. Popular co-op with Russian and European cuisine. Reservations recommended.

McDonalds, off Gorky St., and Pushkin Square. Usually long lines. Now there's even a black market for Big Macs!

Mercury, in Mezhdunarodnaya Hotel. tel. 255-7792. Very plush restaurant and night club, featuring jazz and Las Vegas-type floor shows. Music and dancing. Very expensive. Reserve table.

Metelitsa, 27 Kalinin Prospekt, tel. 291-1130. The "Snowball" is a popular disco. Light snacks. Inexpensive.

Minsk, 22 Gorky St., tel. 299-1248. Byelorussian cuisine.

Moldavia, 6 Bol. Cherkizovsky St., tel. 161-1051. Moldavian cooking. Reasonable.

National, 1 Gorky St. (National Hotel), tel. 203-5590. Elegant 19th-century decor restaurant with nice views of Red Square, serving classic Russian cooking. Folk music and dance bands. Expensive. Popular foreign currency bar is on the second floor.

Okhotnichi, 17/3 Selsk-ohozyaistvenny St., tel. 181-0190. "Hunters" specializes in Russian game and fowl. Shows, music and dancing. Moderate.

Pekin, 1/7 Bolshaya Sadovaya, tel. 209-1865. Chinese food.

Pitsunda, 3 Krzhizhanovsky St., tel. 125-6128. Quiet Georgian restaurant. Try the trout in nut sauce and *chihirtma*, spicy chicken soup. Moderate.

Polonais, 9 Marksistsky, tel. 270-6666. Polish food, music and dancing. Inexpensive.

Praga, 2 Arbat, tel. 90-6171. Old-fashioned atmosphere with Czech and Russian cuisine. Advertizes the "best chicken Kiev in Moscow." Nightly music and dancing. Expensive. Make reservations.

Russkaya Izba, Naberezhnaya 1 (40-minute drive to Ilyinskoye Village outside Moscow), tel. 561-4244. Built to look like traditional Russian *izba* (wooden cottage). Serves authentic old Russian cuisine, such as *pokhlyobka* mushrooms and wild berries. Tea served from samovar. Music by a balalaika band. Expensive. Reserve a day in advance.

Russkiye Pelmeni, 50 Arbat St., tel. 241-8304. Delicious dumplings. Music. Moderate.

Russky Zal, 3 Gorky St., tel. 203-0150. The "Russian Hall" has decor of red velvet and offers Russian food with musical ensembles. Expensive.

Sakhura, 12 Krasnopresnenskaya Emb. (Mezhdunarodnaya Hotel), tel. 253-2894. Excellent Japanese food, prepared by Japanese cooks. Very expensive. Reservations necessary.

Sedmoye Nyebo, in Ostankino TV Tower, tel. 282-2293. The revolving "Seventh Heaven" Restaurant has a great panoramic view of the city. Order a day in advance. Bring your passport.

Slavyansky Bazaar, 25 Oktyabr St. 13, tel. 221-1872. A favoritewith artists in the 19th-century. Chekhov, Tchaikovsky and Tolstoy dined here. In 1898 Stanislavsky and Nemirovich-Danchenko discussed the formation of the Moscow Art Theater. Try the *rasstegai* meat pie and *medok* honey drink. Music and dancing in the evenings. Expensive.

Sofia, 32 Gorky St., tel. 251-4950. Bulgarian food and wine. Dance bands in the evening. Moderate.

Sinyaya Ptitsa, 23 Chekhov St., tel. 299-8702. The "Blue Bird" is a popular jazz club with dancing. Good food. Moderate.

Tbilisi, 1 Generala Tyuleneva, tel. 337-0000. Decorated as a Georgian *patsha* peasant hut. Georgian food and music. Moderate.

Terek, 25 Obruchev St., tel. 331-5388. Popular place with Russian cuisine; orchestra and dancing. Dishes include lamb and baked piglets. Moderate.

Tsentralny, 10 Gorky St. (in Tsentralny Hotel), tel. 229-0241. Founded in 1865, the decor is elegant and ornate. Delicious Russian cuisine, such as *blini* , at moderate prices. Quartet plays baroque music in the evenings.

Turkmenia, 34 Perovsky St., tel. 306-7940. Central Asian Turkmenian food. Music and dancing. Moderate.

Ukrainia, 2 Kutozovsky Prospekt (in Hotel Ukrainia). Ukrainian food, wine and music. Try the *vareniki* meat-filled dumplings. Moderate.

Uzbekistan, 29 Neglinnaya St., tel. 221-3833. Uzbek food and music. Try the *lagman* meat and noodle soup, *manty* spicy lamb dumplings and *plovi* pilafs; even offers camel meat. Nightly music and dancing. Expensive.

Varshava, 2 Oktyabrsky Square (in Warsaw Hotel), tel. 238-1847. Polish food and music, dancing. Try *zrazy* Polish meat rolls. Moderate.

Vilnius, 12 Butlerov St., tel. 336-1502. Some Lithuanian food. Music. Moderate.

Vitosha, 35/2 Khoroshcusky Hwy., tel. 195-4084. Bulgarian food. Reasonable.

Yakor, 49 Gorky Street. The "Anchor" is a fish restaurant.

Zakarpatskiye Uzori, 2 Nizhegorodsky St., tel. 279-4580. Ukrainian restaurant, music and dancing. Reservations advised.

Cafés

Adriatica, 19/3 Ryleyev St., in the Arbat, tel. 201-7302.

Aelita, Exhibition Park of Economic Achievements, Pavilion 76. French breads and pastries, drinks.

Aist, "Stork" 33a Leningradsky Pr., tel. 255-8676.

Angara, 27 Kalininsky Prospekt, tel. 291-2209. Popular dancing spot.

Artisticheskoye, Proyezd Khudozhestvennovo Teatra (across from Moscow Art Theater off Gorky), tel. 292-0673. Popular meeting place before and after theater.

Atrium, 44 Leninsky Prospekt, tel. 137-3008. Russian-European food.

Baskin-Robbins ice cream in the Mezhdunarodnaya Hotel for foreign currency.

Bely Lyebyed. The "White Swan" at 3/18 Sivtsev Vrazhek in the Arbat, tel. 203-1283. Russian and Armenian food. Inexpensive.

Bely Medved, 116 Prospekt Mira. "Polar Bear" has ice-cream.

Bistro 1, 49 Arbat (next to Prague Restaurant), tel. 241-7054. Appetizers, drinks and *shashlik.*

Bistro 3, 4 Chekhov St., tel. 299-3073.

Bistro-Nedelya, 18 Oktyabr St., tel. 288-9398. Open 24 hours. Serves dishes from the Caucasus. Moderate.

Buratino, 31 Arbat, tel. 241-0886. "Pinocchio" cafe is popular with children. Some live animals, games and toys.

Chaihana, 40 Kropotkinsky St., Azerbaizhani tea room.

Gumista, 29 Kalyayevsky St., tel. 258-1315. Reasonable.

Gzhel, 21 Shukhova St., tel. 237-1020. Inexpensive food, music and dancing.

Ivushka, 28 Kalininsky Prospekt, tel. 925-4383. Blues music. Inexpensive.

Khrustalnoye, 17 Kutuzovsky Prospekt, tel. 243-4576. Popular dance spot, pizza served. Inexpensive.

Lasagne, 40 Pyatnitsky St., tel. 231-1085. Italian cuisine.

Lira, 19 Gorky St., tel. 299-8632. Popular dance spot. Good band music. Reasonable.

Margarita, 28 Mahlaya Bronnaya, tel. 299-6534. Tea room with pastries. Hot breakfasts in the morning from 8-11.

Mars, 7 Gorky Street. Quick-food co-op next to Intourist Hotel.

Myikhooa, 2/1 Rusakovsky St., Sokolniki. tel. 264-9574. Chinese food. Inexpensive.

Ogni Arbata, 12 Arbat, tel. 291-4359. "Arbat's Lights" serves lamb *lyula kebab,* steak and beverages.

Okhotnik, 40 Gorky St., tel. 251-4268. "Hunter's" café.

Ooh Kameena, 32 Chernyshevsky, tel. 297-0840. The "Fireside" has European food like pot roasts. Inexpensive.

Ooh Yuzefa, 11/17 Doobinsky, tel. 238-4646. "At Yoseph's" offers European food, a band.

Perekop, 33 Kalanchovsky St., tel. 280-4033. Band music, dancing. Reasonable.

Pokrovka, 4 Chernyshevsky St., Byelorussian food. Reasonable.

Razgooliay, 11 Spartakovsky St., tel. 267-7613. Russian food.

Rioni, 43 Arbat Street. Central Asian grilled dishes, such as *shashlik*. Inexpensive.

Rooslan, 32 Vorontsovsky, tel. 272-0632. Russian and Oriental food.

Ryleyeva 9, 9/5 Ryleyeva in the Arbat, tel. 291-6063. European and Oriental food.

Sayat-Nova, 17 Yasnogorsky St., tel. 426-8511. Tbilisi food; music and poetry readings.

Sever, 17 Gorky Street. Ice-cream parlor.

Sorok-Chetiri, 44 Leningradskoe Hwy., tel. 159-9951.

Sibir 25 Bolshaya Dorogomilovsky, tel. 240-1440. Specializes in Siberian *pelmeni* and other dumplings.

Staroye Foto, 40 Arbat, tel. 241-2202. Quaint cafe in the old Arbat.

U Nikitskih Vorot, Herzen St. and Suvorovsky Blvd., tel. 290-4883. "At Nikita's Gate" is a popular cafe with recorded music.

Uyoot, 1/2 Dmitrovsky Hwy., tel. 216-7096. Serves eggplant, veal, fish, *shashlik* dishes.

Valdai, 19 Kalininsky Prospekt, tel. 291-1034. Specializes in *pirozhki*.

Viktoria, 78 Prospekt Mira, tel. 971-0721.

Vremena Goda, Gorky Park, tel. 237-0827. Popular disco of young crowd. Inexpensive.

Yakimanka, 2/10 Bolshaya Poly-anka, tel. 238-8888. Uzbek food with a band.

Zamoskvorechie, 54 Bolshaya Polyanka, tel. 230-7333. Russian food, variety shows, band and bar. Serves lunch and dinner.

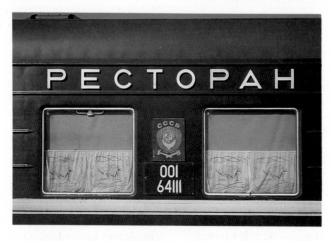

Shops

The easiest and quickest way to purchase souvenirs of your trip to Moscow is to make a stop at a Beriozka foreign currency store. Here one may purchase Soviet goods that are usually cheaper than in ordinary street shops. Each city has large department stores, *Univermag*, an arcade of shops that sell a variety of products for rubles. Speciality shops sell items such as books and records. If you have time, take a walk through a shopping district, such as GUM and Gorky Street. This also gives an idea of how the locals shop and what is available to them.

In most Soviet stores, one must first pay a cashier at the *kassa*, then show the receipt to the salesperson, who wraps and hands over the purchase. If something catches your eye outside a Beriozka, it is advisable to buy it; if you come back the next day, it may not be there. Many goods are not available in large supplies; long lines buy up materials quite quickly. Soviet stores sell items only for rubles and do not accept foreign currency. If shopping in town, make sure you have some rubles. Most stores are open from 10 a.m. to around 7 or 8 p.m. and close for an hour in the afternoon. In purchasing antiques or rugs, official permission is required; many times a duty is levied. Check before buying; the items could be confiscated.

The main shopping areas of Moscow are located along Gorky St., Kalinin Prospekt, the Arbat, and the small side streets (like Stoleshnikov, Petrovka and Kuznetsky Most) behind GUM Department Store on Red Square.

Beriozkas

The largest are found at the Rossiya (at the back) and Ukraine hotels. Others are located in the National, Intourist, Kosmos and Mezhdunarodny. (All Intourist hotels have a Beriozka.) Two Beriozkas are opposite the Novodevichy Monastery and at No. 9 Kutuzovsky Prospekt (near the Ukraine Hotel). A book Beriozka is at 31 Kropotkinsky Street. At No. 60 Dorogomilovsky Street is a food (*gastronom*) Beriozka. The Vneshtorgbank Gold Shop (gold, silver, coins and precious stones) is at 9 Pushkin Street.

Local Soviet Shops

GUM, *Gosudarstvenny Universalny Magazine* (Government Universal Store) on Red Square. Built in the 1880s, GUM is the largest shopping center in Moscow. Merchants once rented out the long rows of small shopping alcoves, now filled with Soviet-made products. Don't let the crowds and lines stop you from strolling inside. **TsUM**, Central Department Store, at 2 Petrovka St., is the next largest store of this type in the city. **Moskva** Department Store is at 54 Leninsky Prospekt.

Antique Shops

China and crystal can be found at 46 Gorky St., 32 Arbat, 56 Dimitrov St. and 99 Prospekt Mira.

Arts and Crafts

46b Gorky St., 12-16 Petrovka, 9 and 24 Kutuzovsky Prospekt, 54 Dimitrov St., 24 Leningradsky Prospekt, 8 25 Oktyabr St., 10/4 Krymsky Emb. (across from Gorky Park), and at 5 Smolensky Embankment.

Meeting the Professor

*T*here is absolutely no necessity to learn how to read; meat smells a mile off, anyway. Nevertheless, if you live in Moscow and have a brain in your head, you'll pick up reading willy-nilly, and without attending any courses. Out of the forty thousand or so Moscow dogs, only a total idiot won't know how to read the word "sausage."

Sharik first began to learn by color. When he was only four months old, blue-green signs with the letters MSPO—indicating a meat store—appeared all over Moscow. I repeat, there was no need for any of them—you can smell meat anyway. But one day Sharik made a mistake. Tempted by an acid-blue sign, Sharik, whose sense of smell had been knocked out by the exhaust of a passing car, dashed into an electric supplies store instead of a butcher shop. The store was on Myasnitsky Street and was owned by the Polubizner Bros. The brothers gave the dog a taste of insulated wire, and that is even neater than a cabby's whip. That famous moment may be regarded as the starting point of Sharik's education. Back on the sidewalk, he began to realize that blue didn't always mean "meat." Howling with the fiery pain, his tail pressed down between his legs, he recalled that over all the butcher shops there was a red or golden wriggle—the first one on the left—that looked like a sled.

After that, his learning proceeded by leaps and bounds. He learned the letter "t" from "Fish Trust" on the corner of Mokhovaya, and then the letter "s" (it was handier for him to approach the store from the tail end of the word, because of the militiaman who stood near the beginning of the "Fish").

Tile squares set into corner houses in Moscow always and inevitably meant "cheese." A black samovar faucet over the word indicated the former owner of Chichkin's, piles of red Holland cheese, beastly salesmen who hated dogs, sawdust on the floor, and that most disgusting, evil-smelling Beckstein.

If somebody was playing an accordion, which was not much better than "Celeste Aida," and there was a smell of frankfurters, the first letters on the white signs very conveniently added up to the words "no inde...," which meant "no indecent language and no tips." In such places there were occasional messy brawls and people got hit in the face with fists, and sometimes with napkins or boots.

If there were stale hams hanging in a window and tangerines on the sill, it meant ...Grr ... grr... groceries. And if there were dark bottles with a vile liquid, it meant ... Wwhi-w-i-wines ... The former Yeliseyev Brothers.

The unknown gentleman who had brought the dog to the doors of his luxurious apartment on the second floor rang, and the dog immediately raised his eyes to the large black card with gold letters next to the wide door with panes of wavy pink glass. He put together the first three letters right away: Pe-ar-o, "Pro." After that came a queer little hooked stick, nasty looking, unfamiliar. No telling what it meant. Could it be "proletarian"? Sharik wondered with astonishment ... No, impossible. He raised his nose, sniffed the coat again, and said to himself with certainty: Oh, no, there's nothing proletarian in this smell. Some fancy, learned word, who knows what it means.

Mikhail Bulgakov, Heart of a Dog

Bookstores

Dom Knigi (House of Books) at 26 Kalinin Prospekt is the largest bookstore; also sells foreign publications, posters and postcards; a must to visit. **Druzhba** (Friendship) has books from socialist countries at 15 Gorky Street. **Inostrannaya Kniga** (Foreign Books), at 16 Kachalov St., sells foreign books and old engravings. **Knigi-Podarki** (Books-Gifts), at 16 Stoleshnikov Pereulok, has gift books. Next door, at No. 14, is a **bukinist** (second-hand bookstore), selling used and rare books. At 6 Kirov St. is **Knizhny Mir** (Book World) with books, prints, posters and postcards. **Moskva** sells books, maps and postcards at 8 Gorky Street. **Planeta** at 8 Vesnin St. and **Progress** at 17 Zubovsky Blvd. both sell books in foreign languages.

Children's Stores

Detski Mir (Children's World), at 2 Prospekt Marxa, is the largest toy store in Moscow. **Dom Igrushki** (House of Toys) is at 8 Kutuzovsky Prospekt. **Mashenka**, 10 Smolensky St., sells girls' clothing.

Cosmetics and Cologne

Christian Dior and Estee Lauder have shops on Gorky Street. Some others are at 6 Gorky, 12 Petrovka and 44 Kalinin Prospekt.

Commissioni (Secondhand Stores)

Samovars, crystal and china are at 32 Arbat, 46 Gorky, 54 Dimitrov, 8 Izmailovsky and 99 Prospekt Mira. Furniture and clocks are at 5 Smolensky and 54 Frunzensky Embankments. Old musical instruments and electronic gear are at 31 Oktyabr St. and 7 Sadovo-Kudrinsky. The **Izumrud** (Emerald) at 23 Lomonosovsky Prospket has jewelry and precious stones.

Crystal, China and Glass

Dom Farfora (House of China) is at 36 Leninsky Prospekt. Others are at 15 Gorky St., 8 Kirov St. and 19 Komsomolsky Prospekt.

Food

Gastronom No. 1 is at 14 Gorky Street. The pre-revolutionary store was known as Yeliseyev's; today, even though the food is sparse, it still has an ornate interior. **Armenia** is at 17 Gorky St. and Georgian food is at 27 Gorky. Other stores on Gorky are at 10 (bread), 12 (waters) and 14 (groceries). **Novoarbatsky Gastronom** is at 21 Kalinin Prospekt. **Russky Pryanik** (Russian Gingerbread) is at 40 Leninsky Prospekt. The **Kulinaria** at the Prague Restaurant on the Arbat sells delicious pastries.

Furs

Fur coats and hats can be found at No. 13 Stoleshnikov Pereulok. Down the street at No. 5 is a used fur store. A **mekha** (fur) shop is also at 13 Pyatnitsky Street.

Gifts and Souvenirs

Podarki (Gifts) is at 4 and 37 Gorky Street. **Suveniri** (Souvenirs) at No. 12 and 45 Gorky, **Azerbaijani** souvenirs

at No. 24, **Olimpiisky** at 37 and **Tadjikistan** products at No. 52. Other souvenir shops are at 24 and 29 Kalinin Prospekt, 9 Kutuzovsky Prospekt, 12 and 16 Petrovka St. and 3 and 39 Leninsky Prospekt.

Jewelry

Yantar (Amber) is at 13 Stoleshnikov Pereulok, 14 Presnensky Val and 14 Gruzinsky Val. **Almaz** (Diamond) is at 14 Stoleshnikov. The **Biryuza** (Turquoise) Store is at 21 Sadovaya Spasskaya. **Zemchug** (Pearl) is at 22 Olimpïisky Prospekt and **Malakhitovaya Shkatulka** (Malachite Box) is located at 24 Kalinin Prospekt. **Agat** (Agate) is found at 16 Bolshaya Kolkhoznaya and **Rubin** (Ruby) at 78 Leningradsky Propsekt. **Samotsveti**

(Semi-Precious Stones) is at 35 and 11 Árbat. Other shops are on Gorky at nos. 12 and 32. The **Jewelery Salon** is on Grokholsky Pereulok 30.

Maps

Kuznetsky Most nos. 9 and 20 (also sells stamps).

Records

Melodiya at 40 Prospekt Kalinin is one of the largest record stores. Others are at 24 Herzen St. and 6 Arbat.

Rugs

Rug stores are located at 9 Gorky St., 11 Stoleshnikov, 4 Gruzinsky Pereulok and 99 Prospekt Mira.

Farmers' Markets (*Rii'nok*)

Here farmers sell their fresh vegetables, fruits, flowers and other wares and produce. Bring a few bags; otherwise the loose strawberries or nuts go into your handbag or pocket! Markets are open from 7 a.m. to about 6 p.m, but a better selection is found in the morning.

Babushkinsky (Grandmothers) is at 30 Menzhinsky Street.

Baumansky is at Baumansky St. 47.

Krestovsky is at 1 Krestovsky Val.

Leningradsky is at Chasovaya St. 11.

Rizhsky is by the Rizhsky Metro stop at 94 Pr. Mira and the **Yaroslavsky** is at 122.

Tsentralny is on Tsvetnoi Blvd. 15 (near the Old Circus).

Zhandovsky 12 Lyublinsky Street.

Katitnikovsky is the pet market and a sight to see! It's held on weekends at 42a Kalitnikovsky Street. Here is also the **Ptichi Rinok**, the Bird Market. Many animals on sale are dogs, cats, rabbits, and an assortment of birds and fish. Try to get there in the morning (opens from 8 a.m. to about 2 p.m.).

Theaters

Bolshoi Opera and Ballet Theater, 1 Sverdlov Square.

Central Children's Theater, 2 Sverdlov Square.

Chamber Musical Theater, 71 Leningradsky Prospekt.

Chamber Yiddish Musical Theater, 12 Tagansky Square.

Children's Musical Theater 5 Vernadsky Prospekt.

Durov Animal Theater, 4 Durov Street.

Gogol Drama Theater, 8a Kazakov Street.

Kremlin Palace of Congresses, the Kremlin (entrance through the Borovitsky Gate).

Lenin Komsomol Theater, 6 Chekhov Street.

Malaya Bronnaya Drama Theater, 4 Malaya Bronnaya Street.

Maly Theater, 1/6 Sverdlov Square.

Maly Theater Branch, 69 Bolshaya Ordynka.

Mayakovsky Theater, 19 Hertzen Street.

Mime Theater, 39/4 Izmailovsky Blvd.

Miniature Theater, 3 Karetny Ryad Street (Hermitage Garden).

Moscow Academic Art Theater, 22 Tverskoi Blvd. (new building); 3 Proyezd Khudozhestvennovo Teatra (old building).

Moscow Puppet Theater, 26 Spartakovskaya Street.

Moscow Regional Drama Theater, 9 25th October Street.

Mossoviet Theater, 16 Bolshaya Sadovaya Street.

Novy Drama Theater, 2 Prokhodchikov Street.

Obraztsov Puppet Theater, 3 Sadovo Samotechnaya (with the puppet clock on building).

Poezia Hall, 12 Gorky Street.

Pushkin Drama Theater, 23 Tverskoi Blvd.

Regional Puppet Theatre, 24 Bolshaya Kommunisticheskaya Street.

Romany Gypsy Theater, 32 Leningradsky Prospekt (in Hotel Sovetskaya).

Satire Theater, 2 Mayakovsky Square/18 Bolshaya Sadovaya Street.

Satiricon Theater, 8 Sheremetyevksky Street.

Soviet Army Theater, 2 Commune Square.

Sovremennik Theater, 19 Chistoprudny Blvd.

Stanislavsky Drama Theater, 23 Gorky Street.

Stanislavsky and Nemirovich-Danchencko Musical Theater, 17 Pushkinskaya Street.

Taganka Drama and Comedy Theater, 76 Chkalov Street.

Theater of Friendship of the Peoples of the USSR, 22 Tversko Blvd.

Variety Theater, 20/2 Bersenevsky Embankment. Also known as the *Estrada*.

Yermolova Drama Theater, 5 Gorky Street.

Yevgeny Vakhtangov Drama Theater, 26 Arbat Street.

Movie Theaters
Kosmos, 109 Prospekt Mira.

Mir, 11 Tsvetnoi Blvd.

Moskva, 2/2 Mayakovsky Square.

Oktyabr, 42 Kalinin Prospekt.

Tsircorama, At Exhibition of Economic Achievement complex.

Zaryadye, Rossiya Hotel.

Zvezdny, 14 Vernadsky Prospekt.

Concert Halls
Andrei Rublev Museum of Early Russian Art, 10 Pryamikov Square.

Cathedral of the Sign, 8 Razin Street.

Central Concert Hall, in the Hotel Rossiya.

Church of the Intercession in Fili, 6 Novozavodskaya Street.

Church of St. Vlasii, 20 Ryleyev Street.

Conservatory Grand Hall, 13 Herzen Street.

Glinka Concert Hall, 4 Fadeyev Street.

Gnesin Institute Concert Hall 30/36 Vorovsky Street.

October Hall of the House of Trade Unions, 1 Pushkinskaya Street. Also known as the *Hall of Columns*.

Olympic Village Concert Hall, 1 Pelshe Street.

Operetta Theater, 6 Pushkin Street.

Ostankino Palace-Museum of Serf Art, 5 1st Ostankinsky.

Rachmaninov Hall, Herzen Street.

Tchaikovsky Concert Hall, 20 Gorky Street, Mayakovsky Square.

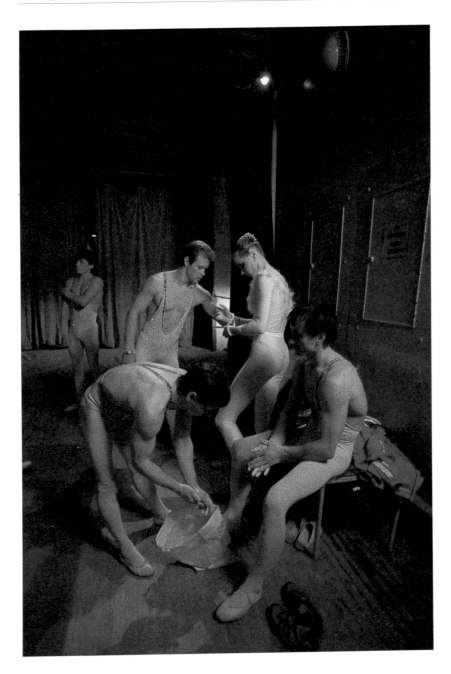

Library
Lenin Library, 3 Kalinin Prospekt.

Circuses
New Circus, 7 Vernadsky Prospekt.

Old Moscow Circus, 13 Tsvetnoi Blvd.

Durova Zoo Circus, 4 Durov Street.

Tent Circus, Gorky and Izmailovo Parks (summer only).

During the year there are performances of the Moscow Ice Ballet and the Circus on Ice.

Sports Facilities
The Aquatic Sports Palace, 27 Mironovskaya Street.

The Central Chess Club, 14 Gogolevsky Blvd.

The Central Lenin Stadium, At Luzhniki.

The Chaika Swimming Pool, 1/3 Turchaninov Lane.

The Dynamo Stadium, 36 Leningradsky Prospekt.

Hippodrome Race Course, 22 Begovaya Street.

Krylatskoye Sports Complex, 10 Pyataya Krylatskaya.

The Moskva Open Air Swimming Pool, 37 Kropotkinskaya Emb. (open year-round).

The Olympic Sports Complex, 16 Olympisky Prospekt.

The Sokolniki Sports Palace, 1 Sokkolnichesky Val.

The Spartak Sports Palace, 23 Maly Oleny Lane.

The Sports and Tennis Palace, 39 Leningradsky Prospekt.

The Young Pioneers Stadium, 31 Leningradsky Prospekt.

Golf Course
Nahabino (outside Moscow). This is the first golf course built in the Soviet Union, designed by Robert Trent Jones II. Open in 1991.

Parks and Gardens
Botanical Garden of the Academy of Sciences, 4 Ostankino-Botanicheskaya Street.

Druzhba Forest Park, 90 Leningradskoye Highway.

Gorky Central Recreation Park, 9 Krymsky Val.

Hermitage Garden, 3 Karetny Ryad Street.

Izmailovo Recreaton Park, 17 Narodny Prospekt (Metro Izmailovo Park).

Kuskovo Forest Park, 40 3rd Muze-inaya Street.

Old Botanical Gardens, 28 Prospekt Mira.

Moscow University Botanical Gardens, Lenin Hills.

Sokolniki Park, 62 Rusakovskaya Street. (Metro Sokolniki).

Terms For Local Stores

Learn the Russian alphabet, so you can sound out these store signs on the street.

aptyeka	pharmacy
bukinist	second-hand bookstore
bulochnaya	bakery
chasy	watches and watch repair
galanteriya	clothing, fabrics and lingerie
gastronom	food store
khozyaistvenny magazin	hardware and kitchen supplies
khudozhestvenny	art gallery
kiosk	small stand
kino	movie cinema
knizhny (knigi) magazin	bookstore
kommissiony magazin	second-hand store
konditerskaya	confectionery—sweets and tea
kulinariya	small take-out delicatessens
magazin	store
mekha	fur shop
loko	dairy products
morozhenoye	ice cream
myaso-Riiba	meat and fish
oboof	shoe store
odezhda	clothing store
ovoshchi-Frukti	vegetables and fruit
podarki	gifts
produkti	produce
remont	repair shop
rinok	farmers' market
shkolnik	school and office supplies
tabak	cigarettes and tobacco
tkani	sewing, fabrics, perfumes
tsvyeti	flowers
univermag	department store
viictavka	exhibit
yarmarka	string of small outdoor kiosks
Gedye' magazeen'?	Where is the shop?
Pakazhee'te	I would like to see. . .

Oo vas yest?	Do you have?
Droogoi' raz'mair?	Another size?
(Raz'mair) bol'she/men'she	(Size) smaller-larger
Deshe'vlye/daro'zhe	Cheaper/more expensive
Droogo'va tsvet'a?	Another color?
Skol'ka e'to stoi'yeet?	How much does it cost?
Mozh'na primyer'eet	Can I try it on?
Menye' e'to (ne) nrav'eetsa	I (don't) like it.
Ya e'to kooplyoo'	I'll buy it.

Clothing and Shoe Size Conversion

Women's Dress Sizes

USSR	44	46	48	50
US	6	8	10	12
European	34	36	38	40

Women's Shoes

USSR	34	35	36	37
US	4	5	6	7

Men's Suits

USSR	48	50	52	54	56
US	37-8	39-40	41-42	43-44	45-46

Men's Shoes

USSR	38	39	40	42	44
US	6 1/2-7	7 1/2-8	8 1/2-9	9 1/2-10	10 1/2-ll

Conversion Table

1 inch= 2.54 centimeters (cm)
1 foot= .304 meters (m)
1 mile= 1.6 kilometers (kms)
1 km= .6214 miles
1 ounce= 28.35 grams
1 pound= .45 kilograms (kg)

1 kilo= 2.2 pounds
1 pint= .57 litres
1 litre= 1.75 pints
1 quart= .946 litres
1 US gallon= 3.785 litres
1 hectare= 2.47 acres

To compute centigrade temperatures, subtract 32 from Fahrenheit and divide by 1.8. To go the other way, multiply centigrade by 1.8 and add 32.

Index

Playing chess in the park (top right); reading the daily newspaper (bottom right); a food store on Nevsky Prospekt (left)

(Preceding pages) Cathedral Square, the Kremlin; Cathedral of the Annunciation (left and top right); Cathedral of the Assumption (bottom right)

Crime and Punishment

They use various horrible methods of torture to force out the truth. One of them involves tying the hands behind the back, drawing them up high, and hanging a heavy beam on the feet. The executioner jumps on the beam, thus severely stretching the limbs of the offender from one another. Besides, beneath the victim they set a fire, the heat of which torments the feet, and the smoke the face. Sometimes they shear a bald place on top of the head and allow cold water to fall on it a drop at a time. This is said to be an unbearable torture. Depending on the nature of the case, some may, in addition, be beaten with the knout, after which a red-hot iron is applied to their wounds.

If a case of brawling is being tried, usually the one who struck first is considered guilty, and he who first brings a complaint is considered in the right. One who commits a murder not in self-defence (they consider the opposite justified), but with premeditation, is thrown into prison, where he must repent under severe conditions for six weeks. Then he is given communion and decapitated.

If someone is accused of robbery and convicted, he is put to torture all the same [to determine] if he has stolen something besides. If he admits nothing more, and this is the first offence, he is beaten with the knout all along the road from the Kremlin to the great square. Here the executioner cuts off one of his ears, and he is put into a dungeon for two years. If he is caught a second time, then, in the manner described above, he has the other ear cut off and is installed in his previous lodging, where he remains until other birds of the kind are found, whereupon they are all sent together to Siberia. However, no one pays with his life for robbery, unless a murder is committed along with it. If, under torture, the thief names those to whom he sold stolen goods, the buyers are brought to court and ordered to make restoration to the complainant. They call such payment vyt, and on its account many are constrained against purchasing suspicious things.

Olearius, Travels in Seventeenth Century Russia